FIGHTING
WORDS

FIGHTING WORDS

EDITED BY
DAVID BLIXT

FOR THE 2015 HISTORICAL NOVEL
SOCIETY CONFERENCE

Published by
Sordelet Ink

Fighting Words

Copyright © 2015 David Blixt

Cover by David Blixt

ISBN-13: 978-0692468272
ISBN-10: 0692468277

Published by Sordelet Ink
www.sordeletink.com

https://www.createspace.com/5553503

CONTENTS

Thanks to:

Dale Girard, Jared Kirby, Dave Doersch, Tom Leoni, and Rick Sordelet

For The *HNS* Writers

"The pen is mightier than the sword if the sword is very short, and the pen is very sharp."

Terry Pratchett

Introduction

By David Blixt

From antiquity to the late 19th Century, swordplay was at the center of the world. I don't mean just duels and warfare. I mean customs and society. The way a man bowed. Why we shake hands in greeting. The reason men's and women's shirts button differently, even to this day – all of this came from swordplay.

Dance is especially important in the history of swordplay. Or rather, swordplay is vital to understanding the history of dance. In a dangerous world, a man had to always remain in practice. So the dance of any given period reflects the fighting style of that period. In the time of longswords, with big sweeping steps and long arcs, the dance is the reel. In rapier-and-dagger fighting of the Tudor era, dance partners held up both hands and switched from one to the other, just as in a rapier duel. The delicate footwork and correct posture for smallsword fighting is exactly mirrored in the 18th century waltz.

The dance of a period comes out of the fighting style of a period. In fact, it is not until we introduce repeating guns that this trend ends (it is also the end of couples-dancing – ever since we started using automatic weapons, men and women have ceased to dance together).

This is what I mean when I say you're writing about swordplay. A woman walking on a man's left in public was to keep his sword-arm free. The length of the sword in Elizabeth's court was a strict 33-inches, because men kept wearing longer and longer swords (overcompensating?) and were constantly whacking each other when they turned.

And language! So many phrases we use today stem from violence. Cloak and dagger. Let the cat out of the bag. Lock, stock, and barrel. Half-cocked. Flash in the pan. Fly off the handle. Even the insult 'gauche' refers to left-handed men, deemed to be devilish for their unnatural way of fighting.

Because fighting was so much at the heart of society, it branched into every aspect

of life. Learning the basic elements of swordsmanship is unbelievably helpful to the
historical author – if only to let you know how easy it is to trip over your sword when
walking up a flight of stairs. Such details are the lifeblood of our art, and are so often
overlooked.

The HNS has offered me a wonderful chance to present some of this knowledge here
in Denver, exploring several different eras of swordfighting. For part of the time,
we'll be picking up swords and learning the basics, just as in the old fight schools and
academies. For the rest of the time, I'll be running through a history of swordplay in
Europe, from the ancient Greeks through the Napoleonic era. I'll talk about the evolution from cutting to thrusting, and how the Romans were far ahead of their time. And
I'll share stories and offer advice on how to write violence.

Like every other element of our stories, it comes from character, and research.

The Rules Of Violence

By David Blixt

There's been a great deal of talk about violence in media (meaning film and video-games), painting all fictional violence with a damning brush. It's an important conversation, and one I'd like to have. But I'm not for toning down the violence in film. I'm for making it better. By which I mean, making it matter.

The trouble is not the violence. The trouble is violence without consequence.

There are many talented writers out there, writing brilliant stories. But a lot of what I see in the Action-Adventure movie world has no weight, because violence has no cost. A guy fires off a million rounds of ammo, mowing down faceless badguys. It can be visually awesome, and it's fun to watch, and you forget it ten minutes later. It has no weight.

For me, all violence should tell a story. That story should never be easy, never be comfortable. It can be enjoyable, sure. Even better, it can be inspiring, heart-pounding, and cathartic.

Clearly I'm a fan of Shakespeare. And Shakespeare learned the rules of his craft from Aristotle, including the importance of catharsis, the cleansing that happens through a shared trial. As an audience, we share the hero's trial. The greater the trial, the deeper the catharsis. That's the theory.

Unlike Aristotle, Shakespeare never wrote down rules, or at least he didn't pass them along to us. But reading his plays, there are some very definite rules at work:

- Instigate an act of violence, and you will receive a violent end

- There is no justification for murder. Ever.

- Justice is for the authority of King, Prince, or God, not the average man

None of this is to say that Shakespeare doesn't have his characters flout these rules. Nor do these rules apply to warfare, where armies meet. But he is absolute in his rules for personal violence. If you commit violence, or if you take the law into your own hands, you are sowing the seeds for your own destruction.

A few examples:

- Romeo attacks Tybalt for murdering his friend, Mercutio. Though in our eyes he's justified, he is taking the law into his own hands. And by killing Tybalt, he is dooming himself and Juliet.

- Titus Andronicus, whose sons have been murdered and his daughter raped, kills the rapists and cooks them into meat dishes to serve to their mother. Revenge is achieved, and perhaps some form of justice, but he is again placing himself in the place of authority, and dies. Unlike Romeo, he accepts this as the cost of his revenge.

- Laertes agrees to kill Hamlet in revenge for the Danish Prince murdering his father Polonius behind the arras. Laertes, of course, is cut with the same poisoned blade he used to cut Hamlet, a lovely ironic touch, mirroring the old phrase 'when setting out for revenge, first dig two graves.'

- Brutus, the best example of all. He tries to save Rome from monarchy by killing his friend and mentor Caesar. He is clearly portrayed as a good and honorable man doing a terrible deed for the best of reasons. But motives cannot change the fact that it is still a terrible deed, and he pays the ultimate price for it.

Then there are those who are not even trying to justify their violent deeds – Macbeth, Iago, Richard – who commit acts of violence to satisfy their ambitions, their jealousies, and their rage at life. None of them live. In Shakespeare, the instigators of violence are always, always, consumed by violence.

In short, there is never violence without consequence. And that's what's missing today - the cost.

Making violence have meaning was much easier to achieve in a world where any gun held only one shot and most of the violence was performed with sword or dagger. In the words of Frank Miller's Batman, 'We kill too often because we've made it easy... too easy... sparing ourselves the mess and the work.' If you're going to kill someone with a sword or knife, there's a certain commitment to the deed, as it will take work. What a good story-teller can do is make taking a life require an effort, re-create that commitment, and never make it casual or easy.

Here's a modern example of violence with consequence – DIE HARD. Not the second, fourth, or fifth installments of the series, but definitely the original, and to some extent the third.

Most everyone agrees that the original DIE HARD is, if not the pinnacle of the Action genre, certainly a touchstone and model to be emulated. But what producers and writers mistakenly focus on is the set-up – one man against twelve villains in a high rise – and not what makes the film so compelling, which is the humanity of John McLane.

In DIE HARD, surviving hurts. The violence is messy, and has unintended consequences. John is so battered by the end that his wife doesn't recognize him. He's been shot, beaten, and had to run (or hop) across broken glass. Of course, this is Hollywood, so they didn't go the extra mile of NOTHING LASTS FOREVER, the book upon which the film is based, and have Holly go out the window with Hans, killed by that damned wrist-watch, the symbol of her success. But at the end there is a real catharsis. John suffered to do what was hard, what was right.

That he did so with grim humor makes him more heroic. His were not James Bond-like coy tag-lines after an enemy's death. McLane's humor was bravado, a way to keep up a brave face against the enemy. But we also see his guard down, in that great monologue where he asks the cop outside to apologize to his wife for him. Also in that moment of pure honesty. "Please, God, don't let me die."

Speaking of Bond, there is a reason I enjoyed CASINO ROYALE more than any other Bond film in years, perhaps ever. I am a huge Bond fan, but have cared less and less for the films over time. I'll still watch the original trio of Connery's films, OHMSS, THE LIVING DAYLIGHTS and maybe GOLDENEYE. But CASINO ROYALE was a return to the Bond of Ian Fleming, the Bond of the books, the damaged, cynical man who kills for his government and who doesn't get the girl. Twice in the books Bond fell truly in love. Both times, the woman he loved died – once by her own hand, once murdered. While the fantasy of Roger Moore's Bond was childishly fun to watch, those films have no weight. They don't matter the way that CASINO ROYALE and SKYFALL do. Because violence has consequences.

In contrast, there's the movie TAKEN. I enjoyed it, and I remember how much of a badass Liam Neeson's character was. But I don't remember his name, or much of anything but the fighting. I remember his daughter being dragged out from under the bed. That was the only human moment in that film.

The trouble with films like TAKEN or the DIE HARD knock-offs, which try to replicate the original's formula, is the indestructibility of the hero. Because the explosions have to be bigger, the violence bigger, there's less and less room for humanity. And it's humanity, not the lack of it, that makes an Action film great. Jason Bourne's search for his identity; Aragorn's reluctance to lead juxtaposed against his natural ability; Tony Stark's growth from naïve weapon-maker to arrogant protector; and of course, the greatest of all Action heroes, Indiana Jones. Remember that scene in Raiders where – well, remember all the scenes in Raiders, because it's a perfect film. But there's no point at which the violence is easy. It can be funny and still be desperate and thrilling. The giant ball at the beginning is hilarious and very scary at the same time, while the great scene on the ship with the 'years/mileage' line is a perfect example of simple humanity and the cost of these adventures.

No, we're not in the age of Shakespeare, and we don't need or want all our heroes to die if they commit an act of violence. But we do need them to be mortal, and we need their deeds to have weight.

So, to my fellow writers, I have this simple suggestion. If you write a scene of violence, don't make it bigger. Make it matter. Don't make it easy, make it hard. Look to character and motivation to root the violence in the people committing it, both for villains and heroes. Because villains are rarely villains in their own mind. Make everyone the hero of their story, make the violence matter as much to them as it should, and make it as surprising and upsetting as it is in life.

Quick Thoughts on Violence in Storytelling

By David Blixt

Violence is a story of desire, and denial. I want something from you. No, you can't have it.

Write a sex scene like a fight scene, and write a fight scene like a sex scene.

Violence is all about character.

The best attacks are linear. The best defenses are circular.

Violence should have a cost.

Fighters like to vocalize during a fight. It helps them remember to breathe.

More fights have been decided by accident than by skill.

Fighting is often like playing cards - it's dangerous to chase a bad hand, and bluff is half the game.

"There are two powers in the world; one is the sword and the other is the pen. There is a great competition and rivalry between the two. There is a third power stronger than both, that of the women."

Muhammad Ali Jinnah

Primary Sources

Below is a list of primary sources for combat, mostly in the form of "Fight-Books", tomes illustrated with plates of the various moves.

Pre-1300

Viking Saga Excerpts
Saxo the Dane (c. Early 13th Century)
MS I.33 (c. 1295)

1300-1399

Manesse at al. – Die Manessesche Liederhandschrift (c. 1300–1315)
Hanko Döbringer's Fechtbuch on the Teachings of Johannes Liechtenauer (c. 1389)

1400-1499

Le Jeu de la Hache (c. 1400)
Fiore Dei Liberi – Flos Duellatorum in Armis (c. 1410)
MS 3542 – Harleian Manuscript or "The Man Who Wol" (c. 1430s)
Gladiatoria (c. 1430)
Sigmund Ringeck – Die Ritterlich Kunst des Langen Schwerts (c. 1440)
Peter von Danzig Manuscript (c. 1452)
Paulus Kal Fechtbuch (c. 1458–1467)
Talhoffer's Fechtbuch (1459)
Talhoffer's Fechtbuch (1467)
Codex Wallerstein (c. 1470)
Paulus Kal – Kunst des Fechtens (c. 1479)
Fillipo Vadi – Liber de Arte Gladitoria Dimicandi (c. 1482–1487)
Hans Lecküchner – Kunst des Messerfechtens (c. 1482)
Hans von Speyer – Handschrift M I 29 (1491)
Mertein Hündsfelder – Fechtlehre mit dem Kurzen Schwert (c. 1491)
Hugues Wittenwiller (c. 1493)
Hans Wurm (c. 1490s)

1500-1599

Anon Lib.pict A.83 (c. 1500)
Marx Walther – Turnierbuch und Familienchronik (c. 1506)
Das Solothurner Fechtbuch (c. 1506–1514)
Das ist ain Hybsh Ring Byechlin (c. 1509)
Albrecht Duerer's Fechtbuch (c. 1512)
Goliath (c. 1510–1520)
Kunst des Ringen (c. 1510)

Jörg Wilhalm (c. 1522)

Jörg Wilhalm (c. 1523)

Ludwig von Eyb – Turnierbuch (1525)

Han Lechencher – DER ALTENN FECHTER ANFENGLICHE KUNST (c. 1531)

Christian Egenolph's Fechtbuch (c. 1531)

Antonio Mancilino – SE OPERA NOVA, DOUE LI SONO TUTTI LI DOCUMENTI (c. 1531)

Additional Manuscript 39564 (c. 1535–1550)

Achille Marozzo – OPERA NOVA (c. 1536)

Hans Czynner – UBER DIE FECHTKUNST UND DEN RINGKAMPF (1538)

Hans Burgkmair – TURNIERBUCH (1540)

Paulus Hector Mair – OPUS AMPLISSIMUM DE ARTE ATHLETICA (1542)

Gaspar Lamberger – DER ROMISCHEN KHAY UNND KU (1544)

Roger Ascham – The Schole of Shootinge (1545)

Paulus Hector Mair – Geschlechterbuch der Stadt Augsburg (1550)

Martin Van Heemskerck – Fechter und Ringer (1550)

Camillo Agrippa – TRATTATO DI SCIENTIA D'ARME, CON VN DIALOGO DI FILOSOFIA (1553)

Hans Lebkommer – FECHTBUCH DIE RITTERLICHE (1558)

Achille Marozzo – ARTE DELL'ARMI (c. 1568)

Jeronimo de Caranza – DE LA FILOSOFIA DE LAS ARMAS (1569)

Joachim Meyer – KUNST DES FECHTENS (1570)

Giacomo Di Grassi – HIS TRUE ARTE OF DEFENCE (Italian edition) (1570)

Giovanni dall'Agocchie – DELL'ARTE DI SCRIMIA (1572)

Henri de Saint-Didier – TRAICTÉ CONTENANT LES SECRETS DU PREMIER LIVRE (1573)

Henrici a Gunterrodt – DE VERIS PRINCIPIIS ARTIS DIMICATORIAE (c. 1579)

Frederico Ghisliero – REGOLE DO MOLTI CAVAGLIERESCHI ESSERCITI (c. 1587)

Christoff Rösener – EHREN TITTEL VND LOBSPRUCH DER RITTERLICHEN (1589)

Codex Guelf 83.4.Aug.8° (1591)

Giacomo di Grassi – HIS TRUE ARTE OF DEFENSE (1594)

Vincentio Saviolo – HIS PRACTICE IN TWO BOOKS (1595)

George Silver – PARADOXES OF DEFENCE (c. 1599)

1600-1699

Luis Pacherco de Narvaez – LIBERO DE LAS GRANDEZAS DE LA ESPADA (1600)

Anonymous Spanish Rapier Work (c. early 17th century)

Salvatore Fabris – SIENZ E PRACTICA D ARME (1606)

Nicoletto Giganti – SCOLA OVERO TEATRO (1606)

Torquato d'Alessandri – IL CAVALIER COMPITO: DIALOGO (c.1609)

Ridolfo Capo Ferro da Cagli – GRAN SIMULACRO DELL'ARTE E DELL'USO DELLA SCHERMA (1610)

Jakob Sutor – NEU KÜNSTLICHES FECHTBUCH (1612)

Antonio Quintino – Discorso or "JEWELS OF WISDOM" (1614)

George Hale – THE PRIVATE SCHOOLE OF DEFENCE (1614)
Hieronyme Calvacabo – TRAITE OU INSTRUCTION POUR TIRER DES ARMES (1617)
Joseph Swetnam – SCHOOLE OF THE NOBLE AND WORTHY SCIENCE OF DEFENCE (1617)
Salvatore Fabris – DELLA VERA PRACTICA & SCIENZA D'ARMI LIBRI (1624)
Girard Thibault d'Anvers – ACADEMIE DE L'ESPEE or "ACADEMY OF THE SWORD" (1630)
PALLAS ARMATA: THE GENTLEMAN'S ARMOURY (1639)
Francesco Alfieri – L'ARTE DI BEN MANEGIARRE LA SPADA (1653)
Charles Besnard – LE MAISTRE D'ARME LIBERAL (1653)
Johann Georg Passchen – VOLLSTANDIGES RING-BUCH (1659)
John Dryden – The Conquest of Granada by the Spartans (1670-1672)
Johannes Georges Bruchius – "OF THE SINGLE RAPIER" (1671)
Nicolaes Petter – KLARE ONDERRICHTINGE DER VOORTREFFELIJKE WORSTEL-KONST (1674)
Alvaro Guerra de la Vega – COMPREHENSION OF DESTREZA (1681)
Sir William Hope – THE SCOTS FENCING MASTER (THE COMPLETE SMALLSWORDSMAN) (1687)
Sir William Hope – ADVICE TO HIS SCHOLAR FROM THE FENCING MASTER (1692)
Sir William Hope – COMPLEAT FENCING-MASTER (1692)
Sir William Hope – THE SWORDSMAN'S VADE-MECUM (1694)
Diederich Porath – PALAESTRA SVECANA (1693)
D. Nicolas Tamariz – CARTILLA Y LUZ EN LA VERDARERA DESTREZA (1696)

1700-1799

Monsieur L'Abbat – THE ART OF FENCING, OR, THE USE OF THE SMALL SWORD (1734)
Capt. John Godfrey – A TREATISE UPON THE USEFUL SCIENCE OF DEFENCE (1747)
Henry Angelo – HUNGARIAN & HIGHLAND BROAD SWORD (1798)

1800-1899

Joseph Strutt – THE SPORTS AND PASTIMES OF THE PEOPLE OF ENGLAND (1801)
Col. Thomas Stephens – BROAD AND SMALL SWORD EXERCISES (1843)
Capt. M. W. Berriman – THE MILITIAMAN'S MANUAL AND SWORD-PLAY WITHOUT A MASTER (1861)
Richard F. Burton – A NEW SYSTEM OF SWORD EXERCISE FOR INFANTRY (1876)
Olivier de la Marche – TRAICTÉ DE LA FORME ET DEVIS COMME ON FAICT LES TOURNOIS (1878)
Major Ben C. Truman – THE FIELD OF HONOR (1884)
Alfred Hutton – COLD STEEL (1889)
Alfred Hutton – OLD SWORD-PLAY (1892)
Jolef Schmied-Kowarzik & Hans Kufahl – FECHTBUCHLEIN (1894)
John Starkie Gardner – FOREIGN ARMOUR IN ENGLAND (1898)

"*Never give a sword to a man who can't dance.*"

Confucius

The Fight Masters

Below are some of the Medieval and Renaissance Fight Masters. While not exhaustive, this list provides an introduction to the people who shaped fighting in Europe from about 1300 to 1900. They are listed in alphabetical order, but you refer to the Primary Sources, you can construct a timeline.

DALL'AGOCCHIE, GIOVANNI: This individual was from Balogna and was the fencing master of Fabio Pepoli, Count of Castiglione. The importance of this Master is in the fact that he explained the guards and blows of Marozzo. His work is dated 1572.

AGRIPPA, CAMILLO: (died 1595?) A famous 16th century Milanese gentleman, renowned as the author of the first treatise to introduce a desirable reduction in the vast number of fencing guards advocated by the masters of his day. Though born in Milan, Agrippa lived and worked in Rome, where he was associated with the Confraternity of St. Joseph of the Holy Land and the literary and artistic circle around Cardinal Alessandro Farnese. He is most renowned for applying geometric theory to solve problems in armed combat. In his Treatise on the Science of Arms with Philosophical Dialogue (published in 1553), he proposed dramatic changes in the way swordsmanship was practiced at the time. He also simplified Achille Marozzo's eleven guards down to four: prima, seconda, terza and quarta, which roughly correspond to the hand positions used today in the Italian school. He is also regarded as the man who most contributed to the development of the rapier as a primarily thrusting weapon. An architect, mathematician, and engineer, he was not primarily a Master of Fence, nor was this his livelihood. Thus he brings a very pragmatic and mathematical viewpoint to fencing that is very different from some others of his time. A contemporary of Michelangelo, the two were probably acquainted (or so Agrippa claims in his later treatise on transporting the obelisk to the Piazza San Pietro).

ANGELO, DOMENICO: (1717-1802) Born Domenico Angelo Malevolti Tremamondo in Leghorn, Italy, Domenico studied fencing in France. Soon after arriving in England he established Angelo's School of Arms in Carlisle House, Soho, London. There he taught the aristocracy the fashionable art of Swordsmanship which they had previously had to go the continent to learn, and also set up a riding school in the former rear garden of the house. He was fencing instructor to the Royal Family. With the help of artist Gwyn Delin, penned the chief work in English literature concerning the use and practice of the small sword. His School of Fencing (1763), considered the foremost text on small sword play, contains some of the best plates on the topic and is quite straight forward in its presentation and techniques. He then handed his school over to a son and established himself at Eton, where his family continued to teach fencing for three more generations.

BESNARD, CHARLES: A renowned seventeenth century French teacher and master of the "Academie Royale d'Arms," best known for his introduction of the "reverence," the practice of formally saluting one's opponent before a bout. Published in 1653, he is alleged to have coined the word flurette, the French word for foil. His book did so much to advance the Art of Fencing in France that it was considered by the French and English to take first place as a school for the science, a position formerly held by Italy.

BONETTI, JERONIMO: Not much is known of this master. He was the son of Rocco Bonetti and was killed by an Englishman named Cheese. He succeeded his father as the master of the fencing school at Blackfriars prior to it being rented to Shakespeare.

BONETTI, ROCCO: Master of a school of fence at Blackfriars in London during the late 1500's. At one time a Captain in the service of Venice, he came to England in 1569. There is some evidence that he was involved in low level espionage, carrying messages at some point during his stay in England. He set up a school in London in 1576, and his patrons included Sir Walter Raleigh and one of the Queen's best swordsmen, Lord Peregrin Willoughby, both men of high stature. His success was not well received by the English Masters, including George Silver. Bonetti was critically injured by Austen Bagger, an Englishman, outside of the school in 1587.

CARRANZA, HIERONIMO DE: (d. 1600) Deemed the father of the Verdadera Destreza, the Spanish science of fence, a fantastical style basing its principals on seemingly irrelevant mathematical principles (1569). It used angles, arcs and related tangents, a knowledge of geometry and natural philosophy. It was claimed that a comprehensive knowledge of his principles must infallibly lead to victory. In 1577, he published a text on the laws of injury and the proper and honorable ways to deal with insults. Carranza is also connected with the literary and artistic School of Seville.

Capo Ferro, Ridolfo: The great sixteenth century Italian master. He appears to have hailed from Cagli in the Province of Pesaro e Urbino, but was active as a fencing master in nearby Siena, Tuscany. With the development of the bota lunga ("elongated blow" or the lunge), he changed the manner of fencing from the round, circling style of his predecessors to that of the direct linear style now mandated in competitive fencing. Although he wrote his theories and system of fencing in 1610, improvements were hardly made upon them by anyone until early in the eighteenth century. Capo Ferro's works are the pinnacle of Italian theory.

Dardi, Filippo di Bartolomeo: (died 1464) was a 15th century Italian fencing master. He was an expert not only on fencing, but also astrology, astronomy, geometry, and mathematics. In 1412, he was licensed as a fencing master and opened a school in Bologna (in via Pietralata). In 1434, he wrote a treatise on fencing and geometry, and was subsequently given a professorship in geometry at the University of Bologna. Though Dardi's treatise has since been lost, he influenced a great number of prominent 15th century masters, including Antonio Manciolino, Achilles Marozzo, Angelo Viggiani, and Giovanni dall'Agocchie. Dardi is often credited as the founder of the Bolognese school of swordsmanship, though there is evidence that he was preceded by earlier masters in the late 14th century.

English Masters of Defence: A guild of professional swordsmen established in 1540, under a patent granted by Henry VIII. Members were trained and tested in many different weapons, advancing through the ranks of *Scholar*, *Free Scholar*, and *Provost* before being tested for the degree of *Master*.

Fabris, Salvator: (1544-1618) A celebrated Italian master of the late sixteenth and early seventeenth centuries whose work dealt entirely with the practical application of swordsmanship in the fencing school, the duel, and the brawl. Born in or around Padua, his youth coincided with the flowering of the Italian school of swordsmanship, with early Italian masters like Achille Marozzo, Angelo Viggiani and Giacomo di Grassi still teaching. He worked as a fencing master in Italy as well as in Northern Europe. After employment with an Archbishop, Salvator entered the service of the king of Denmark, Christian IV from 1601 to 1606. It was the King himself who sponsored the publication of the treatise, putting his court painter, Jan Halbeeck, as well as others like Valeggio (whose signature also appears in the book's plates) at Fabris' disposal to refine the drawings of the book's handwritten edition. Fabris left the King's employment in 1606, and after traveling across Europe, returned to Italy to teach at the University of Padua. His renown at its peak, young noblemen from all over Europe came to Padua to be taught by him. He died at the age of 74 after fighting against malignant fever. On his deathbed, he bestowed his salle to senior student Herman, a German, who was later assassinated by a jealous colleague by the name of Heinrich. The chief significance of Fabris' treatise (1606) was the introduction and definition of the contra postura, as well as the definition and clarification of many previously half defined principles of fence, time, distance, circular parries and their deceptions, the disengagement, feints and opposition.

GIGANTI, NICOLOETTO: (Niccoletto, Nicolat; 1550s–after 1622) was a 16th–17th century Italian soldier and fencing master. He was likely born to a noble family in Fossombrone in central Italy, and later became a citizen of Venice. Little is known of Giganti's life, but in the dedication to his 1606 treatise he counts twenty seven years of professional experience (possibly referring to service in the Venetian military, a long tradition of the Giganti family). The preface to his 1608 treatise describes him as a Mastro d'Arme of the Order of St. Stephen in Pisa, giving some further clues to his career. In 1606, Giganti published a popular treatise on the use of the rapier (both single and with the dagger) titled Scola, Overo Teatro ("School or Fencing Hall"). This treatise is structured as a series of progressively more complex lessons, and is also the first treatise to fully articulate the principle of the stoccata lunga ("elongated thrust" or the lunge). In 1608, Giganti made good the promise in his first book that he would publish a second volume. Titled Libro secondo di Niccoletto Giganti Venetiano, it covers the same weapons as the first as well as rapier and buckler, rapier and cloak, rapier and shield, single dagger, and mixed weapon encounters. This text in turn promises two additional works, on the dagger and on cutting with the rapier, but there is no record of these books ever being published.

GRASSI, GIACOMO DI: One of the three premiere Elizabethan masters. A celebrated Italian master of the sixteenth century whose treatise obtained a great reputation for its clarity and simplicity (1570). Possibly his chief contribution to the science of fence was the consideration and definition of lines of attack, which became indispensable parts of later fencing treatises, modern fencing and stage combat terminology. He also favored a freer employment of the point against the older theories of swordplay. Grassi's work has been recognized as one of the systems most commonly followed in Europe during the last quarter of the sixteenth century.

HUNDFELD, MARTIN: (also Huntzfeld, possibly from Hundsfeld, a village some 20 km east of Würzburg; d. before 1452) An early 15th-century German fencing master. His teaching is recorded by Peter von Danzig in Cod. 44 A 8 and by Hans von Speyer in M I 29. Hundfeld is numbered among the "society of Liechtenauer" by Paulus Kal.

KAL, PAULUS: was a 15th-century German fencing master. He wrote that he studied martial arts under Hans Stettner von Mörnsheim, and was an initiate of the tradition of Johannes Liechtenauer. He was also attached as Schirrmeister to three different courts in his career, serving in various military capacities including commanding men in at least three campaigns. Perhaps his most significant legacy is an honor role of deceased masters included in the Bologna and Munich versions of his treatise, which he styled the Society of Liechtenauer (Geselschaft Liechtenauers). While several of these masters remain unknown, the majority wrote treatises of their own and Kal's list stands as an independent confirmation of their connection to the grand master. Kal's treatise is also interesting in that it represents the first attempt to illustrate parts of Liechtenauer's Record.

LIBERI, FIORE DEI: (Fiore dei Liberi, Fiore Furlano, Fiore de Cividale d'Austria; born c. 1350; died c. 1420s) was a late 14th century knight, diplomat, and itinerant fencing master. He was born in Cividale del Friuli, the son of Benedetto and scion of a Liberi house of Premariacco. He is the earliest Italian master from whom we have an extant martial arts manual. His Flower of Battle (Fior di Battaglia, Flos Duellatorum) is among the oldest surviving fencing manuals. Fiore wrote that he had a natural inclination to the martial arts and began training at a young age, ultimately studying with "countless" masters from both Italic and Germanic lands. Unfortunately, not all of these encounters were friendly: Fiore wrote of meeting many "false" or unworthy masters in his travels, most of whom lacked even the limited skill he'd expect in a good student. He further mentions that on five separate occasions he was forced to fight duels for his honor against certain of these masters who he described as envious because he refused to teach them his art; the duels were all fought with sharp swords, unarmored except for gambesons and chamois gloves, and he won each without injury. Based on Fiore's autobiographical account, he can tentatively be placed in Perosa (Perugia) in 1381 when Piero del Verde likely fought a duel with Pietro della Corona. That same year, the Aquileian War of Succession erupted and Fiore seems to have sided with the secular nobility against the Cardinal as in 1383 there is record of him being tasked by the grand council with inspection and maintenance on the artillery pieces defending Udine (including large crossbows and catapults). There are also records of him working variously as a magistrate, peace officer, and agent of the grand council during the course of 1384. After the war, Fiore seems to have traveled a good deal in northern Italy, teaching fencing and training men for duels. In 1395, he can be placed in Padua training the mercenary captain Galeazzo Gonzaga of Mantua for a duel with the French marshal Jean II le Maingre (who went by the war name "Boucicaut"). Fiore surfaces again in Pavia in 1399, this time training Giovannino da Baggio for a duel with a German squire named Sirano. Fiore was likely involved in at least one other duel that year, that of his final student Azzone di Castelbarco and Giovanni degli Ordelaffi, as the latter is known to have died in 1399. Sometime in the first years of the 1400s, Fiore composed a fencing treatise in Italian and Latin called The Flower of Battle (rendered variously as Fior di Battaglia, Florius de Arte Luctandi, and Flos Duellatorum). He kept expanding and revising this work, so several versions exist. The time and place of Fiore's death remain unknown.

LEBKOMMER, HANS: This German master wrote the earliest known extant book of fence sometime during 1529 to 1536. The title of his book is "Der Altenn Fechter an fengliche Kunst."

LIECHTENAUER, JOHANNES: was a 14th-century German fencing master. No direct record of his life or teachings currently exists, and all that we know of both comes from the writings of other masters and scholars.

LOVINO, GIOVANNI ANTONIO: This individual wrote a treatise in Milan some time during the 16th C. In particular it appears that he wrote and possibly dedicated his work to Henry III of France. Lovino was a Milanese.

MANCIOLINI, ANTONIO: Bolognese. He published his book "Opera Nova" in 1531. Like Marozzo, he covered many aspects of swordplay. Unlike marozzo he did not deal as much with the concept of honor and the duel. manciolino said that honour, law, reasons for the duel, etc. are a matter for the philosopher or the student of law, not the fencer.

MARCELLI, FRANCESCO ANTONIO: This Italian master taught in the mid to late 17th century. He teaches in a baroque rapier style with more parries that utilize dui tempi (two tempos).

MAROZZO, ACHILLE: A Bolognese fencing master who presented the first sound treatise on handling the sword in personal combat (1536). The book was one of the first of its kind, and although he mentions little about the use of the point, his illustrations show that the sword was used for both cut and thrust. His treatise represents the development of double fence and the general practice of swordplay in the late fifteenth and early sixteenth century. Marozzo's study included single dagger, single sword, sword and buckler, case of swords, sword and cloak, sword and dagger, and other combinations. Like most early masters he also covered polearms. Marozzo included a whole chapter on dedicated to honor.

McBANE, DONALD: A late seventeenth, and early eighteenth, century soldier and fencing master, author of The Expert Swordsman's Companion, 1728.

NARVAEZ, DON LUIS PACHECO DE: A student of Carranza who became the master of the Spanish school in the later part of the sixteenth and early seventeenth century. He offered his own reproduction of Carranza's work, where he verbosely expounded the dignified, but unrealistic principles of the Spanish school, basing his system on the imaginary circle.

PALLADINI, ACAMILLO: This master is a contemporary of of 16th C. Italian Masters such as Di Grassi and Saviolo. His work (Discorso sopra l'Arte della Scherma) is relatively unknown and unlike the works of Agrippa and Vigianni is devoid of mathematical and philosophical discussions. the primary elements that are of note in Palladini's work is the extension of the arm and the lunge.

PETER VON DANZIG: was a 15th-century German fencing master. He was counted among the 16 members of the "Society of Johannes Liechtenauer".

SANCT DIDIER, HENRI DE: Born to a noble family in Pertuis in the Provence region of France, son of Luc de Saint Didier, Saint Didier made his career in the French army, ultimately serving 25 years and seeing action in Piedmont, Italy from 1554–1555. He wrote of himself that he "lived his whole life learning to fight with the single sword" and eventually "reached a point of perfection" in his art. He published his book Traite Contenant les Secrets du Premier Livre sur l'Espee Seule etc. in 1573. He is the first known French master that acknowledged the supremacy of Italian theory. He taught how to hold the left hand in single sword some two years before Vigianni. However, he only taught counter attacks; no true parries. His book details how to disarm an opponent by siezing their sword.

SAVIOLO, VINCENTIO: (born c. 1540–1550, d. before 1599) The sixteenth century Italian fencing master who introduced the art of rapier-play to the court of Queen Elizabeth. Born in Padua, he traveled widely in his youth, ultimately learning both the Italian method of rapier fencing and possibly the Spanish system of *la Verdadera Destreza*. Saviolo arrived in England in 1590, and may have taken over the school of Rocco Bonetti. An eclectic, he taught a mixture of Italian and Spanish theory and practice. His book *His Practise, in Two Bookes* in 1595 was the first text on swordplay originally written in English. His system combined many of the newer practices of both the Italian and Spanish schools. He recognized the superiority of the point and taught the use of the thrust over the cut. Teaching in England for seven or eight years, he made quite an impression on the gentlemen of court. There are a number of anecdotes about Saviolo's activities in London, but as these are largely derived from the writings of his hostile critic George Silver, it's unclear how trustworthy they are.

SWETNAM, JOSEPH: (d. 1621) A Seventeenth century English fencing master and (self-described) tutor to the Prince of Whales. He was, by his own word, a Plymouth man who served in the army, primarily abroad. He noted that he studied mostly in London. And, he mentions that he had instruction from English, French and Italian masters. Although his treatise *The Schoole of the Noble and Worthy Science of Defence* (1617) provides no new or innovative developments in the science of fence, it is the first book penned by an Englishman dealing with rapier and dagger fence. He also emphasizes the use of "feigns" (feints). His practice goes back at least twenty years prior to his publication, and it is believed that the style of swordplay presented in his text is close to what may have been used by Shakespeare's players and their contemporaries. Called "the woman-hater", having authored the mysogonistic pamphlet *The Arraignment of Women* in 1615. Died abroad in 1621.

TALHOFFER, HANS: (Dalhover, Talhouer, Thalhoffer, Talhofer; b. ca. ca. 1410-15, d. after 1470) was a 15th-century German fencing master. His martial lineage is unknown, but his writings make it clear that he had some connection to the tradition of Johannes Liechtenauer, the grand master of the Medieval German school of fencing. Talhoffer was a well educated man who took interest in astrology, mathematics, onomastics, and the auctoritas and the ratio. He authored at least five fencing manuals during the course of his career, and appears to have made his living teaching, including training people for trial by combat. In 1433, Talhoffer represented Johann II von Reisberg, archbishop of Salzburg, before the Vehmic court. Talhoffer remained in the service of the archbishop for at least a few more years, and in 1437 is mentioned as serving as a bursary officer (Kastner) in Hohenburg. The 1440s saw the launch of Talhoffer's career as a professional fencing master. His first manuscript, the MS Chart.A.558, was a personal reference book created around 1443. The fencing manual portion is largely text-less and it may have been designed as a visual aid for use in teaching; in addition to these illustrations, it also contains an astrological treatise and a copy of Konrad Kyeser's famous war book *Bellifortis*. Serving the Königsegg family of southern Germany, some time between 1446 and 1459 he produced the MS XIX.17-3 for them This work depicts a judicial duel being fought by Luithold von Königsegg and the training that Talhoffer gave him in preparation, but it seems that this duel never actually took place. Talhoffer's name next appears in the records of the city of Zürich in 1454, where he was chartered to teach fencing in some capacity and to adjudicate judicial duels. The account notes that a fight broke out among his students and had to be settled in front of the city council, resulting in various fines. He seems to have passed through Emerkingen later in the 1450s, where he was contracted to train the brothers David and Buppellin vom Stain. He produced a significantly expanded version of the Königsegg manuscript for them. In 1459, Talhoffer commissioned a new personal fencing manual along the same lines as his 1443 work, but expanded with additional content and captioned throughout. He appears to have continued instructing throughout the 1460s, and in 1467 he produced his final and most extensive manuscript, Codex Icon 394a, for another of his noble clients, Eberhardt I von Württemberg.

THIBAUT, GIRARD: (ca. 1574–1629) was a 17th century fencing master and author of the 1630 rapier manual Academie de l'Espée, one of the most detailed and elaborate sources ever written on fencing. Thibault was born in or around 1574 in Antwerp, son of Hendrick Thibaut and Margaretha van Nispen. Hendrick Thibaut came from a well-known family in Ypres, living in Ghent and Antwerp before going into exile in the northern Netherlands (Henrick's eldest son, Christiaen, founded the noble family Thibaut van Aegtekerke). Thibault first studied swordsmanship in Antwerp under Lambert van Someron, who taught between the years of 1564 and 1584. In 1605, Thibault was a wool merchant in Sanlúcar de Barrameda, south of Seville on the Guadalquivir river, and the hometown of Jerónimo Sánchez de Carranza. There, he took an interest in swordsmanship, studying the Spanish rapier system of Destreza. Thibault died in 1629, a year before his masterpiece was finally published (despite the date on the title page of 1628, it was not published until 1630).

VIGGIANI, ANGELO: (Angelo Viziani, Angelus Viggiani; d. 1552) was a 16th century Italian fencing master. Little is known about this master's life, but he was been Bolognese by birth and seems to have been an initiate of the tradition of Filippo di Bartolomeo Dardi. He might also have been connected to the court of Charles V, Holy Roman Emperor. Viggiani first proclaimed the superiority of the thrust over the cut (1560). According to the preface, the Viggiani's dying wish to his brother Battista was that his treatise not be published for at least fifteen years. Thus, though it was completed in 1551, the first edition wasn't printed until 1575, when Lo Schermo was published, first in Venice, then the following year in Bologna (a presentation manuscript was completed in 1567 as a gift for Maximilian II, King of the Romans and later Holy Roman Emperor). Viggiani taught of the superiority of the thrust over the cut. His guard position lead to further developments of using a single sword in combat by always coming on guard with the right foot forward. He is also the father of the lunge which he called the punta sopramano (A "thrust over the hand" or the demi-lunge) which was an advancing of the right foot with the sword arm fully extended and the left arm lowered backward to provide a counter balance.

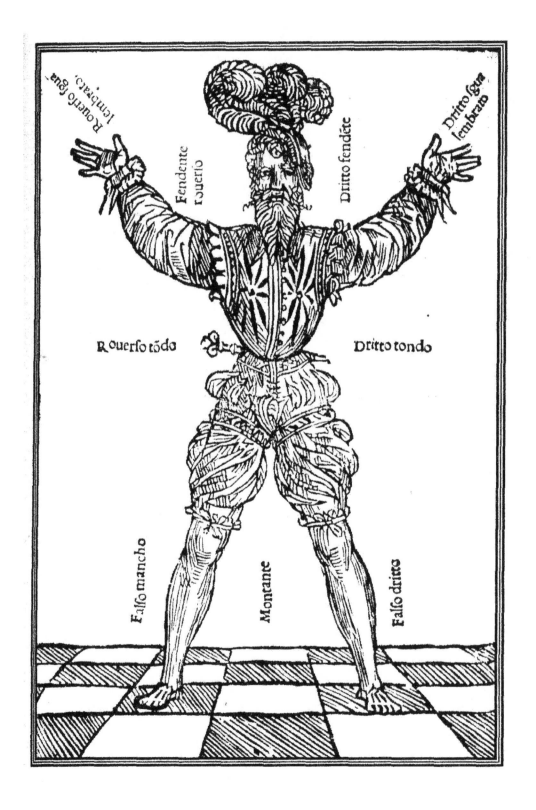

THE SWORDS

"Without a sign, his sword the brave man draws,
and asks no omen, but his country's cause."

Homer

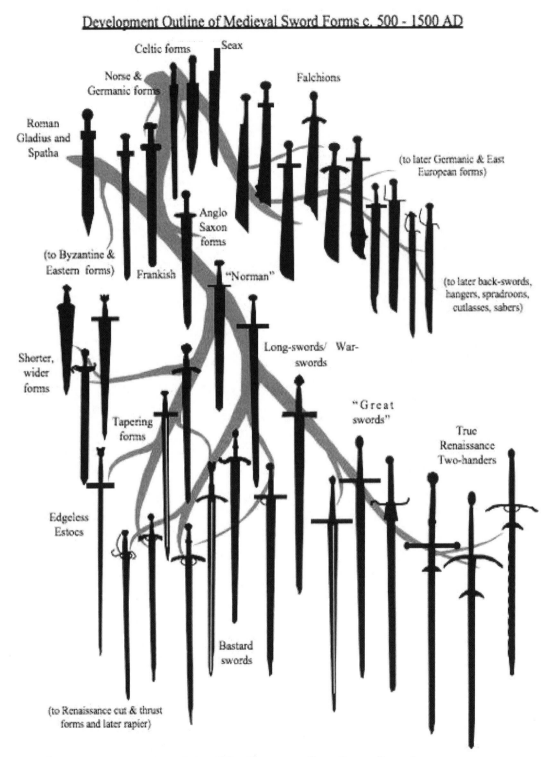

Development Outline of Medieval Sword Forms c. 500 - 1500 AD

Celtic forms

Seax

Norse & Germanic forms

Falchions

Roman Gladius and Spatha

(to later Germanic & East European forms)

Anglo Saxon forms

(to Byzantine & Eastern forms)

Frankish

"Norman"

(to later back-swords, hangers, spradroons, cutlasses, sabers)

Shorter, wider forms

Long-swords/ War-swords

"Great swords"

True Renaissance Two-handers

Tapering forms

Edgeless Estocs

Bastard swords

(to Renaissance cut & thrust forms and later rapier)

An outline cannot completely show all the relationships among all sword types. Some elements cross over among different classes, such length and hilts between tapering hexagonal or diamond blade shapes. This chart emphasis blade function and not simply hilt design.

Medieval & Renaissance Sword Forms: An Evolution

Medieval swords existed in great varieties over a number of centuries. Both experimentation and specialization in design was constant. But certain common characteristics can describe the "generic" medieval sword as a long, wide, straight, double-edged blade with a simple cross-guard (or "cruciform" hilt). It might be designed for one or two-hands. The typical form was a single hand weapon used for hacking, shearing cuts and also for limited thrusting. This style developed essentially from Celtic, Germanic, Anglo-Saxon, and late Roman (the spatha) forms. The Viking and early Frankish forms (the "spata") are also considered to be more direct ancestors. Medieval swords can be classified (typically by hilt design) into a great many categories by curators, collectors, and military historians. However, students & re-creationists today should prefer the actual historical terms. At the time, long bladed weapons were simply referred to as "swords", or for the longer ones often a "sword of war", "war-sword" (French Espée du Guerre or Epee du Guerre), or even a "long-sword". Various languages might call them by schwert, svard, suerd, swerd, espada, esapadon, or epee. When later worn on the belt by mounted knights they might be called an Arming-sword. Arming-swords were also considered "riding-swords" (also parva ensis or epee courte). It is this single-hand form which is so closely associated with the idea of the "knightly sword" (c. 1300). The challenge of armor in the Age-of-plate, forced many blades (both single-hand and longer) to be made narrower and pointier, but also thicker and more rigid. Ffrom at least the late 1300's in England, a single-hand blade of this form was referred as a "short swerde". In 15th century Germany it was the Kurczen swert. At this same time, as a result of the increased use of thrusting techniques some blades adopted guards with knuckle-bars, finger-rings, and/or sides-rings which lead to the compound-hilt. In later Elizabethan times, older one-handed medieval type blades became known as "short-swords" while the larger variety were still referred to as "long-swords". The term "short sword" was used later by 19th century collectors to refer to any style of "shorter" one-handed swords typically from ancient times on.

MEDIEVAL SWORDS

The Broadsword

A term popularly misapplied as a generic synonym for medieval swords or any long, wide military blade. The now popular misnomer "broadsword" in reference to Medieval blades actually originated with collectors in the early 19th century –although many mistranslations and misinterpretations of Medieval literature during the 19th & 20th centuries have inserted the word broadsword in place of other terms. They described swords of earlier ages as being "broader" than their own contemporary thinner ones. Many 17th-19th century blades such as spadroons, cutlasses, and straight sabers are classed as broadswords as are other closed hilt military swords. The weapon known as the true broadsword is in fact a form of short cutlass. The term "broadsword" does not appear in English military texts from the 1570s - 1630s and noes not show up in inventories of sword types from the 1630's, and likely came into use sometime between 1619 and 1630. Descriptions of swords as "broad" before this time are only incidental and the word "broad" is used as an adjective in the same way "sharp" or "large" would be applied. Leading arms curators almost always list the broadsword specifically as a close-hilted military sword from the second half of the 17th century. Those cage and basket hilted blades used by cavalry starting in the 1640's were in form, "broadswords". During this time a gentleman's blade had become the slender small-sword, whereas the military used various cutting blades. Today, arms collectors, museum curators theatrical-fighters, and fantasy-gamers have made the word broadsword a common, albeit blatantly historically incorrect, term for the Medieval sword.

Long-Swords

The various kinds of long bladed Medieval swords that had handles long enough to be used in two hands were deemed long-swords (German Langenschwert/ Langes Swert or Italian spada longa). Long-swords, war-swords, or great swords are characterized by having both a long grip and a long blade. We know at the time that Medieval warriors did distinguished war-swords or great-swords ("grant espees" or "grete swerdes") from "standard" swords in general, but long-swords were really just those larger versions of typical one-handed swords, except with stouter blades. They were "longer swords", as opposed to single-hand swords, or just "swords". They could be used on foot or mounted and sometimes even with a shield. The term war-sword from the 1300's re-ferred to larger swords that were carried in battle. They were usually kept on the saddle as opposed to worn on the belt. A 15th century Burgundian manual refers to both "great and small swords". As a convenient classification, long-swords include great-swords, bastard-swords, and estocs. In the 1200's in England blunt swords for non-lethal tournaments were sometimes known as "arms of courtesy". There is a reference to an English tournament of 1507 in which among the events contestants are challenged to "8 strookes with Swords rebated". Wooden training weapons were sometimes called wasters in the 1200's or batons in the 1300's and 1400's. Knightly combat with blunt or "foyled" weapons for pleasure was known as à plaisance, combat to the death was à lóuutrance.

Great-Swords

Those blades long and weighty enough to demand a double grip are great-swords. They are infantry swords which cannot be used in a single-hand. Originally the term "great-sword" (gret sord, grete swerde, or grant espée), only meant a war-sword (long-sword), but it has now more or less come to mean a sub-class of those larger long-swords/war-swords that are still not true two-handers. They were even known as Grete Swerdes of Warre or Grans Espees de Guerre. Although they are "two hand" swords, great-swords not are the specialized weapons of later two-handed swords. They are the swords that are antecedents to the even larger Renaissance versions. Great-swords are also the weapons often depicted in various German sword manuals. A Medieval great-sword might also be called a "twahandswerds" or "too honde swerd". Whereas other long-swords could be used on horseback and some even with shields, great swords however were infantry weapons only. Their blades might be flat and wide or later on, more narrow and hexagonal or diamond shaped. These larger swords capable of facing heavier weapons such as pole-arms and larger axes were devastating against lighter armors. Long, two-handed swords with narrower, flat hexagonal blades and thinner tips (such as the Italian "spadone") were a response to plate-armor. Against plate armor such rigid, narrow, and sharply pointed swords are not used in the same chop and cleave manner as with flatter, wider long-swords and great swords. Instead, they are handled with tighter movements that emphasize their thrusting points and allow for greater use of the hilt. Those of the earlier parallel-edged shape are known more as war-swords, while later the thicker, tapering, sharply pointed form were more often called bastard-swords. One type of long German sword, the "Rhenish Langenschwert", from the Rhenish city of Cologne, had a blade of some 4 feet and an enormous grip of some 14 to 16 inches long, not including the pommel.

Bastard Swords

In the early 1400's (as early as 1418) a form of long-sword often with specially shaped grips for one or two hands, became known as an Espée Bastarde or "bastard sword". The term may derive not form the blade length, but because bastard-swords typically had longer handles with special "half-grips" which could be used by either one or both hands. In this sense they were neither a one-handed sword nor a true great-sword/two-handed sword, and thus not a member of either "family" of sword. Evidence shows the their blade were typically tapered. Since newer types of shorter swords were coming into use, the term "bastard-sword" came to distinguish this form of long-sword. Bastard-swords typically had longer handles with special "half-grips" which could be used by either one or both hands. These handles have recognizable "waist" and "bottle" shapes (such grips were later used on the Renaissance two-handed sword). The unique bastard-sword half-grip was a versatile and practical innovation. Although, once again classification is not clear since the term "bastard-sword" appears to have not been entirely exclusive to those swords with so-called "hand-and-a-half" handles as older styles of long-sword were still in limited use. Bastard-swords varied and they might have either a flat blade or narrow hexagonal one for fighting plate-armor. Some were intended more for cutting while others were better for thrusting. Bastard swords continued to be used by knights and men-at-arms into the 1500's. Their hilt style leads toward the shorter cut & thrust sword forms of the Renaissance. Strangely, in the early Renaissance the term bastard-sword was also sometimes used to refer to single-hand armingswords with compound-hilts. A form of German arming sword with a bastard-style compound hilt was called a "Reitschwert" ("cavalry sword") or a "Degen" ("knight's sword"). Although these might have been forms of single-hand estoc.

The familiar modern term "hand-and-a-half" was more or less coined to describe bastards swords specifically. The term "hand-and-a-half sword" is often used in reference to long-swords is not historical and is sometimes misapplied to other swords (although during the late 1500's, long after such blades fell out of favor, some German forms of this phrase are believed to have been used). While there is no evidence of the term "hand-and-a-half" having been used during the Middle Ages, either in English or other languages, it does appear in the 16th century. In his 1904 bibliography of Spanish texts, D. Enrique de Leguina gives a 1564 reference to una espada estoque de mano y media, and a 1594 reference to una espada de mano y media. In the Ragionamento, the unpublished appendix to his 1580, Traite d Escrime ("Fencing Treatise"), Giovanni Antonio Lovino describes one sword as una spada di una mano et mana et meza (literally "hand and a half sword") which he distinguishes from the much larger spada da due mani or two-handed sword (the immense Renaissance weapon). The term spadone was used by Fiore Dei Liberi in 1410 to refer to a tapering long-sword and Camillo Agrippa in 1550 called the spadone a war sword. Later it was defined by John Florio in his 1598 Italian-English dictionary as "a long or two-hand sword".

Two-handed Swords

The term "two-hander" or "two-handed sword" (espée a deure mains or spada da due mani) was in use as early as 1400 and is really a classification of sword applied both to Medieval great-swords as well Renaissance swords (the true two-handed swords). Such weapons saw more use in the later Middle Ages and early Renaissance. Technically, true two-handed swords (epee's a deux main) were actually Renaissance, not Medieval weapons. They are really those specialized forms of the later 1500-1600's, such as the Swiss/German Dopplehander ("double-hander") or Bidenhander ("both-hander") or Zweihander / Zweyhander are relatively modern not historical terms. English ones were sometimes referred to as "slaughterswords" after the German Schlachterschwerter ("battle swords"). These weapons were used primarily for fighting against pike-squares where they would hack paths through lobbing the tips off the poles. In Germany, England, and elsewhere schools also taught their use for single-combat. In True two-handed swords have compound-hilts with side-rings and enlarged cross-guards of up to 12 inches. Most have small, pointed lugs or flanges protruding from their blades 4-8 inches below their guard. These parrierhaken or "parrying hooks" act almost as a secondary guard for the ricasso to prevent other weapons from sliding down into the hands. They make up for the weapon's slowness on the defence and can allow another blade to be momentarily trapped or bound up. They can also be used to strike with. The most well-known of "twa handit swordis" is the Scottish Claymore (Gaelic for "claidheamh-more" or great-sword) which developed out of earlier Scottish great-swords with which they are often compared. They were used by the Scottish Highlanders against the English in the 1500's. Another sword of the same name is the later Scots basket-hilt broadsword (a relative of the Renaissance Slavic-Italian schiavona) whose hilt completely enclosed the hand in a cage-like guard. Both swords have come to be known by the same name since the late 1700's. Certain wave or flame-bladed two-handed swords have come to be known by collectors as flamberges, although this is inaccurate. Such swords developed in the early-to-mid 1500's and are more appropriately known as flammards or flambards (the German Flammenschwert). The flamberge was also a term later applied to certain types of rapiers. The wave-blade form is visually striking but really no more effective in its cutting than a straight one. There were also huge two-handed blades known as "bearing-swords" or "parade-swords" (Paratschwert), weighing up to 12 or even 15 pounds and which were intended only for carrying in ceremonial processions and parades. In the 1500's there were also a few rare single-edged two-handers such as the Swiss-German Grosse Messer or later sometimes called a Zwiehand sabel.

The Estoc

A form of long, rigid, pointed, triangular or square bladed and virtually edgeless sword designed for thrusting into plate-armor was the estoc. Called a stocco in Italian, estoque in Spanish, a tuck in English, Panzerstecher or Dreiecker in German, and a kanzer in Eastern Europe. They were used with two hands and similar to great-swords (but were unrelated to later rapiers). They were used in two hands with the second hand often gripping the blade. Some were sharpened only near the point and others might have one or two large round hand guards. Rapiers are sometimes mistakenly referred to as tucks, and there is evidence that during the Renaissance some rapiers may have been referred to as such by the English. In French "estoc" itself means to thrust.

The Claymore

Identified with the Scot's symbol of the warrior, the term "Claymore" is Gaelic for "claidheamh-more" (great sword). This two-handed broadsword was used by the Scottish Highlanders against the English in the 16th century and is often confused with a Basket-hilt "broadsword" (a relative of the Italian schiavona) whose hilt completely enclosed the hand in a cage- like guard. Both swords have come to be known by the same name since the late 1700's.

The Falchion

A rarer form of sword that was little more than a meat cleaver, possibly even a simple kitchen and barnyard tool adopted for war. Indeed, it may come from a French word for a sickle, "fauchon". It can be seen in Medieval art being used against lighter armors by infidels as well as footman and even knights. The weapon is entirely European and not derived from eastern sources. More common in the Renaissance, it was considered a weapon to be proficient with in addition to the sword. The falchion is similar to the German Dusack (or Dusagge), and has been dubiously suggested as possibly related to the Dark Age long knife, "seax" (scramanseax), and even later curved blades such as sabres (or sabels). Similar to an Arabian "scimitar", the falchion's wide, heavy blade weighted more towards the point could deliver tremendous blows. Several varieties were known, most all with single edges and rounded points. A later Italian falchion with a slender sabre-like blade was called a "storta" or a "malchus". Another similar weapon in German was the saber or machete-like Messer. Large two-hand versions, called Grosse Messers, with straight or curved single-edged blades were known by 1500.

RENAISSANCE SWORDS

Cut & Thrust Swords

The term "cut and thrust sword" is a general one which can be applied to a whole range of blade forms (field swords, side swords, arming swords). However, the Renaissance military sword is generally characterized by a swept or compound-hilt, a narrow cut-and-thrust blade with stronger cross-section, and tapering tip. A direct descendant of the medieval knightly sword, the cut and thrust sword was used by lightly armed footmen as well as civilians in the 16th and 17th centuries. During this time they were employed against a range of armored and unarmored opponents. They were popular for sword & buckler and sword & dagger fighting. They utilized an innovative one-handed grip fingering the ricasso (a dull portion of blade just above the guard). Renaissance cut & thrust swords should not be referred to as "early Renaissance swords" since they were actually in use throughout the period. Military and civilian forms of them existed before, during and after the development of the rapier. For example, similar blades (with and without ricassos and compound hilts) saw use in the English Civil War and even later. They should also not be referred to as "sword-rapiers" or "early rapiers", although in a sense, some of them were. Renaissance cut & thrust swords were their own distinct sword type. Although sometimes considered a "transition" form, this is inaccurate as they were both the ancestor and contemporary of the rapier for which they are often misidentified. Some forms of cage & basket hilts blades are occasionally referred to as "riding swords" by collectors and curators, and sometimes even as "broadswords". However, the 16th century Italians did sometimes distinguish between spada da cavallo, or a blade for horsemen, spada da fante, an infantry sword for foot-soldiers, and later spada da lato (side sword), a civilian cut-and-thrust sword, a form of which only later became the rapier (in modern times sometimes called a stricia).

The Back-Sword

The back-sword or Backe swerd was a less-common form of single-edged renaissance military cut & thrust blade with a compound-hilt (side-rings or anneus, finger-rings, knuckle-bar, etc.). Most popular in England with a buckler or target from at least the 1520's, it was long enough for both mounted and infantry and favored because its single-edge designed allowed for a superior cutting blow. It was also popular in Germany. Back-swords may be related to later single-edged European blade forms and came in a variety of hilts and lengths. They also include later Hangers and hunting swords, as well as Mortuary-hilt and Walloon-hilt broadswords.

The Schiavona

A form of agile Renaissance cut & thrust sword with a decorative cage-hilt and distinctive "cat-head" pommel. So named for the Schiavoni or Venetian Doge's Slavonic mercenaries and guards of the 1500's who favored the weapon. They are usually single edged back-swords but may also be wide or narrow double edged blades. Some have ricasso for a fingering grip while others have thumb-rings. The Schiavona is often considered the antecedent to other cage hilt swords such as the Scottish basket-hilted "broadsword".

The Katzbalger

A form of one-handed sword with a shorter blade and "S" shaped guard. It was favored by pikemen and the Swiss/German Landesknetchs for fighting close in amidst pike-squares. Many were originally longer, wider blades which were cut down and remounted. The name likely derives from a word associated with cat- gut or cat-skin. Their lengths varied from short to mid-sized.

The Rapier

Popular in the late 16th and early 17th centuries, the rapier was a dueling weapon whose form was developed from cut and thrust swords. Its use was more brutal and forceful than the light sport fencing that we know of today. Originally, starting about 1470, any civilian sword was often referred to as simply a "rapier", but it quickly took on the meaning of a slender, civilian thrusting sword. There is also an English document from the 1500's that uses the term "rapier-sword" for advising courtiers how to be armed, indicating the understanding that there were new slender blades coming into civilian use. Eventually developing into an edgeless, ideal thrusting weapon, the quick, innovative rapier superseded the military cut & thrust sword for personal duel and urban self-defense. Being capable of making only limited lacerations, earlier varieties of rapier are still often confused with the cut and thrust swords which gave gestation to their method. As a civilian weapon of urban self-defense, a true rapier was a tip-based thrusting sword that used stabbing and piercing, not slashing and cleaving. True rapier blades ranged from early flatter triangular blades to thicker, narrow hexagonal ones. Rapier hilts range from swept styles, to later dishes and cups. It had no true cutting edge such as with military swords for war.

The Flamberge

terms411.jpg (3404 bytes)An unusual waved-bladed rapier popular with officers and upper classes during the 1600s. It was considered to look both fashionable and deadly as well as erroneously believed to inflict a more deadly wound. When parrying with the flamberge, the opponent's sword was slowed slightly as it passed along the length. It also created a disconcerting vibration in the other blade. The term flamberge was also used later to describe a dish-hilted rapier with a normal straight blade. Certain wave or flame-bladed two-handed swords have also come to be known by collectors as "flamberges", although this is inaccurate. Such swords are more appropriately known as "flammards" or "flambards".

The Small Sword

Sometimes known as a "court-sword", a "walking-sword", or "town-sword", small-swords developed in the late Renaissance as a personal dueling tool and weapon of self-defense. Most popular in the 1700's it is sometimes confused with the rapier. It consisted almost exclusively of a sharp pointed metal rod with a much smaller guard and finger-rings. Its blade was typically a hollow triangular shape and was much thicker at the hilt. Most had no edge at all, and were merely rigid, pointed, metal rods. They were popular with the upper classes especially as decorative fashion accessories, worn like jewelry. In a skilled hand the small sword was an effective and deadly instrument. Until the early 1800s it continued to be used even against older rapiers and even some cutting swords. It is the small-sword rather than the rapier which leads to the epee and foil of modern sport fencing.

Curved Blades

While it is the straight-bladed cruciform sword style that for both war and duel was perfected in Europe as no where else, curved swords were hardly unknown. Many forms were known from the ancient convex-bladed Greek kopis and Iberian falcatta, to the laengsaex curved Viking blade, as well as the short-sword/long-knife seax or scramsax. There is also the Medieval falchion and the German curved Messer, Grossmessr, and bohemian Dusask The Italians used the curved storta, the straight bladed but curved-edge braquemart and the curved badelair (baudelair, bazelair, or basilaire) as well as the short curved braquet. Finally, wide varieties of sabers, sabres, sabels, and cutlasses were used from at least the mid-1500's. Indigenous European curved sword forms such as the Czech tesak, Polish tasak, and Russian tisak were used since at least the 7th century.

Daggers

A common long dagger, "poignard" (poniard), or "pugnale" was a favored companion, carried en-suite with a sword or rapier as a backup weapon or even on its own. The dagger was lightweight, deadly, and elegant. Used primarily as a defensive weapon, dagger fighting was an art itself. Technically, a poniard was square or triangular shaped with no edge, while a dagger had a knife-like blade. Generally, daggers in the Middle Ages were employed point down, pommel up, while those in the Renaissance were used point up with the thumb placed on the hilt. Many later daggers for use with rapiers had elaborate guards and were specially designed for trapping and parrying.

Bucklers

The buckler (or Italian "rondash" or "bochiero") was a small, agile hand-shield. Used since medieval times, bucklers were round or even square, approx. 8-20" and made of metal, wood, or metal trimmed wood. A single handle (or enarme) was used to hold it in a fist grip and smack, deflect or punch at blows and thrusts. The edge could also be used to strike and block. Some had long metal spikes on the front to attack with. On some later bucklers metal hooks or bars were placed on the front to trap the point of an opponent's rapier. More popular for a method of 16th sword & buckler fighting, they declined in use during the early 17th century as they were inconvenient for urban wear and faster rapiers outmaneuvered them.

The Targe

A targe/targa (or Italian "rondella") was a small wooden shield with a leather cover and leather or metal trim. Some were also covered with metal studs or spikes. Unlike bucklers, targes were worn on the arm as with typical shields. They were also usually flat rather than convex. Though associated with the Scots, the word "targe" actually comes from small "targets" placed on archery practice dummies. Some forms of medium sized steel shields from the Renaissance are often classed as targes. In England in the 1500s & 1600s, "target" was a common term for any small shield.

Longsword

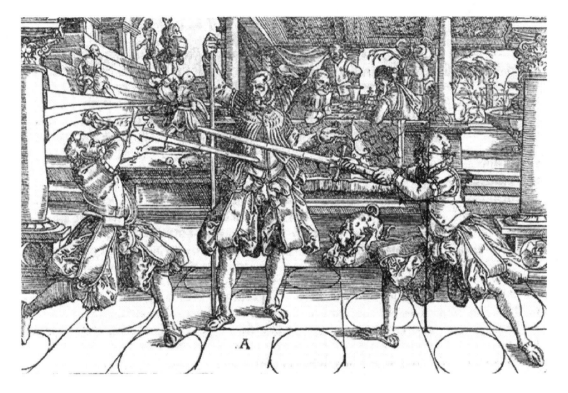

Divisions of the Sword to the Weak and Strong

The Sword is firstly divided in two parts, namely from the grip to the middle of the Blade which is known as the Strong, from the middle to the most forward, is the Weak furthermore is the sword divided in four parts how the figure below this shows.

With the inward part, that is the haft, and (with it) the work with the pommel and cross and haft will be understood, in the next part, thereafter will the work with cutting and pushing and what belongs to the Strong be understood, to the third part of the sword should be noted the alterable work of the Weak and Strong after opportunity and liking. Which alone is extremely weak for you to work properly to the Openings. *(Meyer 1560, Maurer translation 2012)*

THE RAPIER

"Understanding is a three-edged sword. Your side,
my side, and the truth."

J. Michael Straczynski

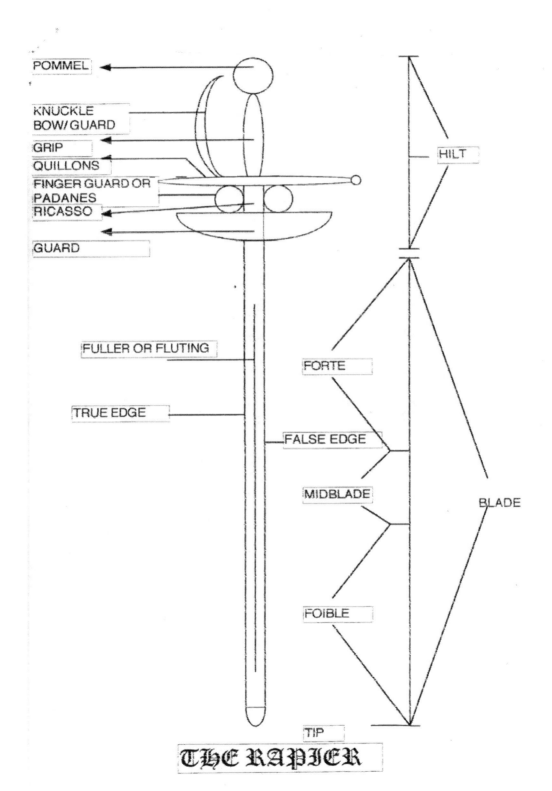

POMMEL

KNUCKLE
BOW/GUARD

GRIP

QUILLONS

FINGER GUARD OR
PADANES

RICASSO

GUARD

HILT

FULLER OR FLUTING

FORTE

TRUE EDGE

FALSE EDGE

MIDBLADE

BLADE

FOIBLE

TIP

THE RAPIER

A Brief Glossary of Italian Rapier Concepts

By Tom Leoni

Introductive Remarks

"Sword" or "Rapier"? Interestingly enough, the Italians, perhaps the highest exponents of the "classical" rapier, had no specific term for this kind of weapon. Continuing a tradition that had started centuries before late-16th-early17th century fencing masters such as Salvator Fabris, Francesco Alfieri and Ridolfo Capoferro, any sort of sword appearing in Italian manuals was simply called….spada ("sword"). One of the few exceptions was the Spadone, essentially a long-sword primarily for war rather than a duelling or urban self-defense tool.

So, lacking an explicit indication from the authors, what makes certain Italian sword manuals "rapier" manuals? Is it the physical style of the sword, sporting a rather long, slim, tapering blade and a complex hilt? Is it the style of swordsmanship, featuring mostly in-line, single-blow attacks? Is it that other Countries' Maestri identified any Italian swordsman of the time as a rapierist just by virtue of being Italian?

The answer to these questions is nebulous. The original Italian edition of Di Grassi (Venice, 1570), for instance, was written in the tradition of the Bolognese *spada da filo* or *spada da lato* (side-sword or short sword). In Di Grassi's manual, the blades are short, slender, and tapering with simple hilts of side-rings. Di Grassi's manual was not a "rapier" text, but a fencing manual clearly in the Bolognese cut-and-thrust tradition. But when it was translated into English, it "became" a "rapier" manual. Conversely, the work of the Milanese master Camillo Agrippa a few decades earlier is decidedly rapier in style, although it features almost the same late-medieval cruciform sword.★

I believe the correct approach, as followed by modern Renaissance martial arts revivalists, should be to take all aspect of "rapier" – the physical sword and the swordsmanship style – into consideration. As with all *post factum* definitions, we should not be too strict in our demarcation of the parameters of what, in this case, makes a rapier a rapier.

There were many types of sword and many different ways of using the same type. Perhaps my most satisfactory answer to this dilemma is this. A rapier is like the old definition of obscenity –you know it when you see it. For now, I will confine my discussion (and my terminology) to the authors that are recognized as the primary classical Italian "rapier" authors: Giganti, Capoferro, Alfieri and, above all, Fabris.

★*George Silver in 1599 lamented how a certain "Giacomo" was spreading Italian rapier fencing in England like a sort of foreign plague. If, however unlikely, he was indeed referring to an aged Giacomo Di Grassi and his "conservative" cut and thrust style, we might wonder what would he have said of Fabris?*

The Sword And Its Parts

"The knowledge of the sword is the first half of fencing: it teaches us to become familiar with the sword in order to handle it properly." (Capoferro, Chapter III)

Italian rapier masters insisted that the knowledge of the sword is an essential element of successful fencing. Hence the need to name and classify its many components.

FORTE This is the half of the blade closer to the swordsman's hand. It is the defensive part of the sword with which virtually all successful parries are executed. The forte has no offensive role in traditional Italian rapier theory, so much so that Capoferro states that it would not matter whether it sported an edge at all.

DEBOLE (FOIBLE) This is the half of the blade incorporating the tip. It is the offensive part of the sword with which all attacks are executed. According to traditional Italian rapier theory, this section of the blade should almost never be employed defensively, especially against cuts. The one exception is noted below under terza.

TEMPERATO This word is employed by Alfieri to describe the middle section of the blade.

FILO DRITTO (TRUE EDGE) The edge of the sword on the same side as one's knuckles. This is the part of the blade with which most parries and cutting attacks are performed, according to virtually all classical Italian rapier masters.

FILO FALSO (FALSE EDGE) The edge of the sword opposite the true edge. The role of this part of the blade is somewhat more limited than that of the true edge. However, there are some cuts that are delivered with this edge, primarily ascending diagonal cuts (falsi, see section below on cuts). As far as defensive play, Capoferro concedes that in rare cases, the false edge may be used in parries.

PIATTO (FLAT) The "side" of the sword, i.e. the flat part of the blade on either side, between the two edges. This part of the sword has no active role in traditional Italian rapier play, as no offensive or defensive action involve it directly.

FINIMENTO, FORNIMENTO, (THE GUARD OF THE HILT) This is the part of the hilt consisting of differently-shaped bars and branches or (later) of the cup. Its role extends beyond the obvious one – the protection of the hand. Fabris makes a very successful use of the guard's mass and width to literally shut the opponent's blade out of line in the course of an attack.

The sections of the blade (using Fabris' four quarters)

PRIMA (FIRST) In the division of the blade, this is the quarter closest to the swordsman's hand. It is the strongest part of the blade and, for this reason, it is the preferred part of the sword with which to execute parries. The prima and the seconda have no offensive role in traditional Italian rapier play.

SECONDA (SECOND) In the division of the blade, this is the quarter that goes from the end of the first part to mid-sword. This section of the sword, like the previous one, is exclusively used for defense, although it is not as strong as the prima. The reason for this is both structural and mechanical. Structurally, any well-made blade tapers progressively from the hilt to the tip, thus becoming increasingly flexible; mechanically, the greater the distance between any point along the blade and the swordsman's hand, the less the leverage when meeting another blade. The prima and the seconda together constitute the sword's forte (see definition above).

TERZA (THIRD) In the division of the blade, this is the quarter that goes from mid-blade to half-way to the tip. It is almost entirely useless for parries (especially against cuts), although it can be successfully opposed to the fourth part of the opponent's blade when parrying a thrust. Its primary role is an offensive one: when used together with the fourth part in adding a "slicing" motion to the percussive action of a cut, it can make such a blow very effective, as Fabris reminds us in chapter 3.

QUARTA (FOURTH) In the division of the blade, this is the fourth incorporating the sword's tip. Its role is essentially offensive, as it is the part responsible for delivering both thrusts and cuts (see above). The terza and quarta together constitute the sword's debole (see definition above).

Why divide the blade in so many parts?

Although Italian masters disagree as to the exact number of parts into which to divide the blade (e.g. Capoferro = 2; Fabris = 4; Alfieri = 5), they all place an enormous emphasis on the need for the swordsman to know that each section has its own peculiar role. In other words, these masters viewed the sword as a highly sophisticated tool possessing many parts, each one of which, in turn, possessed its specific function. For instance, Fabris, who divides the blade into four sections, assigns to each a specific degree of usefulness as far as defense or offense; had he only distinguished between debole and forte, many of the subtleties inherent in his style would not be possible. Even Capoferro, who, in his usual pragmatic style states that it is enough to divide the blade between forte and debole (two sections) though later in the book finds the need to further subdivide the debole. Alfieri, who divides the blade in five parts, de facto utilizes the sword in a similar manner to Fabris, even finding it necessary to explain how Salvator Gran Maestro divided the blade.

The Guards

In 1553, the Milanese Camillo Agrippa did away with the myriad of fancy-named guards of *spada da lato* and codified four guards that were to remain the mainstay of fencing for at least another two centuries. For this and many other reasons, Agrippa may be considered one of the true pioneers of the rapier style.

GUARDIE (GUARDS) Postures of the feet, body, arm(s) and sword possessing the desired characteristics to fulfill various tactical purposes of defense and offense. Italian rapier guards derive their properties from the position of the sword-hand (prospettiva, or "perspective").

PRIMA (FIRST) Any guard featuring the thumb-down position in the sword hand. The reason why it is called "first" is because it is the first natural position the hand assumes after pulling the sword from the sheath and pointing it towards the opponent. The *prima* is an inherently high guard, so it tends to defend the upper body and the head rather well, although it leaves the legs exposed. For this reason, Fabris prefers the *prima* in sword and dagger rather than sword alone. Defensively, this guard is particularly effective against cuts. Offensively, the *prima* is very formidable, since the thrusting attacks launched from this position proceed naturally downward, thus possessing great momentum. The *prima*'s main drawback is the fact that it tends to tire the arm.

SECONDA (SECOND) Any guard featuring the palm-down position in the sword hand. Since the blade's true edge naturally faces to the outside, this guard is particularly effective to shut the opponent out of line to that side. Although not as high as the prima, the seconda provides excellent defense to the upper body without tiring the arm as much as the previous guard. Offensively, many good attacks can be performed from this guard, since it lends itself to flexibility as far as forming angles and, therefore, can take advantage of even the most unusual openings the opponent may offer. As an interesting aside, Capoferro, in Chapter X of *Gran Simulacro*, vilifies the *prima* and the *seconda* to the point that Alfieri finds himself compelled to refute him rather harshly 30 years later.

TERZA (THIRD) Any guard featuring the knuckles-down position in the sword hand. This is probably the preferred position in classical Italian rapier, with Capoferro going as far as to state that the *terza* is the only guard (until the last chapter of his book, which has the strong flavor of an afterthought). Although virtually no parries are executed in terza (as the true edge faces downwards), it is a very flexible guard since the hand is half-way between the seconda and the quarta and can therefore quickly turn to either side to fulfill most defensive requirements. Ditto for attacks, few of which are actually carried out with the hand in third. Another of the many advantages of this guard is that it is the least tiring for the sword arm.

QUARTA (FOURTH) Any guard featuring the palm-up position of the sword hand. Fabris prefers *quarta* over all other guards, although in virtually all his examples of attacks, the fencers start out in *terza*. The main advantage of *quarta* is that it covers the inside line splendidly. Once the arm gets used to this position, the *quarta* is indeed an excellent guard. Offensively, it is the most-used hand-position in classical Italian rapier, with the austere Capoferro stating that the hand should always be in *quarta* when performing a typical lunge. Indeed, attacks in fourth are suitable for both the inside and the outside, thanks to the ease with which angles can be formed with the hand thus situated.

Mista, bastarda (Mixed, bastard) Any guard in which the hand and the arm are situated in between two (adjacent) of the above four positions. The most important mixed guard in Italian rapier is the one introduced by Alfieri, which shares of the third and the fourth.

Quinta, Sesta (Fifth, Sixth) Guards found in Capoferro's illustrations (marked by the letters E and F, page 44), otherwise not further described or identified by him or any of the classical Italian rapier masters.

Other terms pertaining to Guards and Posture

Dentro (Inside) The area to the left of the sword when in guard (assuming fencer is right-handed). Thus when two fencers face each other "to the inside", it means that each will see the opponent's sword to the left of his own. Fencing to the inside is the more used method in classical Italian rapier.

Fuori (Outside) The opposite of inside, i.e. the area to the right of the sword when in guard (assuming fencer is right-handed).

Over the right (or left) foot Any guard, unless specified, is formed with the right foot forward ("over the right foot"). According to classical Italian rapier theory, placing oneself in guard over the left foot (especially without a companion weapon) is counterproductive for two reasons: 1) it places the left leg in danger, since the forte of the sword is not nearby to protect it and 2) it leads to slow attacks because the right foot has to travel a greater distance as it passes forward. Fabris states that guards over the left foot are safest in sword and cloak, as the latter hangs low to protect the whole left leg.

Counterguards

Fencing, like chess, is not a static game, and one must adapt his play to the moves of the opponent in order to maximize effectiveness and minimize danger. Therefore, depending on what posture and strategy the opponent adopts, one should tailor his own to suit every particular situation. Hence the need of counterguards, or "counterpostures" (literally: postures to counter the opponent's guards).

Fabris devotes two whole chapters to the counterguard as one of the mainstays of his style (chapter 4 on sword alone and chapter [3-deest] of sword and dagger). According to Fabris, a counterguard (or counterposture) is a subtle adjustment of any of the main guards made to ensure that the line between the opponent's tip and one's body is completely covered by the forte of the sword. Counterpostures are to be formed outside the measure in order to ensure good defense once the "danger zone" is entered.

Nicoletto Giganti, in his Chapter 1, plainly states that while inexperienced fencers stand in guard, good ones stand in counterguard.

Some Masters' idea of a counterguard (e.g. Cavalcabo) is a guard itself rather than its adjustment. For example, he advocates using the fourth guard against a first, a second against a second, etc. By contrast, Fabris and Alfieri can tailor most guards to oppose any posture by the opponent by means of slight adjustments of the sword-arm and the angle of the wrist.

Regrettably, the concept of counterguards is one of the most overlooked in modern rapier studies.

Measures (Misura)

LARGA (WIDE, LARGE) The distance where, by lunging forward with the right foot, the opponent can be reached with the tip of the sword.

STRETTA (NARROW) The distance where, by bending the body forward, the opponent can be reached with the tip of the sword (without moving the feet). Both the larga and the stretta are widely used in Italian rapier, with the first being a "safer" distance (albeit conducive to slower attacks) and the second possessing the opposite benefits and drawbacks.

FUORI MISURA (OUT OF MEASURE) The distance between two opponents where neither can reach the other in a single tempo.

STRETTISSIMA (EXTRA-NARROW) Identified by Capoferro as the distance where, while in the misura larga, one can wound the opponent in the sword or dagger-hand (see also *mezzo tempo*).

PERFETTA (PERFECT) Identified by Alfieri as a sub-species of the *misura larga* where the necessary lunge to reach the opponent is not so long as to disrupt one's form and balance.

ROMPERE DI MISURA (BREAKING THE MEASURE) The act of retreating from one of the measures to out of measure.

GUADAGNARE LA MISURA, ENTRARE IN MISURA (GAINING THE MEASURE) The act of proceeding from out of measure to the misura larga, or from the misura larga to the *misura stretta* (close).

It is important to understand that the concept of "measure" is not absolute; rather, it is relative to one's size and ability. It oftentimes happens that two fencers of different height and skill face each other at a given distance and one is in measure, the other is not. This is because the first can reach the second by lunging with the right foot (by virtue of his longer limbs and/or his more developed ability) while the other is too small or unskilled to do so from the same distance. Needless to say, the first enjoys a tremendous advantage. So, say all the Italian Masters, practicing long and accurate lunges is a vital part of the swordsman's exercises in order to "shorten the measure" for oneself.

Advantage Of The Sword

Definition: a fencer has the advantage of the sword when his blade is situated in such a way as to enjoy the mechanical advantage of the lever when intersecting the opponent's. Key: when the two blades intersect, the one that is met closer to the hilt has the advantage. Example: if fencer A places the second part of his blade against B's third part, A enjoys the advantage of the sword.

The advantage of the sword is extremely important in classical Italian rapier, and all the attacks, defenses, guards and counterguards depend on this subtle hinge-point.

TROVAR DI SPADA (FINDING THE SWORD) The art of placing one's blade against the opponent's (without actual contact!) so as to enjoy the advantage of the sword. "He who has more of his sword into the opponent's (no matter by how little) will have the advantage of the sword" (Fabris, Chapter 9). Between two experienced fencers, the one who manages to find the opponent's sword usually enjoys an enormous defensive and offensive advantage.

Synonyms: *trovar di spada, occupare la spada, guadagnare la spada, acquistare, coprire*, etc.

FREE SWORD, KEEPING THE SWORD FREE (SPADA LIBERA) Preventing the opponent from finding one's sword. This can be accomplished by attempting to gain the advantage oneself, by keeping the sword away from the opponent's (especially feasible when fencing with a companion weapon) or by breaking the measure. Keeping the sword free is essential towards succeeding in a bout, according to Fabris.

PERDER LA SPADA (LOSING OF THE SWORD) If A finds B's sword, B has "lost the sword". Not a situation to find oneself in, according to classical Italian rapier theory.

Footwork

PIE' FERMO (FIRM-FOOT) This term applies to all offensive footwork where at least one foot remains static (exception: the girata). The typical lunge with the right foot falls within this category, as the left foot remains in its place.

PASSATA (PASS) A series of resolute steps towards the opponent (usually starting with the left foot) in the course of an attack. One of the advantages of the passata is that the first step reduces the distance from the opponent considerably; another is that its momentum oftentimes unsettles the opponent. All Italian rapier Masters consider the passata an extremely important technique to have in one's repertoire, although Fabris tells us that the lunge "a pie' fermo" was the more commonly used in anger.

PASSO GRANDE, PASSO PICCOLO (WIDE, SMALL STEP) The distance between feet while in guard. Fabris is an advocate of the small step, since it is conducive to a longer, more explosive lunge and keeps the right leg more protected. Capoferro's guards, on the other hand, feature a much wider step, with Alfieri being somewhere in the middle.

Passo straordinario (Extraordinary step) The distance between feet while performing a typical lunge – i.e. bringing one's feet more than a wide step apart. The theory on steps and their measures is explained in great detail by Agrippa.

Girata The act of turning one's body out of line while stepping forward in the course of an attack. Most commonly, a girata is performed by either stepping to the left with the right foot or by crossing the left foot behind the right one. The main drawback of these types of footwork is that the sword loses the "support" of the feet and body and can therefore be more easily pushed aside.

Timing

Tempo 1) A motion of the opponent within the measures that creates a momentary opportunity to attack. The concept of tempo incorporates elements of both time and motion. A tempo (Italian = time) is finite and must therefore be longer in duration than the time required for the attack. 2) The act of performing a single movement (e.g. 1-tempo parry-counterattack = the act of parrying and delivering a counterattacking blow in the same movement. Also called un tempo, stesso tempo).

Contratempo The art of beating the opponent as he tries to take advantage of a tempo you created. E.g.: you make a movement within the measures (= you "make a tempo"); he attacks (= "attack of tempo"), but, by doing so he himself makes a tempo; you are able to strike at him (with or without parrying) and save yourself.

Mezzo tempo (Half-tempo) Identified by Capoferro as the situation when one can make a quick strike at the opponent's sword hand. (See *Misura strettissima*).

Attacks

Ferita (Wound) Any action resulting in harming the opponent. This includes all cuts, thrusts, lunges or defensive counteractions (such as the "stop-thrust", an action described as early as Agrippa).

Distesa (lunge) A type of ferita a pie' fermo (see definitions) consisting of performing an extraordinary step with the right foot. Different Maestri call it by different names, although there is little or no technical difference between them. Capoferro's botta lunga, for instance, establishes some rather "fixed" canons as far as the length of the step, the placing of the limbs and the position of the hand. Fabris' distesa, instead is tailored to the specific situation as far as distance, placement of the body and position of the hand.

Passata (Pass) See definition above.

Punta One of the many terms for "thrust" (see below).

Taglio, also "coltellata" Cut (see sub-species below).

Thrusts

Stoccata (generic for thrust) This term is applied rather loosely to mean a thrust or even a lunge. Fabris utilizes this term (although not exclusively) to describe all thrusts, qualifying it with the position of the hand; e.g. stoccata di quarta = thrust with the hand in fourth position. Another common synonym is punta. Some Masters (e.g. Capoferro), restrict the meaning of "stoccata" to a thrust delivered with the hand in third.

Imbroccata (thrust from the first guard or position) This term is generally used to describe a thrust executed from the prima.

Other terms (*punta dritta, riversa*) Some Masters mention these other thrusts as sub-species proceeding, respectively, from the second and the fourth guards.

Cuts

These are blows of the edge as opposed to stabs with the point. Depending on the circumstance and blade used, they may or may not be intended as wounding actions.

Classification according to general direction:

Mandritto (Fore-hand) Any cut proceeding right-to-left (assuming the fencer is right handed).

Riverso (Back-hand) Any cut proceeding left-to-right (assuming the fencer is right handed). This cut is very dear to Alfieri, who employs it as an alternative tactic on most of his attacks.

Classification according to specific direction:

Tondo A cut proceeding on a perfectly horizontal plane. It can land at 3 o'clock of the target (mandritto tondo) or at 9 o'clock (riverso tondo).

Squalembrato A descending diagonal cut. It can land at 1–2 o'clock of the target (mandritto squalembrato) or at 10–11 o'clock (riverso squalembrato).

Fendente A descending vertical cut landing at circa 12 o'clock of the target. Depending on whether it proceeds slightly from the right or from the left, it can be mandritto fendente or riverso fendente.

Sottomano (Underhand) This is an ascending cut landing just right of 6 o'clock of the target. It is mentioned by Fabris and Alfieri.

Montante (Ascending) This is the common name assigned to a vertical ascending cut. Fabris and Alfieri, who also mention the sottomano, classify the montante as a cut landing just left of 6 o'clock of the target.

Ridoppio (literally = redoubled) In a strictly rapier context, this cut is mentioned by Capoferro as being a rapid succession of two generic mandritti: the first one to the opponent's sword (to get it out of the way), the second to his body.

Falso This is an ascending diagonal cut delivered with the false edge of the sword. It was used extensively by the 16th-Century Bolognese masters of Spada da filo such as Marozzo and Manciolino, but it makes an appearance on classical Rapier manuals. Falso dritto is the one landing at 5 o'clock of the target; falso manco the one landing at 7 o'clock.

Classification according to delivery method:

Dalla spalla (From the shoulder). This method of delivering any of the above cuts can be further sub-divided into two categories:

· Letting the shoulder swing the whole arm as it delivers the cut (similar to a tennis stroke). This gives the cut great momentum, but has the serious drawback of leaving the body open for a rather long time. For this reason, Fabris considers it the worst kind of cutting technique in rapier play.

· Keeping the arm and the wrist locked forward as the cut is delivered from the shoulder; in this manner, the motion of the arm (and the sword) is more controlled, although it does not give the cut quite the same impetus as the previous one. But the fact that such a cut never brings the sword completely out of line makes this delivery method one of the preferred one by Fabris and Alfieri. Also, the narrower motion is compensated by the fact that the whole weight of the arm contributes to the momentum of this cut.

Dal gomito (From the elbow) Any of the cuts can be delivered by keeping the shoulder (and the arm) locked and by just swinging the forearm and the wrist. This type of cut, although not making as wide an arc as the first one delivered from the shoulder, still brings the sword quite far out of line. For this reason, Fabris advises against it.

Dal polso, dal nodo della mano (From the wrist) This cut is delivered by keeping the whole arm locked forward (shoulder and wrist) and by swinging the sword in a small arc from the wrist. This type of cut is quick and does not open up the line too much; it is therefore one of Fabris' preferred methods of delivering cuts.

Stramazzone This cut, very dear to the pre-eminent 16th-Century Bolognese Maestri, is delivered from the wrist, and it makes the sword describe a whole circle not dissimilar to that described in a modern moulinee. Although Fabris does not use the term, he would include the stramazzone in the repertoire of cuts delivered from the wrist (and therefore advisable).

In order to specifically classify a cut, Maestri tended to use all three identifying criteria: general direction, specific direction and delivery method (not unlikely biology's Family,

Genus and Species). For example, a wide swinging cut landing horizontally on the opponent's right side should be classified as a riverso tondo from the shoulder.

Trading Sides

CAVAZIONE (TRADE) The act of "trading sides" with the opponent's sword, i.e. bringing the sword from the inside to the outside or vice-versa. This can be done both under and over the opponent's sword. It is similar (but not analogous) to the modern "disengage". One of the main differences is that the classical Fabris trade is almost always executed in the course of a forward thrust; the motion, therefore, ends up being "corkscrew-shaped", since it combines a forward motion and a semi-circular one.

One of the most serious modern misconceptions about the trade or cavazione is that of equating it with a circular parry. This idea originated in the 19th Century, when the first fencing historians such as Castle researched old martial arts texts in order to find the supposed "family tree" of contemporary fencing techniques. The classical Italian rapier cavazione is not a parry, although it can incorporate one if the tactical situation calls for it.

CONTROCAVAZIONE (COUNTERTRADE) The act of nullifying the effect of an opponent's trade by performing one of your own, thereby ending on the same side of his sword as before the whole operation started.

RICAVAZIONE (RE-TRADE) The act of nullifying the effect of an opponent's countertrade by performing one additional trade, thereby ending on the same side as after the first trade.

MEZZA CAVAZIONE (HALF-TRADE) The act of interrupting a trade in the middle, ending in most cases with the sword underneath the opponent's.

COMMETTERE DI SPADA (COMMITMENT OF THE SWORD) The act of performing a trade, then returning the sword on its original side.

Other Actions

ATTACCARE DI SPADA (ATTACHING SWORDS) The act of pushing forcefully against each other's blade in order to – eventually – shove the opponent's sword out of the way. This, according to Fabris, is a very poor technique that can make a sword bout degenerate into a wrestling match. For this (and many other reasons), Fabris advocates never to make contact with the opponent's blade unless forced to parry.

CEDERE DI SPADA (YIELDING OF THE SWORD) The act of ceding to the pressure of the opponent's blade while attaching swords (see above), in order to let the opponent's sword fall out of line while your own goes to the attack. Fabris advocates this technique as the best one to adopt in the event of an attachment of swords.

Schivar di vita (Voiding) The act of voiding the opponent's sword by bringing one's body out of line (e.g. with a side-step). Knowing how to void is one of the most essential aspects of 16th–17th-Century Italian swordsmanship (not just rapier).

Finta (Feint) The act of giving the opponent the impression of attacking a part of his body in order to cause him to create an opening as he goes for the parry. A feint generally involves a "fake" target (where one initially pretends to strike) and a "real" one (where the attack eventually lands). Fabris, who perhaps has the best section on feints, admonishes us that the "fake" target should nonetheless be a realistic one, in case the opponent does not fall for the feint and fails to move for the parry.

Chiamata, invito (Invite) The act of deliberately making a tempo or offering an opening to the opponent in order to lure him to attack – and then beat him with a contratempo (see definition). Be careful not to make too wide an opening as you perform an invite, says Fabris; otherwise, the likelihood of a "double" is very real.

Mutazione (Mutation) A movement or change of posture performed outside the measures. The same thing performed within the measures becomes a tempo (see definition).

Conclusion

In this glossary, I have listed most components of classical Italian rapier play. For the sake of brevity, I have omitted their specific tactical *raison d'etre* as well as the description of their proper technical execution. For a deeper insight on any of these terms and their tactical/technical context, please refer to the following primary sources:

Salvator Fabris, Lo schermo, overo Scienza d'armi, Copenhagen, 1606
Francesco Alfieri, La scherma, Padova, 1640
Ridolfo Capoferro, Gran simulacro dell'arte e dell'uso della scherma, Siena, 1610
Camillo Agrippa, Trattato di scienza d'armi, Roma, 1553

Smallsword Parts

"There are only two forces in the world, the sword and the spirit. In the long run the sword will always be conquered by the spirit."

Napoleon Bonaparte

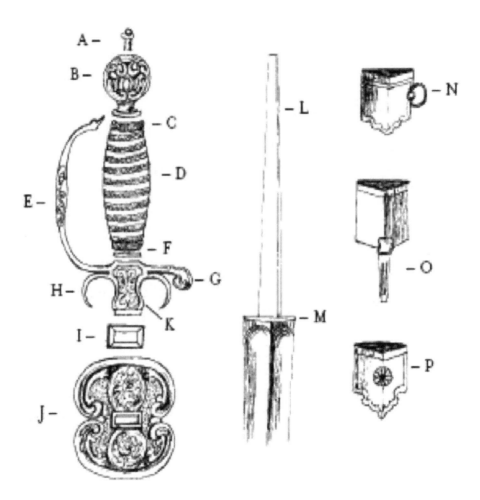

A. Pommel nut
B. Pommel
C. Ferrule (Turk's head) on grip
D. Grip
E. Knuckle guard (knuckle bow)
F. Grip washer
G. Quillon connected to quillon block or cross
H. Arms of the hilt
I. Ricasso washer
K. Ricasso
J. Shell guard
L. Tang of the blade

M. Heel or shoulders of the blade
N. Upper section of the furniture of the scabbard, mounted with a ring
O. Upper section of the furniture of the scabbard, mounted with a hook
P. Upper section of the furniture of the scabbard, mounted with a button

[Taken from "The School of Fencing"
edited by Jared Kirby, 2005]

The weapon most linked to modern fencing, it is the deadliest of swords. Not particularly sharp along the first two-thirds of its blade, it is flexible in its upper third so it may bend and do more damage once it enters the body. A thrusting weapon.

The Smallsword is composed of two principle parts: the Blade and the Hilt.

• The Blade —made of steel with a variety of cross sections (typically triangular). The blade is divided into three distinct parts:
1. The Forte, that 1/3 of the blade closest to the guard which is the strongest part.
2. The Middle, the place of the blade that delineates its equal division.
3. The Foible, which is the weakest part.

• The Hilt — is composed of three parts:
1. The Guard (Coquille), can be in a variety of shapes such as round, oval, solid figure-eight or hollow figure-eight.
2. The Grip or Handle, is straight and may have a variety of wrappings (leather, wire, etc). It should be of a length to position the pommel at the wrist of the swordsman.
3. The Pommel (Pommeau), holds the weapon together and serves as a counter-weight.

Many of the terms used in Smallsword fighting can be found in the Glossary.

THE GLOSSARY

"The sword is the axis of the world and its power
is absolute."

Charles de Gaulle

A few notes on these definitions.

First, a massive heap of gratitude to Dale Girard, who complied the vast majority of these terms for his Fight Master's Companion. His work is meant as a reference guide for theatrical fight directors. I have done my level best to remove theatrical terms from the text, but there may be a stray allusion to a John Wayne punch or Errol Flynn-style swordplay, to make this a purely historical guide. That said, with so many years covered, the numbering system most often referenced is the modern accepted one, purely for ease of understanding.

Secondly, the Romans. I love Rome, and certainly I don't want to ignore the Romans, But were I to include every Roman military and gladiatorial term, this volume would be three times the size. This collection of terms is primarily focused on Medieval, Renaissance, and Enlightenment combat. There are a few basic words, such as Gladius here, but for the most part I have avoided the Romans, who should (and probably do) have their own volume.

Thirdly, the Germans. While so many of the fightbooks we have today were written by Germans, and therefore use German terms, seldom do those terms reach the mainstream of the fighting world. Thus for this volume I have kept mostly to the language of the sword - Romance languages. For anyone interested, I will be happy to e-mail a separate list of German fight terms.

Finally, please forgive any infelicities in the editing. This was a labor of love, done in my spare moments over the last six months. It will not be perfect.

-DB

A

A Propos: An opportune moment to launch an attack.

Abate: a.) To beat the edge or point of a blade back; to turn the edge, to take off the edge, to blunt. A dulled, blunted or rebated blade.
b.) To beat down, throw down, demolish, or destroy. c.) To bring down (a person) physically, socially, or mentally; to depress, humble, degrade; to cast down, and/or deject.

Absence of Blades: a.) A state in which the sword blades are not in contact. See Free. b.) (also Absence of the Blade) An event where blade contact is avoided, either deliberately by refusal to engage, or in deceiving the opponent's attempt to find the blade.

Abuse: Offense, insult, injury.

Accomplice: (also Complice) Cooperator, fellow in arms.

Accomplish: To equip or be armed perfectly.

Achieve: To gain or succeed; to kill, to finish.

Acquired Parry: Another name for the Circular or Counter Parry due to the practice necessary to master the action.

Across: a.) The mark of an unskilled tilter who, instead of delivering a "head on" hit with the point of the lance, breaks the lance "across" his opponents breast plate. In tilting it was thought disgraceful to break the lance across the body of the adversary, instead of by the push of the point.
b.) Said of any guard in swordplay that aligns the blade of the weapon across the body, directing its point to the side opposite which the hand and hilt are placed.

Adjudicate: To act as a judge, or court of judgment.

Adjudication: The act of adjudging or determining the quality or state of something.

Adjudicator: One who determines the quality or state of something, or awards the prize in a competition. A judge.

Adjustment Step: a.) A small step intended to correct or realign the feet. Usually done very quickly. i.e. Recovery Forward from a Wide Stance. b.) Any step that is not part of a step definition or choreography and is performed for the explicit reason to fix a problem with either distance or angle.

Advance: (also *Fencing Step*) Footwork carrying the body forward by moving the lead foot first, followed with the lag foot (without crossing them). The opposite of *Retreat*. "The act of stepping forward toward your adversay, while on guard; the left foot instantly following the right so as that your primative posture is still preserved."

Advance-Lunge: See *Patinando*.

Adversary: An opponent or antagonist in single combat.

Affondo: (It.) An extending step thrust. See *Lunge*.

Affront: To face one's opponent in defiance. To stand.

A-field: (also *Afield*) a.) On or in the field of battle. b.) To or into the field; hence, to battle.

After-Cut: A cut on the riposte. See *Riposte*.

Aggressor: The person who sets upon, attacks, or assails another; the one executing the violent action.

Aids: (Also *Last Fingers*) The last three fingers on the sword hand which assist or aid the manipulators (thumb and forefingers).

Aim: a.) To point or direct a weapon. b.) The direction of a missile or of anything compared with it. c.) The point or target to which a weapon or missile is directed. d.) To cry "aim" is an expression borrowed from archery to encourage the archers by crying out aim, when they were about to shoot, and then in a general sense to applaud, to encourage with cheers.

Ala Stoccata: (It.) At the thrust.

Alarm: (Also *Alarum*) a.) Originating from

the cry of a medieval Italian sentry, who, upon spotting the approach of an enemy, would call out All'arme! literally meaning "To arms!" Anglicized originally to *Alarme*, the actual cry or call to arms, finally becoming the name of the call itself. b.) A summon to arms, notice of approaching danger. c.) To call to arms, to combat. d.) A state of war, hostile attack. e.) Combat, contention.

ALERT: A term derived from the Italian *all'erta, erta* meaning watchtower, hence, on watch.

ALIGNMENT: Essentially good posture, where the various parts of the body - head, shoulders, arms, ribs, hips, legs, feet - are all in correct relative position to one another. Proper alignment (sitting or standing) serves as the axis from which all movement begins.

AL LA MACCHIA: (*ala mazza*) Renaissance term for a less-formal rough-and-tumble duel "out in the woods", often by groups as well as individuals.

ALTA GUARDIA: Alferi's term for *Prima Guardia*.

ALTA LINEA: (It.) See *High Line*.

ALTO: (It.) Used in reference to the target at the upper part of the opponent's body; at the shoulder or chest level.

AMBUSCADO: An ambush, snare, trap; a surprise attack.

AMBUSH: a.) A covert to surprise the enemy. b.) The troops or persons posted in a concealed place.

ANGELO SLIP: A Slip Right which is preceded by a small lateral step with the right foot to the right.

ANGRIFF: (Ger.) See *Attack*.

ANNELETS: A term for the "arms-of-the-hilt", protective quillons rings over the *ricasso*.

ANNEU: The side-ring (ring guard or "port") on a compound-hilt.

ANSWER: a.) A Riposte. b.) To meet an aggressor in a fight; to return a hostile action.

ANSWERING BEAT: See *Return Beat*.

APPEL: (Fr.) (Literally "a call") a.) A stamping or slapping of the floor with the sole of the lead foot generally executed immediately before an attack or feint with the blade, often accompanied by a loud shout. The action is highly characteristic of both the historic and modern Italian school of fence. b.) (Small Sword) "A sudden beat with your right foot, by raising and letting it falll on the same spot, previous to, or at the instant of, making a feint against an adversary; thereby startling him and obaining some opening to deliver your intended thrust."

APPUNTATA: (It.) A remise made in the lunge position, coordinated with a tap of the front foot on the floor.

ARM BAR: A type of joint lock that immobilizes the arm, by trapping the hand or wrist and applying pressure to the elbow, or shoulder joint, bending the arm backward against itself.

ARM LOCK: A hold applied to the arm to immobilize it, or as a lever to be used for a throw. Generally seen with the arm bent and held behind the victim's back. See *Joint Lock* and *Arm Throw*.

ARM THROW: a.) A wrestling or grappling technique that uses the aggressor's arm for leverage in order to take them off balance and bring them down from an erect or standing position. b.) The use of the arm or a part thereof as the fulcrum for a throw in wrestling or judo. To throw (an adversary) by a maneuver in which the arm is used. See also *Arm Bar and Arm* Lock. c.) See *Irish Whip*.

ARM(S): Equipment of war, both offensive and defensive; things used in combat. a.) "In arms" - sword in hand; ready to fight. b.) To furnish with weapons of offense or defense; to take up arms; to arm oneself. c.) The exercise or employment of arms; war; combat. d.) The statutes about the use of arms and the use of arms and the forms of dueling. e.) The practice or profession of arms. f.) An armed knight; a soldier; a knight. g.) To furnish with anything that will add strength or security. h.) Heraldic insignia, i.e. "Coat of Arms."

ARMS-OF-THE-HILT: The finger rings extending from the quillons to the blade, often attached to a ring guard, they are mistakenly often called the *pas d'ane* although this has long been proved incorrect.

ARMED: Furnished with arms or armor; equipped for combat or war. Hence the term "Armed to the teeth" used to describe one who is fully or completely prepared for battle.

ARM-GAUNT: Being said of a horse that has been made lean by bearing arms in battle; hence, warlike, high-spirited.

ARMING SWORD: (Also *Armying Sword*) A cut and thrust fighting sword; part of a knight's equipment for war.

ARMOR: (U.S.) See *Armour*.

ARMOUR: (also *Armor*) a.) The habit worn to protect the body in battle.

b.) The whole apparatus of war, offensive as well as defensive arms.

ARMOURER: (also *Armorer*) a.) Manufacturer of weapons. b.) Someone who has care of the arms and dresses their master in armor.

ARMOURY: (Also *Armory*) Place where instruments of war are deposited.

ARMS OF THE HILT: See *Pas d'Ane*.

ARNIS: (Ph.) (also *Escrima* and *Kali*) The martial art of the Philippines. When the Philippines were invaded by the Spanish in 1521, the invaders, although armed with the sword and dagger, required guns to subdue their fierce opponents. The deadly fighting skills of Filipino warriors nearly overwhelmed them, and they dubbed the native fighting style escrima; meaning skirmish. Escrima was subsequently outlawed, but the techniques did not disappear. The conquered people disguised their art and practiced it in private and in the form of religious plays, known as moro-moro. The climax of these plays were often mock battles with blades of some kind. The blade fighting forms and footwork of these "mock" combats were identical to those used in escrima. These plays featured Filipinos, sometimes costumed as Spanish soldiers wearing Arnes, the harnesses worn for armor. The *"arnis de mano"* expression is said to have come from the Spanish description of this leather harnesses used by the moro-moro actors. The word arnes soon became corrupted to arnis, and the name stuck. "Arnis de Mano" now literally means "hand art." The ban on the practice of arnis and escrima has of course been lifted, and the art has flourished in its homeland. Arnis eventually came to the west, some of its practices introduced by Bruce Lee. Many arnis techniques being incorporated into his own style Jeet kune do. Historically, arnis incorporated three related methods: *espada y daga* (rapier and dagger), which employs a long blade and short dagger in the old Spanish style; *solo baston* (single stick); and *sinawali* (to weave), which uses two sticks of single length, twirled in a "weaving" fashion for blocking and striking (the term derives from sinawali, the bamboo matting woven in the Philippines). It is the patterns of sinawali that makes arnis dif¬ferent from western styles of swordplay. Like the Elizabethan form of rapier, and rapier and dagger, however, counter attacks are a general practice. The mere avoidance of an attack is seen as futile. If you avoid one attack, another is sure to follow. It is better to counter at the same time, to foil any further attacks. Unlike judo and karate, there are no fixed or exacting stances or footwork in arnis. The knees are slightly bent with the weight often balanced on the balls of the feet. The combatant flows from one position to another, always balanced and centered. The essence of arnis is not prearranged, but instant adaptation to change.

ARREBATAR: (Sp.) A cutting attack from the shoulder with the entire arm. See *Shoulder Cut*.

ARRESTSTOSS: (Ger.) See *Stop Thrust*.

ARRET: A *Stop Thrust* or *Stop Cut*.

ARTICULATION OF MOVEMENT: To form or fit individual actions into a systematic whole while maintaining the clarity of their individual purpose.

ARTICULATION: Specific movement created

by the bending and flexible certain joints.

ARTE DELLO SPADONE: Fiore Dei Liberi's name for his craft of the long-sword, symbolized by four virtues or qualities as represented by the Wolf (carefulness or prudence), the Tiger (swiftness or speed), the Lion (courage or bravery), and the Elephant (strength).

ASCENT: *(Small Sword)* "The act of the wrist's ascending inwards , on performing the parades of carte, semicircle, and prime."

ASSAIL: To attack.

ASSALTO: (It.) An attack.

ASSASSIN: a.) A term derived from the Arabic *hashishin*, literally meaning "hashish eater." During the First Crusade a band of men were brought together under the leadership of a young Iranian student, Hassan ben Sabah, who titled himself "Sheikh al Jebal," and who took it upon himself to start a holy war against the Crusaders and other Christians. The men were fanatical killers, motivated more from personal gains than religious zeal. The reward for a job well done was the administering of "a certain potion," says Marco Polo, "which cast them into a deep sleep, and when they awoke, they found themselves in a garden, all full of ladies and dam¬sels, who dallied with them to theirs heart's content, so that they would have what all young men would have." The potion given to these men was hashish, hence the term hashish eaters. b.) One who undertakes to put another to death by treacherous violence. The term retains so much of its original application as to be used chiefly of the murderer of a public personage, who is generally hired or devoted to the deed, and aims purely at the death of his victim.

ASSAULT: a.) A violent informal bout between fencers, with the intention to injure one another. b.) *(Small Sword)* "Where you engage an adversary with foils, as is single combat with swords, using such efforts and academical rules, either offensive or defensive, as your judgment may direct, for the purpose of succeeding in the execution of your designs, or in baffling those of your adversary." c.) Attack; onset. d.) A fencing bout (generally in an exhibition) performed without keeping score.

ASSAY: To test the composition of an ore or metal, hence, to try the `metal' of anyone in a fight. a.) To assault or attack someone. b.) A challenge.

ASSEMBLY: The term used by Errol Flynn for the *Corps-a-Corps,* particularly the Rabbit Ears Grasp.

ASSISTED HEAVY PARRY: The action of a parry, joined by a second weapon into a Heavy Parry; both weapons taking the opposing blade to the floor.

ASYMMETRY: A lack of proportion or balance in time, space or energy, opposed to conventional balance.

ATAJO: (Sp.) In the Spanish schools, the idea of taking control of the opponent's blade, essentially a *prise de fer.*

A-TILT: To run, ride, or perform in a joust or tournament; an encounter on horseback with the thrust of a lance. "Breake a Launce, and runne a-Tilt at Death."

ATTACK INTO THE ATTACK: (also *Time Hit*) To attack one's opponent as they begin an attack.

ATTACK OF FORCE: See *Attack on the Blade.*

ATTACK ON PREPARATION: An offense that is made as the opponent prepares their attack, whether the preparation is made with the sword or footwork, separately or together.

ATTACK ON THE BLADE: (also *Attacks of Force*) a.) Actions used to remove or displace the opponent's blade before an effective offensive action can be launched. Attacks on the Blade are generally broken into three major categories; Beats, Pressures and Flowing. b.) Offensive actions made against an opponent's weapon. These may include the Beat, Bind, Coule (Glide), Croise, Envelopment, Froissement, and Press. c.) Actions used to remove or displace the opposing blade before an effective offensive action can be launched. These may include any Prises de Fer (Bind,

Envelopment, and Croisé) as well as a Glissade, Beat or Press.

ATTACK WITH OPPOSITION: An attack maintaining a strong controlled contact with the opponent's blade which may deflect it out of line.

ATTACK, COMPUND: *(Small Sword)* "The offensive attempts against an adversary, by deceiving with feints, counter disengagements, glizades and repelling every feint and thrust he may attempt against you." See also *Compound Attack.*

ATTACK, SIMPLE: *(Small Sword)* "The offensive attempts against your adversary, when engaged in an assult, by simple moverments." See also *Simple Attack.*

ATTACK: a.) A simple or compound offensive action intended to hit one's opponent. b.) The act of falling upon with force and/or arms; an onset; an assault.

ATTACO: (It.) See *Attack.*

ATTAQUE SIMPLE: (Fr.) See *Simple Attack.*

ATTAQUE: (Fr.) See *Attack.*

AUSFALL: (Ger.) see *Lunge.*

AUSTRALIAN COUPÉ: A movement that takes the blade around ("Down under") the partner's blade point in the Low line. Also see *Coupe.*

AVANCÉS: The targets of one's opponent nearest to you; the sword arm and lead leg.

AVANTAGE: The slight bow or bend in the foible of a fencing blade which "trains" the blade to give on a hit rather than pierce, allowing the blade to arch as denoted in the classically executed hit.

AVOIDANCE: A movement of the body and/or feet backward or to the side in order to dodge an attack. See also Slipping a Punch.

AX KICK: (also *Axe Kick*) A descending vertical or diagonal kick generally associated with the martial arts that strikes downward with the heel much like a blow with an ax.

AZIONI VOLANTI: Avoiding blade contact on the attack and instead thrusting by deceptive motion.

B

BACK BLOW: (also *Backe Blow*) A backhanded cutting attack prescribed by early seventeenth century fencing master Joseph Swetnam which was delivered from the left the height of the left shoulder to either the right side of the head or the right leg. The attack could be made two ways, either as a simple straight attack ("a plaine Dunstable way") from left to right, or with a feint to the left changed to a backhanded strike with a molinello around the head. Swetnam deemed the back blow from the feint attack the best of the two. See also *Cross Blow.*

BACK STANCE: (also Back-stance) (MA) An offensive or defensive stance in which the majority of the body weight is taken on the rear foot. The front foot may lie flat, or the heel may be raised off the floor.

BACK: a.) The "back" or false edge of a blade. b.) The rear or dorsal part of the human body. Generally used in reference to the rear portion of the upper torso. c.) The rear of an army. d.) Said originally of a sword or knife that was of good and solid steel from its true edge to its back, hence, said of a man, true and solid, front to back. e.) To go, or cause to go, backward or in reverse. See *Backpedal.*

BACKE PACE: Di Grassi's term for a passing step backward. "The like is ment by the pace that is made directly backwardes: but this backe pace is framed more often streight then croked." See *Pass Back.*

BACK-EDGE: See *False Edge.*

BACKPEDAL: a.) The checking of a forward movement, the reversing of an action. b.) To travel backward from an opponent, or opponents, through passing steps or consecutive retreats, though still facing them. c.) *(Boxing)* To withdraw from conflict or combat; running or moving backward. "They sprout bad punching habits while concentrating on blocking, parrying, back-pedalling and the like."

BACKSTEPPE: In English swordplay, a simple step backward with the rear leg, sometimes followed by the lead leg.

BACKSWORD GUARD: a.) The guard or hilt of a back-sword. See Backsword. b.) An offensive/defensive posture assumed with the back-sword. A ward in back-sword play. c.) The specific ward prescribed by early seventeenth century fencing master Joseph Swetnam for back-sword play. "Carrie your Sword-hilt out at the armes end, and your point leaning or sloping toward your left shoulder, but not joyning with your enemies weapon, . . . but so long as you lie in your guard, let there be three foote distance betwixt your weapons, but if your enemie do charge you, either with blow or thrust, carrie your Sword over your bodie against your enemies assault, and so crosse with him according to the Picture, beare also your point stedie over your bodie, something sloping towards your left shoulder; I meane the point must goe so farre as the hilt . . ." d.) An alternate term for the Casstle-Guard as taught by English Fight Master Joseph Swetnam. See *Castle-Guard*.

BACKSWORD MAN: (also *Backswordsman*) A person who fences or fights with the back-sword; one who prefers the style or use of a backsword.

BACKSWORD: A popular eighteenth century contesting sword similar in style to a basket-hilted claymore, with a single cutting edge where the false or back edge is blunted except for a few inches at the tip, where it is double edged. Also sometimes referring to a stick with a basket-hilt used instead of the sword in practice.

BACKSWORDING: a.) The practice of the backsword. b.) Cutting attacks delivered from the elbow or wrist, made with the false or back edge of the blade.

BACKWARD LUNGE: (also *Echappement*) An evasive by distance which removes the body from cutting attacks across the belly or chest with grand lunge straight backward. The action does not lower the body into a duck or surrendering ground to one's opponent.

BACK-WOUNDING: Wounding in the back or from behind; back stabbing.

BALANCE: a.) A state of equilibrium where the combatant's weight is equally divided between both feet. See Center. b.) The total composition of a scene so that it is esthetically pleasing to the observer.

BALDRIC: A belt or girdle of the Baroque period, usually of leather and richly ornamented, that hung from one shoulder, across the chest and under the opposite arm, usually from the right shoulder to the left hip, supporting the wearer's sword and scabbard.

BALESTRA: (It.) (also *Jump-Lunge*) A compound piece of footwork designed to quickly cover a great deal of ground by combining a jump forward and the grand lunge. There are two counts in this action; one (jump), two (lunge). The first action leading instantly into the second. The Balestra is an aggressive action generally meant to end with an attack. This term suggests the historic link between fencing and the formal ballet, which is said to have been influenced by the fencing positions.

BALISONG: (also *Filipino Butterfly Knife* and *Butterfly Knife*) Literally translated, "bali" means to break, and "sung" means horn. The early handles were carved out of animal horns. This was the "broken horn" knife. The original knife took its name from a small barrio called Balisung, in the Batangas region of the Philippines. The people of that town are noted solely for producing this knife. The knife is one of the ancient weapons of Arnis, the ancestral art of the Malaya-Polynesian fighting systems. It is a non-typical folding knife with two half-handles that safely store the blade when closed and can be quickly pivoted around to form a sturdy grip. See Butterfly Knife.

BALLESTRA LUNGE: See *Balestra*.

BALLOW: A provincialism for cudgel.

BANDEROLE: (also *Bannerole* and *Bandarole*) A small ornamental streamer, with cleft end, that attached to the lance of a knight.

BANDEROLE: (Fr.) A diagonally executed chest cut.

BANDITTO: (also Bandetto) Outlaw, robber.

BANG: a.) A stroke or blow. b.) To beat, thump; to strike.

BARBED: Having the breast and flank protected by armor.

BARD: (also Barbe) a.) Full horse armor, which could include a shaffron, crinet, peytral, crupper and flan¬chards. b.) Armor composed of metal plates. c.) A common slang name for William Shakespeare - "The Bard."

BARDED: a.) To be armed, or in armor composed of metal plates. b.) A horse armed and ready for battle.

BARGE: To bump heavily into someone or something. To knock roughly against; to go roughly and heavily through or into someone or something.

BARONIAL HALL: A term for a sequence of parries and ripostes executed with restrictive footwork as if the routine were being executed atop a long narrow table like that which would be found in "Baronial Hall." The footwork consists of breaking an advance or retreat into two separate actions so that the attack and parry can be executed on the extension of one foot and the riposte on the recovery. The action is also known as the Errol Flynn "Tah-Tahs." The vocalized rhythm of the "tah-tah" indicates the count for the two actions of parry and riposte on one piece of footwork. The action is an old cinematic swashbuckling technique, but is still used at times in modern theatrical swordplay.

BAROQUE: a.) An excessively ornate style of architectural decoration which arose in Italy in the late Renaissance and became prevalent in Europe during the 18th century. b.) This term and rococo are not infrequently used without distinction for styles of fight choreography characterized by excessive flourishes, oddity of combinations, or eccentric guards, parries, postures and so on.

BARRAGE: A succession of offensive action, with or without a weapon, by one combatant against another. Usually these actions are hard and fast.

BASE FOOT: The foot used for support or balance while the other is used in some technique such as a kick, flip or throw.

BASE: A term used for a strong placement of the feet for centered movement. See *Four-Point Stance*.

BASKET-HILT: (also *Basket Hilt*) a.) The most common cavalry sword of the seventeenth century consisting of narrow plates of steel curved into a shape resembling a basket, designed to provide defense for the combatant's hand. In the late sixteenth and early seventeenth century it was considered "crude" in form in comparison to the rapier. Thus, it was often given to comic characters on stage. The educated gentleman now accepted the rapier and by this period the broadsword was the stage weapon of oafs and clowns. In Ben Jonson's Bartholomew Faire, the clown character of Cokes carries a basket hilt, and in *A Tale of a Tub*, Jonson has gone as far as to name one of his more doltish characters "Basket Hilts." b.) Used as a term of contempt, suggesting a swordsman whose sword, and hence style were old-fashioned. "a worn-out practicer of sword-tricks."

BASSA LINEA: (It.) See *Low Line*.

BASSO: (It.) Literally "low" or "lowered." Generally used in reference to the lowest immediate target on the opponent's body; at the thigh or knee.

BASTARD GARDANT WARD: George Silver's term for a ward in short sword play assumed like a low Seconda or Terza across, but with the point angled down towards the combatant's left foot. The ward is not to be used in general blade-play, but is intended for the specific purpose of engaging the opposing blade with a parry and close for a disarm or other in fighting technique. ". . . bastard gardant fyght wch is to Carrye yor hand & hylt below yor hed, brest hye or lower wt yor poynt downwarde towarde yor left foote, this bastard gardant ward is not to be used in fyght, ecept it be to Crosse yor enemyes Ward at his comynge in to take the grype of him or such other advancement, as in divrs placs of ye sword fyght is set forth."

Bastard Sword: (also *Hand-and-a-Half Sword*) A contemporary term, now used to describe a sword that may be wield¬ed by one or both hands.

Bastinado: To beat or cudgel.

Bate: a.) A quarrel or fight. b.) To beat back or blunt the edges of a blade or weapon. A blunted or dulled weapon; rebated. c.) To reduce, remit or undervalue.

Bate-Breeding: (also *Breed-bate*) Occasioning quarrels.

Bateless: Not to be blunted.

Battaile Axe: See *Battle Axe*.

Battement: (Fr.) A beat attack. See *Beat*.

Batter: To beat with successive blows, and hence to bruise, to shake, to demolish.

Battery: a.) Assailing with blows. b.) Unlawful beating of another. c.) A grouping of artillary pieces for tactical purposes. d.) A term for the guns of a warship.

Battle-Axe: (also *Battle-Ax*) A heavy axe used in combat to crash and split the opponent's armor.

Battre de Main: (Fr.) To parry with the hand. See *Hand Parry*.

Battuta Klingenschlag: (Ger.) See *Beat*.

Battuta: a.) (It.) A distracting smack to move the adversary's blade off line or evoke a response. See *Beat*. b.) Muslim traveler and explorer of the 14th century.

Bear Hug: A grasp or hold made upon an opponent where both arms are wrapped about their torso (often pinning the victim's arms at their side), generally executed from behind.

Beat Attack: (also *Battrement*) A controlled tap with the forte or middle part of one's blade against the middle or weak part of the opponent's blade to remove a threat, open a line for attack, or to provoke a reaction. An action that deflects the opponent's weapon in preparation for either an offensive or defensive action. See also *Beat*.

Beat Away Disarm: A disarm executed by using the mechanics of the beat away. The disarm may be secure or loose, but is more frequently secured.

Beat Away: (also *Quillon Bash*) A type of beat attack that knocks the opposing blade away after the successful completion of a blocking parry. Not a beat parry, this is an aggressive action with the hilt of the sword and not the forte of the blade. After the opposing blade has been stopped by a successful parry, and while it remains engaged, the hilt of the sword is punched towards the parried blade. The marked action of the hand and hilt deflects the opposing blade by "bashing" or knocking it aside.

Beat Out: See *Beat Parry*.

Beat Parry: a.) A parry made by striking the opponent's blade sharply aside, removing the attacking blade and allowing for a immediate riposte. As the blades are about to join, the hand and wrist of the parry punches out about two to four inches, deflecting the opposing blade by "striking" it sharply aside. The beat must be executed at the last possible moment. This form of parry and immediate riposte seems to be in keeping with the references to the parry offered in period fencing manuals. b.) A defensive action of the blade that breaks an attack by knocking the opposing weapon out, away from its intended target. "Therefore all blowes shalbe beaten outwards toward that side or parte of the bodie which is least to the end it may the sooner avoide daunger. And those blowes that come on the right side must be beaten towards the right side:

and those on the left side must in like manner be voided from the same side."

Beat Through: a.) A Beat Parry executed with an Expulsion. b.) A parry in which the defending blade parries, knocks the opposing blade aside, and moves into preparation for a cutting attack in one action. c.) A *Beat Aside* or *Shunt* executed from the horizontal, high-line parry of five.

Beat to the Punch: An expression in boxing and pugilism used for a form of "time," where a combatant hits an opponent first, although the oppo¬nent's punch started at the same time, or even before. See also Stop-Hit or Counter Punch.

Beat: a.) A sharp, controlled tap against the middle or weak part of the opponent's blade to open a line of attack or to provoke a reaction. See *Beat Attack*. b.) *(Small Sword)* "(in the French *batre*) Is particularly applied to the act of abruptly striking, with the fort of your blade, the foible of your adversary's, so as to embarrass him and get openings to thrust." c.) To strike, knock, or batter. d.) To drive a person back, away, off, from, to, into, or out of, a place or thing with repeated blows. e.) To drive a person back, away, off, from, to, into, or out of, a place or thing with arms or else by superior force. f.) To conquer in combat or at play.

Beat-Aside: (also *Rising* or *Intercept Parry*) A defensive action that beats the offensive blade aside during the execution of an attack. This parry is generally used in defense against a descending vertical or diagonal cutting attack. The defending blade is brought up to intercept the attacking blade and knock it aside before it lands on its "intended" target.

Beat-Away: A defensive action made with the sword which literally smacks into the attacking blade and knocks it away.

Beating the Bind: (also *Change Bind*) A beat attack executed by the victim of a bind by disengaging around the aggressor's guard, in the same direction as the bind, and then instantly snapping their blade against the middle or foible of the opponent's blade, beating it blade aside.

Beating: a.) To deliver blows; to strike repeatedly. b.) Receiving blows, a cudgeling.

Beats: Attacks on the blade that utilize percussive shock to laterally remove the opposing weapon.

Beaver: (also *Bevor, Bavier* or *Buffe*) a.) The lower portion of the face-guard of a helmet, when worn with a visor, occasionally serving the purpose of both. b.) Sometimes used as a term for the entire helmet.

Before: Referring to the dagger placement in a cross parry where the dagger is situated to the front of the rapier, on the side towards the other combatant. Opposite of *Behind*.

Behind: Referring to the dagger placement in a cross parry where the dagger is situated to the back of the rapier, being placed on the side away from the other combatant. Opposite of *Before*.

Bell: a.) The body of a helmet. A possible source for the term "having one's bell rung." Used as a expression indicating being struck up-side the head or helmet. b.) See *Bell-Guard*.

Bell-Guard: The cup or bell shaped guard of the Spanish rapier; possibly deriving its name from not only from its bell like shape, but also the bell like sound it would emit upon being hit by the opponent's blade.

Belly Cut: An attack made with the edge of a bladed weapon, intended to land on, or cross the plane of, the recipient's stomach. b.) A term used in sabre fencing for a cutting attack made to the non-weapon bearing side of the body at roughly waist level. In a proper on guard stance the foot of the weapon bearing side is carried forward, slightly turning the belly to the inside and exposing it to the cut more than the non-weapon bearing hip. Opposite of a *Flank Cut*.

Belt: a.) The imaginary line about a boxer's

waist, at the approximate level a belt would be worn, at the level of the navel. Hitting below the belt is a foul in boxing. b.) To beat with, or as with, a belt. c.) A jarring blow. d.) See *Sword Belt*. e.) A distinct ranking within the Martial Arts designated by color.

BENT ACTION: A term used by George Silver for the condition of activity, at work, in practical or effective operation of the body and weapon that is inclined, or turned in some direction with impetus or concentrated energy. See also *Action*.

BERSERK: Originally a frenzied Viking warrior who entered into battle bare of any armor, wearing only a simple shirt or bearskin coat, his aim was the killing of as many enemy as possible with little regard to personal survival.

BERSERKER: a.) A wild Norse warrior of great strength and ferocious courage, who fought on the battle-field with a frenzied fury known as the "berserker rage." b.) Often applied to a lawless thug or highwayman. c.) Now used to describe a frenzied, furious, or madly violent person.

BEST: To have the advantage; the position of superiority in combat.

BESTED: To have been beaten; to have lost a battle, combat or contest.

BESTRIDE: a.) To stand over a fallen combatant and defend them. b.) To stand over a fallen opponent as their victor.

BETHUMP: To cuff.

BICORNIO: See *Posta di Bicornio* ("Two Horned Guard").

BILBAO: The Spanish town famed for its immaculate sword blades, at one time rivaling even those of Toledo.

BILBO: A blade, originally from the Spanish town Bilbao, known for its temper and elasticity; a well tempered sword. A test to establish the quality of such a blade was to see if it could be bent from hilt to point and then return to true.

BILL: a.) A military weapon, dating from the thirteenth century, used chiefly by the infantry. Derived from a forest clearing tool, the bill varied in form from that of a simple concave blade with a long wooden haft, to one with a kind of concave ax with a spike at the back and its shaft terminating in a spear head. During the sixteenth and seventeenth century bills were often painted or varnished in different colors- hence `brown bill.' b.) To post or issue a public challenge. c.) a formal posted announcement of an English student's public "Playing" of his "Prize".

BIND AWAY: (also *Throw Off*) An active bind that throws or flings away the opposing blade, and the combatant who wields it.

BIND OVER: An active bind that continues its circular path down to the floor. The action generally begins with a low line parry, followed by a dynamic bind that carries the blades up, over and down to the floor on the opposite side. The objective of this action is to disarm the opponent or to pin their weapon, making its immediate use impossible.

BIND: a.) A *pris d'fer* that carries the opposing weapon from a high line to a low line, and vice versa, diagonally across the line of engagement. The Bind can be executed both in a passive and active form. The passive action is executed from the hand and wrist with the forte of the blade against the opposing blades foible. An active bind can use the whole arm, controlling the opposing blade with the forte or mid-blade. b.) (Small Sword) "Binding the sword is the act of crossing your adversary's blade with pressing the fort of yours on the feeble of his, and by a sudden jerk of the wrist securing or binding his blade, so as to be covered either from a time thrust or an interchanged thrust. It is generally performed from the guard or engagement of carte, when your adversary holds his wrist low on guard. A thrust thus delivered on the act of binding, is termed the thrust of flanconnade. See Flanconnade."

BINDUNG: (Ger.) See *Bind*.

BISH-BASH-BOSH: A vocalized rhythm for swordplay used by the late English actor Sir Laurence Olivier.

BITE THE BULLET: Before the use of anesthesia the military surgeon would give a wounded soldier a leaden musket ball to bite down on to keep the soldier from screaming, as the surgeon probed the wounds for bullets, ampu¬tated limbs, etc. It is believed that soldiers who were flogged for disciplinary reasons were also given a bullet to bite, hence the modern connotation of gritting your teeth and bearing a rather unpleasant situation.

BITING: A pinching, ripping or cutting attack made with the teeth, usually delivered to exposed skin or other such sensitive body areas.

BLADE: a.) The essential part of a cut and/or thrust weapon that covers its entire expanse, running threw the hilt and extending from the guard to the extreme tip of the weapon. The basic blade is broken down into the following parts: tip, foible, middle, forte, shoulders and tang. Many blades, like the rapier, have a ricasso between the forte and tang. The cutting edge is divided into the true and false edge. The blade being the primary part of a weapon, it is often used as the name for the whole weapon. "The blade of a Sword or Foil is divided into three parts, viz. the fort, the medium and the foible; or the shoulder or strength, the middle, and the feeble; the shell is at one extremity, and the point is at the other." b.) A term for a fencer or a swordsman.

BLANK: (also Blank Cartridge) Ammunition that contains paper or plastic in place of the bullet.

BLEAR: To blur or blind the eyes, to hoodwink or deceive.

BLIND SIDE PUNCH: See *Sucker Punch*.

BLIND: a.) A drunken bout or orgy; a binge. b.) To act without previous investigation of the circumstances; to plunge without regard to the risks involved; i.e. "to go it blind." c.) The unguarded, weak or assailable side of a person or thing, weakness; i.e. Blind Side.

BLOCK: a.) An action used to stop or deflect an oncoming attack. Such actions can be made in four ways: 1 Opposition: where the defending hand or arm is brought up as a solid wall or shield against the attack; 2 Displace: where the defending hand or arm intercepts the attack and diverts or redirects the energy of the blow away from its intended target; 3 Beat: where the defending hand or arm deflects the attack by "striking" it sharply away from its intended target; 4 Offensive: where the defending hand or arm strike into the attack intending to hit and disable rather than block or displace. Any of these defensive actions can be made on either side of the body and in all lines. b.) (also Parry) A defensive action made with the hand or arm intended to stop a punch or similar attack. A block can be made on either side of the body and in all lines. These may be a Circular Block, Cross Block, Descending Block, Inside Block, Opposition Block, Outside Block, Parallel Block, Redirection Block, Rising Block, Transfer Block, Wing Block, or X Block. See *Parry*.

BLOCKED PUNCH: A move that deliberately stops the incoming punch. It can be executed either with one arm, or both, but should avoid striking bone, or the inner elbow joint, as this could cause the fist to continue traveling forward. Usually this move is executed with open palms, but also can be effective on the major muscle groups of the forearm.

BLOCKING PARRY: (also *Standard Parry, Opposition Parry* and *Parry by Opposition*) A parry made by moving the sword to close the line in which the opponent makes an attack. Such a parry is performed in double time with the parry as one action, separate from the second action of a counter attack or riposte. The defensive action, being separate, may be performed alone, without a riposte.

Blocking: a.) Laying out of action or movement in a scene with the actors and/or camera. b.) The defensive action of stopping or deflecting an attack. See *Parry*.

Blood Groove: (also *Blood Gutter*) A misnomer created to explain the grooving and/or fluting of a blade, which falsely supposed these grooves were devised to allow the blood to drain from one's opponent. See *Fuller* and *Fluted Blade*.

Blood Gutter: See *Blood Groove*.

Bloody Mary: A form of spring loaded switch-blade knife where the blade is housed in the grip and can be extended or retracted, like a sewing machine needle, with the flip of a switch.

Blosse: (Ger.) See *Opening*.

Blow: Violent application of the hand, fist, or an offensive weapon.

Blunt: Having no edge; a bated or dulled blade.

Blunts: Dull cut & thrust practice blades which were rebated (or "bated") with rounded edges and tips (they were sometimes called "foils" or "foiled blades").

Boar's Thrust: An attack devised in the late seventeenth century by fencing master Donald McBane. The Boar's thrust was only used by McBane "when he had a mind to kill," being a thrust punched upward into the body after the sword hand was suddenly dropped to the level of his knee.

Boar's Tooth: See *Posta di Dente Chingiale*.

Bob and Weave: A boxing term for an evasive action that combines the techniques of a duck and a slip. The "bob" is used to avoid a head punch, and the fighter bobs forward and down, toward the aggressor. The "weave" is the circling of the body to the left or right, usually in the direction the punch. Immediately after completion the fighter should be ready to counter-punch. Such a technique can be accompanied by footwork, but it is not essential to the action.

Bob: a.) To drub, to thump. b.) To move up and down, jerkily or repeatedly.

Bodkin: a.) A short pointed weapon; a dagger, poniard, stiletto, lancet. b.) An arrow point designed for piercing armor.

Body Blow: Any attack, armed or unarmed, that is landed, or appears to land, to the body of a fighter.

Bolt: a.) A short arrow with a quarrel at one end. Commonly used in the cross-bow.

Botta: (It.) An attack from its beginning to its completion; a blow or thrust.

Botta Dritta: (It.) *botta*, blow or thrust, *dritta*, right/right hand. a.) A pronated thrust from the right; the straight thrust.

Botte de Paysan: A two-handed stab made by grabbing the blade near the middle with the free hand and closing-in to knock aside an opponent's weapon.

Botta-in-tempo: ("*attack in time*") An attack while the adversary's preoccupied with a parry, bind, or feint.

Botta Lunga: (It.) (also *Grand Lunge*) (Literally "Elongated Blow") The classi¬cal movement which replaced passing (as a means of reaching an opponent and attacking them) early in the seventeenth century. The lead foot being propelled forward (as far as the combatant can conveniently manage) by straightening the lag leg. The sword arm is thrust forward, the rear arm is snapped backward, and the trunk and pelvis are turned slightly forward. The honor of having first described the grand lunge goes to Giganti, however, Capo Ferro explained the mechanics of the lunge in greater detail, fixing the principles of the science, making him the founder of the modern school of fence.

Botta Segrete: (It.) The "secret attack." Most masters of the sixteenth century Italian school claimed to have developed a secret attack to which there was no possible defense. No such attack ever existed, or has hence been discovered, but much like the philosopher's stone and the fountain of youth the secret attack was believed in, and thus these secret attacks were often sold, for a great price, to "select" students.

BOTTE SECRETE: See *Botta Segrete*.

BOTTOM MAN: See *Base Man*.

BOUT: a.) The spell of activity between two fencers engaged in personal combat. b.) The spell of activity between any two combatants, boxers, pugilists, etc. c.) A wrestling match ending in a decisive fall.

BOX DRILL: a.) A drill or exercise that takes a series of attacks through the parry pattern of the Defensive Box. See also *Offensive/Devensive Drill*. b.) A drill or exercise consisting of cutting attacks delivered to the four points of the Box Target (right and left chest, and the right and left hip or thigh.)

BOX TARGET: A target system in on-line swordplay with four on-line body targets that when joined with imaginary lines form a box. These targets are generally right and left chest and right and left thigh. The right chest is parried by 3 or 6 the left chest by 4, the thighs parried on the right by 2 or 8, and on the left by 1 or 7. The box target, like all on-line targets, are for point-work.

BOX: a.) To strike or punch with the hand; to fight with fists; a slap, strike, blow, cuff or punch with the hands or fists. b.) See *Boxing*. c.) See *Defensive Box*. d.) See *Box Target*.

BOXER: One who engages in boxing; a professional fighter; a pugilist.

BOXING: The action of fighting with fists; now usually applied to a pugilistic encounter in which the hands are covered with well-padded leather gloves. The art or sport of fist fighting; pugilism.

BRABBLE: To quarrel about trifles; a noisy quarrel or brawl.

BRABBLER: A brawler or quarreler; a noisy fellow; a ruffian.

BRACE: A term for a part of the suit of armor referred to as the vantbrace.

BRAIN: To kill a person with a blow or stroke, of the hand or with a weapon, that caves in the skull; literally beating out the brains.

BRANDISH: To shake, to flourish a sword, dagger or like weapon.

BRAQUEMAR: A term applied to many broad bladed swords.

BRAVAZZO: (also *Branando*) A swashbuckler, a swaggerer, a cutter, quarreller, rostier, raffine, ruffian.

BRAWL: a.) A noisy quarrel; a row; a squabble. b.) Brandle, also a dance.

BRAWLER: a.) One who participates in a brawl. b.) A term in boxing for a fighter who uses a very physical approach that includes leaning on his opponent, muscling in, and sometimes even such illegal tactics as butting.

BRAWLING: (also *Brawling Style* and *Brawling Type*) A term for the hand to hand combat style which represents the actions of people who are not expert fighters or martial artists, but nonetheless are familiar with violent confrontations.

BREACH: a.) The gap battered in the wall of a besieged town or fortress, through which the besiegers might charge in - unless the defenders stepped into the breach to repel them. b.) The space between the several parts of a solid body parted in violence; figuratively: a wound, a hurt.

BREAK A LEG: Theatrical slang for good luck. It is possibly derived from a superstition that it was bad luck to wish someone good luck, so the worst possible thing is wished to avoid a jinx. But old-fashioned European bows were made by extending the front leg and bending the back one. From this position, the bowing party is able to move directing into an attacking position. Hence "Break a leg" means "take a bow".

BREAK THE GAME: To interrupt the opponent's actions by either retreating out of distance or intercepting their feinting blade prior to the finale of their attack.

BREAK: a.) The separation of two fighters (generally boxers or pugilists), by an official, when they are clinched together and all action has stopped. b.) A term for the sudden or violent separation or splitting of bones. c.) A quarrel or fight.

Breaking Ground: Any action of footwork that surrenders ground to the opponent.

Breaking the Measure: (*rompere di misura*) Retreating from within the measure to out of measure.

Breastplate: Armor for the front of the upper torso, the chest.

Breed-Bate: One who causes quarrels.

Broach: A tapering pointed rod of wood or steel; a lance, spear or bodkin. To pierce, impale, to stick on a spit or such a pointed weapon.

Broad Ward: (also *Broad Warde* and *Wide Ward*) a.) The second guard position dictated by Di Grassi which is assumed with the hand at chest level, arm drawn directly backward so the hand is directly outside the torso, blade parallel to the floor its point directed at the opponent or across the body to their right. "This second warde from the effecte shall be called the broad or wide warde, because the arme widning and stretching it selfe directlie as much as posible from the right side, beareth the sword so farre off from the bodie, that it seemeth to give great scope to the enimie to enter, albeit in truth it be nothing so. For although the hand & the handle of the sworde, be both farr from the bodie, and quite out of the streight line, yet the poynt of the sworde, from which principallie procedeth the offence, is not without the saide lyne: For it is borne so bending towarde the left side that it respecteth directlie to strike the enemie and being borne in that sorte, it may verie well both strike and defend. And when the poynt of the sword is borne out of the streight lyne, as the hand and handle is, then a man is in daunger to bee hurte easelie by the enemie, the which happeneth not when the poynt is bending, for in such order, it is as a barre and defence to the whole bodie." b.) A sword

and dagger guard taught by English fencing master Joseph Swetnam which parallels his Perfect Guard of rapier and dagger play. See *Perfect Guard*.

Broadsword Grip: a.) The Broadsword is gripped firmly with the lead hand near the cross-guard and the rear hand (when being used) gripping the pommel in the middle of the hand leaving the little finger just off the pommel. This provides a levering action to control the weapon. By wringing the hands together as if wringing out a towel a controlled cut can be made that looks powerful. b.) The manner of holding a Broadsword. See *Sword Grip*. c.) The Handle of a *Broadsword*.

Broadsword: (also *Broad Sword*) A term now apply to almost all swords of the Medieval period. Most often applied to the Armying sword of the Middle Ages. The label "Broadsword," however, is only accurate when used in comparison to the narrower bladed weapons of the sixteenth, seventeenth and eighteenth centuries. Histori¬cally the swords of the Middle Ages had many different names, but the term "broadsword" was not one of them.

Brochiero: (It.) A variety of hand shield or buckler.

Broil: a.) Tumult, noisy quarrel, contention. b.) War, combat, battle.

Bruising Irons: A slang term for battle maces and other such weapons of weight.

Buckler: (also *Bokeler*) a.) A small round shield generally used in conjunction with the broad bladed swords of the Middle Ages and early Renaissance. "As the forme of the Buckler is round and small, and ought to be a shield & safegard of the whole bodie . . ." In England the buckler was usually carried by a handle at the back and used, not so much for a shield as for a warder to catch or beat aside the blow of one's opponent. It was constructed of strong iron plate and could be round, square or occasionally trapezoidal. Its edge was further reinforced with a strip of metal riveted all around it while a hook or spike sometimes projected from its boss. In close combat, the buckler with a spike could serve as an offensive weapon. A lantern was often suspended from the hook to help light the bearer's way at night. The buckler could range in size from ten inches to thirty inches in diameter, the larger bucklers were generally strapped to the arm (These bucklers are generally referred to as Targets). The buckler accompanied by the short sword were the national weapon of England until the late sixteenth century. b.) A shield secured to the left forearm in the manner of the target. Most sources tend to state otherwise. c.) To act as a buckler, to shield, defend, ward off blows. d.) (Shield Boss) In referring to the buckler, many fifteenth and sixteenth-century fencing manuals refer to the spike or point emitting from the center of the buckler. Such a spike proved profitable in close-quarter combat. "It shall be also verie profitable, that in the midst of the Buckler, there be a sharpe poynt or stert of Iron, to the end the enimie may be stroken therwith when occasion serveth." See *Mustachio*.

BUFF: Leather clothing or jerkin.

BUFFET: a.) A blow or stroke, now usually given with the hand. To beat, thump, cuff or knock about. "The buffeting of fists was cliché, common in the Bible, etc. In the old romances duels of strength were sometimes tried in buffets; Richard I killed Austria's son in one of these. Buffets where aimed at the head, each party having to stand still in turn." b.) To fight or contend.

BULLDOG: (also *Bull-Dogging*) a.) A "cowboy" or Western term for an unarmed attack made in a manner similar to the leaping attack of a bulldog. Generally applied to an airborne attack, often from above, where one combatant leaps at the other and they collide torso against torso; where they wrestle with, and throw the victim to the floor. b.) Antiquated slang for a cannon or other

firearm. In modern use, a particular kind of revolver.

BUM IN THE FACE: A slang term used for the *Grand Volte*.

BURGONET: A close-fitting helmet.

BUTCHER OF A SILK BUTTON: Believed to be a reference to the well known Italian master of fence, Signior Rocco Bonetti, "who was so excellent in his fight, that he would have hit anie English man with a thrust, just upon anie button in his doublet."

BUTT END: The trailing end of the staff in the En Guard position.

BUTT STRIKE: a.) An attack or blow delivered with the butt end of the quarterstaff. Also applied to any such attack with the butt end of a rifle or gun stock. b.) An attack or blow delivered with the pommel or butt end of knife. See also *Pommel Strike*.

BUTT: a.) To strike with the head like a horned animal. b.) To hit an opponent with the head or shoulder. In boxing such a technique is a major foul, leading to disqualification with repeated use. See *Head-Butt*. c.) The back end of a quarter-staff or polearm. See *Butt End*. d.) An archery target. e.) The back or pommel end of a knife. See *Pommel*.

BUTTERFLY GUARD: A guard or shell, on certain eighteenth century small swords, consisting of two ellipsoidal parts on either side of the blade that form a shape roughly resembling a butterfly.

BUTTERFLY KNIFE: (also *Filipino Butterfly Knife* and *Balisong*) One of the ancient weapons of Arnis, the ancestral art of the Malaya-Polynesian fighting systems. A nontypical folding knife as it has two half-handles that safely store the blade when closed as well as quickly pivoting around to form a sturdy grip. Because the two half-handles operate independently, the knife can be opened quickly with one hand without the use of springs. The term "butterfly" is a reference to both the wing-like independence of the half-handles and the flashy way that the wings can be displayed when opening the knife.

BUTTOCK: (also *Buttocking*) The use of the hip or buttock as the fulcrum for a throw in wrestling. To throw (an adversary) by a maneuver in which the buttock or hip is used.

BUTTON: a.) The round flat metal disk used to blunt the tip of the competitive fencing blades of the foil and epee. Historically the resemblance of this protective device to a bud or the protuberant receptacle of the rose lead to the fencing foil to be called a "fleuret" by the French. b.) A term sometimes used for the capstan rivet. c.) The pay-off or climax of a piece of business or a gag that ties the whole piece together and closes the bit.

C

CUSHION: A small circular pad of foam, leather or felt placed on the inside some sword hilts to prevent the fingers from jamming against the guard.

CADENCE: a.) The rhythm of a sequence of interrelated movement that has a definite beginning and comes to a definite end or point of rest and gives the sense of harmonic completion. A fencing tempo. b.) The rhythm of a series of fencing movements.

CAGE: To corner or trap an opponent as if in a cage.

CALIVER: A light kind of musket or harquebus, introduced during the sixteenth century. The lightest portable fire-arm, excepting the pistol, fired without a rest.

CAMBIAMENTO: (It.) See *Change of Engagement*.

CAMINEERING: A change of engagement or in the line of threat/attack.

CAPA: See *Cloak*.

CAP-A-PE: (also *Cap-a-Pie*) Literally "from head to foot."

CAPSTAN RIVET: A small rivet forged from the tang of the blade, capping or crowning the top of the pommel, joining and locking the hilt of the sword to its blade.

CAPULUS: The Latin name for the hilt of the Roman sword. Often ornate.

CARBONADO: Originally applied to meat cut for broiling. The term was then applied to anything cut or hacked like broiling meat.

CARELESSE GUARD: (also *Lazie Guard*): A deceptive looking guard in rapier and dagger play, taught by seventeenth century English Fight Master Joseph Swetnam, assumed with the sword bearing hand and hilt resting upon the thigh with the blade across the body to the inside, its point resting on the ground. The dagger hand and arm hang limp at the side, its blade positioned behind the rapier blade. In such a guard the combatant looks careless or lazy, leaving what appears to be the whole body wide open. In reality, however, it is a viable guard with a strong defensive action.

Carriage: a.) The manner of carrying one's body, bearing, mien. b.) The sword carriage. The complicated waist belt and suspension rigging for the Elizabethan rapier. c.) The loop attached to the sword- belt, through which one passes their sword.

Carte Guard: (also *Quarte*) (Small Sword) "Anciently the fourth, is now one of the principal guard-postures (the other is called Tierce Guard). The greatest elevation of the point on guard should be nearly fifteen degrees; if the polint is elevated more, it will make too great a cross in the juncture of the blades. The greater the cross of the blades, the more easily are thrusts parried , as the curves formed by the point in parrying will be greater; but it will at the same time impede the approach towards the body- Hence the smaller the cross of the blades, when in contact or guard, the more dextrous should the movements be, to render thrusts effectual."

Carte Parade: (also *Quarte*) (Small Sword) "Anciently the fourth, is now the first of the upper parades. It throws off all simple thrusts made inwards to the upper part of the body. It is performed from the medium guard, by a gradual turn of the wrist ascending inwards- the point receding to its original direction."

Carte Thrust Inside: (Small Sword) "The natural thrust corresponding to the parade of carte. It is an upper thrust, and the opposition to your adversary's blade is inwards, so as to be covered on the longe by seeing the point over your arm."

Carte Thrust Over the Arm: (Small Sword) "The natural thrust corresponding to the parade of tierce: it is the opposite thrust to carte inside; for the opposition to your adversay's blade is outwards- This thrust is a good substitute for tierce thrust, it being rather aukward in execution, and as such is seldom or never practiced."

Cartel: A hand delivered written notice of challenge describing the cause of the offence that provoked a duel of honor.

Cartoccio: (It.) The *Passata Sotto*.

Carve: a.) A deep and severe cutting stroke delivered by pushing the edge of the knife into the flesh and cutting loose a piece of flesh by turning the edge of the knife and usually letting the flat of the blade travel down the length of a bone. b.) To cut; to hew.

Case of Rapiers: Two rapiers or swords used together in double fence, each weapon serving both offensive and defensive actions. "There are also used now adaies, aswell in the scholles, as in the lists, two Swordes or Rapiers, admitted, and approved both by Princes, and the professors of this art, for honourable and knightlie weapons, albeit they be not used in the warres." The case of rapiers were generally of a special design so they could be carried in the same scabbard.

Case: A set of something; a matched pair; two of something; twins.

Casque: A head-piece, a helmet.

Castle-Guard: (also *Back-Sword-Guard*) A sword and dagger guard placement, taught by English Fight Master Joseph Swetnam, assumed with the sword hand and hilt at roughly waist level on the sword-bearing side of the body (in a placement similar to Terza Guardia), its blade angled up and across the body at roughly 45★. The dagger is held forward at arms length its hand and hilt at cheek level, the blade directed up and across the body at roughly 45★. The dagger blade is placed in front of the rapier's, with both blades forming an inverted "V" (like a roof above the head and body) closing the high lines to attack.

Cat is out of the Bag: The "cat," cat-o'-nine-tails, used to punish and discipline sailors, was stored in a cloth sack or bag, hence, once the cat was removed from it's bag there was generally hell to pay.

Cat Stance: (MA) A basic stance where virtually all the body-weight is on the rear foot, with the front foot merely touching the floor.

Cause: See *First* and *Second Cause*

Cavalry Hanging Parries: Hanging parries rolled around the head and held behind either the lead shoulder (*Outside Cavalry Hanger*) or unarmed shoulder (*Inside Cavalry Hanger*) as well as many variations for "style." See also *Hanging Parries.*

Cavating: (Small Sword) "A dextrous motion of the wrist in shifting your blade from one side of your adversary's to the other.- It is a synonymous term to disengaging, changing or shifting, and in this Treatise is more frequently termed disengagement- The nicety of the whole art partly consists in the dextrous shifts or disengagements of the blade from one side to another; as without it no feint can be executed. See *Disengaging.*

Cavation Umgehung: (Ger.) See *Disengage.*

Cavatione di Tempo: (It.) Fabris' term for the *Time Disengagement.* "When the enemy tries to engage your sword, or to beat it aside: without letting him engage or beat it, you must take a cavatione di tempo,"

Cavatione: (It.) (also *Cavazione*) Literally "drawing away." Fabris' term applied to the disengage. More than likely originally applied to the action of the sword, removing of the blade backward from the opposing weapon, but today it is applied to the semi-circular motion of the point around the opposing guard. See *Disengage.*

Cavazione: (It.) See *Disengage.*

Cavé: (Fr.) See *Angulation.*

Ceding Parry: See *Yield Parry.*

Cedute: (It.) A ceding parry. See *Yield Parry.*

Center Line: An imaginary line bisecting the body in equal halves, right and left.

Center of Percussion: a.) That point on a blade where in angular transfers of energy the maximum efficiency is obtained (similar to the sweet spot in tennis). Usually not the middle of the implement, depending upon the axis of rotation and the mass distribution of the unit. b.) See *Middle*

Center: a.) The point or position of equilibrium or balance within the body. b.) To place oneself in a state of equilibrium that allows for movement in any direction at any given moment. "The third & fourth govrners is a twyfold mynd when you press in on your enemye, for as you have a mynde to go forwarde, so you must have at yt instant a mynd to fly backwarde upon any action yt shalbe offered or don by yor advrsarie."

Central Guard: (also Neutral Guard) Misleadingly called a "guard," the central guard places the hand and the blade at mid body along the center line, thus opening both inside and outside lines to possible attack. The neutral position of the hand equally distributes the lines of attack. See also *Lines.*

Cercle: A late seventeenth century term for a half-circular parry generally ending in the parry of seven. See Circular Parry.

Chagrin: "Originally," says Robert Claiborne, "a piece of heavy, rough leather used to polish sword-blades and the like; then, the abrasive spiritual effects of rough experiences and, finally, the resulting spiritual soreness. If you're chagrined, you feel rather as if someone had gone over you with emery paper."

Challenge: A summon to a fight or contest, especially to single combat.

Challenger: One who calls upon another to fight; one who defies; one who challenges another, especially to single combat.

Chamber: a.) That part of the bore of a gun in which the charge is placed. In old revolvers, each of the barrels and in new, each of the compartments of the breaching which contains the charge. b.) To contain or hold as in a chamber of a fire-arm; hence the ready placement of a punch, kick, slap or other such blow prior to discharge. A wind-up or preparation for an attack; armed or unarmed. See also *Wind-Up*.

CHAMPION: a.) A class of proxy fighters used to engage in trials by combat for one side or the other. These men, often criminals, were often employed to accuse men who were considered threats to the crown, generally on the understanding that if they won, they would thereby save their own lives. b.) A fighting man; a man of valor; a combatant; a stout fighter. c.) One who fights on behalf of any person or any cause. d.) To challenge to a contest; to bid defiance to.

CHANGE BEAT: (also *Indirect Beat*) a.) A beat attack that is executed after the successful completion of a *Changement*. The *Beat*, accompanied by a *Changement* allows the initiator of the action to manipulate the direction their partner's blade is knocked.

CHANGE BIND: A changement (disengage/coupé) executed by the victim of a bind, in the same direction as the bind, bringing the blade to the other side of the opposing weapon, re-engaging and executing a counter bind. The action consists of a bind, changement and counter bind.

CHANGE DOWN: A half-disengage executed from the high line into the low line.

CHANGE OF ENGAGEMENT: a.) The act of engaging your opponent in a new line. b.) To release contact of the blades and reestablish contact in a new line. See also *Changement*.

CHANGE OVER: A changement executed from a free guard position that passes the point over an opposing weapon into a new line. The change over is executed from the hand, wrist and forearm in the pattern of an inverted "V." The point is either passed directly over the tip of the opponent's rapier, returning to the same side of the body, or over the opponent's sword and head to the opposite side of their body.

CHANGE PARRY: See *Circular Parry*.

CHANGE STEP: The second step of a Half Passe where the feet change so that the opposing foot kicks out either forward (Half Passe Forward) or backward (Half Passe Backward), and steps to either a linear step, Thwart, Cross or Slip.

CHANGE UNDER: A changement executed from a free guard position that passes the point under an opposing weapon into a new line. The open line can either be around the hilt of the opposing rapier, on the same side of the body, or under the hilt on the opposite side of the body. The action of passing the point under the opposing guard was a common occurrence is swordplay and appeared in most treatises on the topic. Saviolo in 1595 tells his student to "turne his Rapier hand, that the pointe bee conveighed under his masters weapon, which being done, promptly and readily his point will be towards the belly of his master"

CHANGE UP: A half-disengage executed from the low line into the high line.

CHANGEMENT: a.) The practice of changing, joining, freeing, removing and replacing the blades. Any action of the blade, from a free or engaged guard position, that moves the blade to a new line of engagement. Each type of changement has a particular name and function. b.) An action of the blade that carries it from one line of engagement to another.

CHAPE: (also *Drag*) Metal plate or mounting of a scabbard; especially that which covers the point.

CHAPELESS: A scabbard without a chape.

CHARGE: a.) The order or signal of attack. b.) The attack itself. c.) To attack.

CHASING THE BLADE: An improper defensive action in swordplay where the parry is reached out, extending beyond the regular placement of a parry.

CHECK PARRY: (also *Check*) A type of replacement parry that "checks" the parried blade, allowing the primary parrying weapon to free itself for a counter attack. See *Replacement Parry*.

CHECK: a.) The process of curbing, or restraining the offending hand, arm or leg after a successful block. The defending hand or arm remains in contact with the opponent's (without gripping, locking or holding) in order to sense their movements, feel or control the placement of the offending limb, and use that to both offensive and defensive advantage. These actions (Bind, Envelopment and Transport) command the opposing hand or arm and may retain it or remove it with the action of an Expulsion. b.) An action in armed or unarmed combat that follows a block or parry with one hand by an immediate second action that curbs, or restrains the attacking arm while freeing the original arm for a counter strike.

CHECKING THE BLADE: a.) (also *Check* or *Check Parry*) The process of curbing, or restraining the offending blade while freeing another weapon for a counter strike. By not quitting the opposing blade, the parrying weapon can feel where the offending blade is and use that to both offensive and defensive advantage. b.) The process or procedure of examining the blade of a weapon for any imperfections that might be deemed a hazard in practice or performance.

CHEEK CUT: A horizontal or descending diagonal cut, generally executed from the wrist or elbow, directed at the opponent's cheek.

CHEEK TO CHEEK: a.) A classic piece of stock swordplay business consisting of repeated cheek cuts delivered on the exchange. This can be a pattern of cuts or thrust (although usually cuts) delivered to either cheek (parried in a high 3 or 4), which is parried and riposted with an attack to the same shoulder on the opponent. The pattern is generally repeated over and over with various pieces of footwork thrown in to try and make it look interesting. b.) A different classic piece of stock swordplay business bearing the same name, but consisting two cutting attacks delivered from one side of the face to the other. A common piece of business in the old swashbuckling films. c.) A term for close quarters. See *Corps-a-Corps*.

CHEST CUT: A term used in sabre fencing, for a cutting attack made to the non-weapon bearing side of the body at roughly chest level. In a proper on guard stance the foot of the weapon bearing side is carried forward, slightly turning the body to the inside (exposing the weapon bearing shoulder while removing the non-weapon bearing shoulder) and thus exposing the chest and breast bone to the cut more than the non-weapon bearing shoulder. Opposite of a *Shoulder Cut*.

CHEST: a.) A target in fencing, on either the right or left side of the body at approximately rib or arm-pit level, below the top of the shoulder and above the flank. b.) An on-line target in swordplay, generally referring to the center of the upper torso at the level of the sternum.

CHEVALIER: A knight.

CHIP: (Wrestling) A technical term for a trip, a trick, or special mode of throwing one's opponent.

CHIPPING: (Wrestling) The base of a wrestler is like a pyramid, wide and strong on the bottom narrow and sharp at its top. Seemingly immovable and untoppleable. But if you chip away at that wide base, narrowing the foundation, the pyramid will tumble like so many loose stones. The principal of chipping is to knock out the feet from under the wrestler either by kicking out the foot or entangling their legs.

CHIVALEAROUS: (also *Chivalrous*) Becoming a knight.

CHIVALEARY: (also *Chivalry*) a.) Knighthood. Deeds and qualities of a knight. b.) The body or order of knights.

CHIVALROUS: Like, or having the characteristics of, a medieval knight or man-at-arms. To be doughty or valorous.

CHIVALRY: a.) The contemporary name for the "men-at-arms", or mounted and fully armed fighting-men, of the Middle Ages. b.) As a historical term for the medieval men-at-arms. Occasionally applied poetically or idealistically to "cavalry" or "horsemen" in general, especially when chivalrous gallantry is attributed.

CHOKE: a.) To hinder breathing by obstructing the windpipe with a piece of food or foreign matter in the throat. b.) To hinder breathing by obstructing the windpipe; to decrease or stop a person's intake of air; to strangle; to suffocate. This may be accomplished with one or both hands, the arm or any object that can crush the windpipe. c.) A narrowing in size toward the muzzle in the bore of a gun.

CHOP: a.) To cut with a quick and heavy blow by bringing down the blade of the knife sharply on the surface of an object, hacking as with an ax or cleaver and then promptly pulling the blade out and back in the direction from which it originated. b.) (also *Karate Chop*) An open-handed strike, associated with martial arts, made with the outside edge (little finger side) of the hand and the fingers tensed. See also Knife Hand.

CIRCLE LEFT: A passing action in footwork that carries the combatant clockwise around the imaginary circle.

CIRCLE PARADE: (Small Sword) "One of the lower round parades, derived from the simple parade of semi-circle- It secures the lower part of the body within; baffles the inward counter disengagements and feints- It is frequently called doubling semicircle, as the point forms an exact circle from that parade. The course of the point is from right to left , drop'd to an angle of forty-five degrees from guard point." See also *Circular Parry.*

CIRCLE RIGHT: a.) A demi-lunge to the right that advances a combatant counterclockwise on the imaginary circle. The circle right is used in conjunction with the demi-volte in order to move the combatant continuously around the circle while keeping the sword arm to the inside towards one's opponent. b.) Any footwork that carries the combatant to the right on the imaginary circle.

CIRCLE STEPS: (also *Circular Paces*) Previous to the linear style of fencing generated by the introduction of the lunge, fencers, especially the Spanish, circled around one another like two animals about to fight. After the introduction of the lunge, the "circle steps" were predominantly a feature of the Spanish school. In the seventeenth century Spanish school, the 'mysterious circle' was the geometrical basis of all footwork and distance. Many masters however, still practiced and taught various forms of evasions and passes on the circle well into the nineteenth century. See *Circular Paces*

CIRCLES IN THE AIR: A dexterity exercise with the sword that has the combatant draw circles with the point of the sword in both a clockwise and counter-clockwise direction. The size of the circles are diminished after each set, placing focus on the command of the weapon's point.

CIRCLES: (Small Sword) "In general are compound movements with the point or blade in pursuit of your adversary's blade- All round parades form exact circles with the point from right to left or vice versa."

CIRCULAR BLOCK: a.) A defensive action made with the hand or arm that goes from above the belt to below the belt, or vice-versa, in a semi-circular path on the same side of the body. b.) A block that goes from above the belt to below the belt, or vice-versa, in a semi-circular path on the same side of the body. c.) See *Circular Parry.*

CIRCULAR FEINT: a.) (also *Tour d'epee*) An offensive movement of the blade where the point of the weapon describes a complete circle, finishing in the same line it had begun in, made to resemble a disengage- coupé on an attack. b.) Taking a circular step either to the left or right with a feint attack, then springing from the advanced foot and reversing with a step and attack from the opposite direction of the circle.

CIRCULAR PACES: a.) (also *Circle Steps*) The ninth and tenth direction of footwork determined by the ten directions of movement in Spanish swordplay; these are the *Circular Pace Right* and *Circular Pace Left*.

CIRCULAR PARRY: (also *Counter Parry* and sometimes "*Twiddle*") Any parry which the point of the weapon describes a com¬plete circle with the hand and weapon finishing in the position in which they started. The point of the blade describes a circle during the movement while the guard remains in the same relative position. The blade finishes the parry in the same position as that from which it started. The Circular Parry was one of the principle forms of defense in historical swordplay. The sweeping action of the blade was believed to defend the entire body from the aspects of a thrust. A form of "Universal Parry."

CIRCULER HALFE PACE: Giacomo di Grassi's term for the *Demi-Volte*.

CIVIL SALUTE: See *Salute*.

CIVILIAN SWORD: Any sword worn by someone not in the military. The rapier was one of the first swords to be considered primarily a civilian weapon. The Spanish name Espada Ropera, literally means, "dress sword"; and within a few decades of its first appearance in the 1480's the rapier had become an essential part of every Spanish and Italian gentlemen's proper attire; regardless of his actual skill at swordplay.

CLAPPERCLAW: (also *Clapper-claw*) To scratch or claw with the open hand and nails; to beat, thrash, drub. The exchanging of blows; a rough and tumble.

CLAPPERDUDGEON: a.) The hilt of a dagger. b.) An insulting reproach, a term for a beggar born.

CLASSIC STANCE: a.) The traditional on guard stance for competitive fencers. See *Three-Point Stance* and *Two-Point Stance*. b.)

A term in boxing for the basic placement of the body taught to most beginners: "left foot flat, forward, and slightly turned in, heel of right foot off the floor, upper body turned slightly left, right hand high and close to chin, left just below eye level."

CLATTER: The rattling noise of weap¬ons.

CLAW HAND: (MA) An open hand attack with the fingers splayed and crooked generally associated with the Martial Arts.

CLAYMORE: (basket hilted) A form of 18th century Scottish cut & thrust sword relative of the Italian *schiavona*.

CLICHÉS: "In the early days of printing, illustrations were carved on wooden blocks," says Robert Claiborne, "which were then inked and run through the press. With faster presses and bigger editions, wood wouldn't stand up; instead, the block was used to make a cast metal plate, called a *cliché* or *stereotype*. Since clichés were reused from time to time, some clever newspaperman transferred the term to stereotyped expressions that were also reused - too often."

CLINCH: a.) A struggle or scuffle at close quarters where fighters have used both hands and arms to lock onto one another while fighting. See Corps-à-Corps. b.) In unarmed combat, where fighters have locked onto one another while fighting in close. c.) See Bear Hug.

CLOAK AND DAGGER: a.) A style of armed combat that uses a dagger as the primary offensive weapon and a cloak, generally wrapped about the opposite arm, for defense. b.) Involving or suggesting of espionage.

CLOAK AND SWORD: A sixteenth century alternative to rapier and dagger, the cloak being used in the left hand for defense while the rapier was used in the right hand for offense. The cloak was generally wrapped twice around the left arm, leaving a section to hang loose in order to entangle a thrust or block a cut. It was advised that the left leg was kept back, so that the cloak had no resistance behind it.

CLOBBER: To pound mercilessly; to hit with force.

CLOSE FIGHT: To fight at the half-sword; fighting inside measure.

CLOSE MEASURE: Fencing measure used when working offensive/defensive blade-play in the close. The blades extend beyond the combatants by roughly three to four inches. Torsos roughly four feet apart. Tighter measure makes it difficult to safely continue blade-play.

CLOSE QUARTERS: a.) When two combatants are inside normal measure, by accident, design or confines of fencing space, but can still wield their swords correctly. b.) Immediate contact with the foe. c.) Said of a battle or combat where the participants are close enough for hand to hand combat.

CLOSE TO THE OBLIQUE: See *Zone*.

CLOSE: a.) To cover or shut a line of engagement (by the defender's weapon) against an attack. b.) (also *Enter*) The technique of stepping inside measure, usually into an offensive action, to gain tactical advantage for both defensive and offensive actions. c.) (also *The Close, Foot-to-Foot, At the Half-Sword,* and *Close Quarters*) The rough and tumble portion of swordplay when two combatants are inside normal measure, by accident, design or confines of fencing space, but can still wield their swords correctly. In this position they can strike with the unarmed hand, kick and punch their opponent.

CLOSED LINE: Refers to a line of engagement when the defender's weapon has covered or blocked the line to an attack.

CLOSED: (also *Covered*) Said of a line of attack, when the defender's blade placement prevents an attack to that particular line.

CLOSED-HAND TECHNIQUES: Offensive and/or defensive techniques made in armed or unarmed combat executed with a closed hand or fist. Opposite of *Open-Hand Techniques.*

CLOSES: It would appear that by the end of

the sixteenth century the practice of closes and grappling in swordplay were being cut back as techniques taught in the fencing schools. This is mentioned in Silver's manual and shown in the decreasing amount of grappling techniques appearing fencing manuals after 1600. "Besides, there are now in these dayes no gripes, closes, wrestlings, striking with the hilts, daggers or bucklers, used in Fence-schooles."

CLOSING LINES: The act or placement of the weapon(s) where one or more of the lines of attack open to the adversary are blocked off, or "closed." Such placement of the blade masters all attacks in that line unless the adversary somehow displaces the guard.

CLOSING PARRY: The most common defensive action with the sword which opposes the energy coming in or closes the line of attack (target area) to it. See also *Opposition Parry.*

CLOTHES LINE: (also *Clothesline, Clothesline*) Slang for a straight arm attack that catches the victim horizontally across the chest or neck, having the similar effect of running into a tight rope or clothes line.

CLOVER: See *Four-Leaf Clover.*

CLUB: a.) A heavy stick. b.) In Elizabethan England, during any public fray the cry was "Clubs! Clubs!" by way of calling for persons with clubs to part the combatants:

CLUMP: A term from sword and cloak play for a cape tossed over the head, covering or wrapping the opponent's face.

COBB'S TRAVERSE: (also *Cobs Traverse*) A euphemism for running away from a fight; or sometimes running backward; or back-pedaling from an encounter named for an Elizabethan fencer and well-known brawler by the name of Cobb. ". . . those that had seene anie go backe too fast in his fight, would say, he did tread Cobs Traverse."

COCCIA: (It.) The guard or hilt of the weapon.

COCK: a.) The part of a lock of a gun that strikes fire. b.) A term for the "wind up" or "control point" in armed and unarmed combat. To draw the arm or weapon back like the hammer of a gun; ready to release and strike. See also *Chamber* and *Wind-Up*.

Cockstep: In the English style a koc stappis or kocstep, a forward skipping step of the lead foot, similar to the *Balestra* of later fencing.

COCKY: During the Victorian era, the term "cock" was deemed uncouth and as such the cockroach became a "roach" and the common barnyard cock became a "rooster." The term cocky, for some reason, remained unedited meaning a pert or arrogant man seeming to display the machismo of a crowing cock.

CODOLA: (It.) See *Tang*.

COIN CARRIER: An exercise designed to help the combatant develop fluid horizontal movement in footwork by placing a coin either on or under the initiating foot and then carrying the coin forward with the foot.

Cold Blood: The codes of dueling established in the Elizabethan period had gentlemen meet at dawn, after tempers had cooled, they had rested, and were in their right mind. With the heat of the moment passed, they could then rationally come to terms or settle their differences as gentlemen.

COLD STEEL: (also *Cold Iron*) Slang for a cut and thrust weapon. Now generally applied to any sharp sword.

COLDCOCK: (also *Cold-Cock*) To knock someone unconscious. The source of this term is obscure; it could well have derived from musket combat where, at close quarters there may not have been time to reload and a soldier was forced to take down his opponent with the butt end of the musket without firing. The hammer of a gun being referred to as a "cock," a man who dispatches his opponent with his musket without firing could be said to have cold¬cocked his victim. Another plausible source is offered by Robert Claiborne, "my own guess,"

he says, "is that it refers to the piece of lead pipe once used for such a purpose, which was roughly the shape of a cock [a vulgar term for the penis] but - being metal - was cold, not warm." I'm sure there are other possible origins, that being as it may, the term is still with us today and a person can coldcock another with the butt of a musket, a lead pipe, or anything...

COLICHEMARDE: (also *Conichemarde* and *Konigsmark*) A blade that came into fashion between 1680 and 1690, first in France, then in Germany and England. The name "colichemarde" is believed to be a very bad phonetic rendering of its supposed inventor the Swedish Count Konigsmark. The blade was characteristically wide at the forte, for about eight inches from the hilt, then it narrowed quite suddenly, being extremely light and flexible for the remainder of its length. This highly perfect form of blade was used between 1680 and 1720, where it seems to have very suddenly gone out of fashion, being replaced by the small sword.

COLLAPSE: A relaxed fall or faint completed with a lifeless, unconscious body.

COLLAR: a.) A piece of armor designed to protect the neck; the neckpiece of a hauberk or similar piece of armor. b.) Something to be worn about the neck, hence, to grab someone by the throat, wearing one's hands about their neck.

COLPI DRITTI: ("right strokes") Vadi blows from the right side used to defend.

COLPO D'ARRESTO: (It.) See *Stop Thrust*.

COLUMN OF CONFLICT: The third, or middle column of a side-by-side fight plot, used to indicate the Phrase number of the choreography and to indicate the direction of offensive and defensive action between the combatants.

COMBAT: An encounter or fight between two armed persons; personal combat, a duel. To fight or do battle.

COMBATANT: a.) One who fights; a fighter, a warrior. b.) One who is armed and ready to fight. One who is contending in a fight.

COMBINATION: a.) The delivering of two or more offensive actions in quick succession to one another. b.) (Boxing) Throwing two or more punches that are strung together in a pattern and issued in rapid succession. The classic one-two combination is a left jab followed by the right cross.

COME OFF: To retire or retreat from an engagement. To leave the field of combat.

COMING TO THE CLOSE: Angelo's term for getting within distance and seizing the opponent's blade.

COMING TO THE POINT: In a disagreement between two gentlemen, if they matter could not be resolved by discourse they would be forced to come to the point -- meaning literally to settle the argument with swords. This is where "ala stocatta [the thrust] carries the day."

COMMAND: (also Commanding the Blade) Controlling the opposing blade during the execution of a pris d'fer and remaining engaged upon completion. Opposite of Expulsion.

COMMANDING: (also *Commanding the Sword*) a.) See *Command*. b.) The manipulation of the opposing blade for a disarm or offensive advantage. A beat, pressure or *pris d'fer*. c.) Coming to the close and seizing the opponent's blade.

COMPASS BLOW: a.) A cut delivered from a molinello. b.) (also Compasse Blow) A term used by early seventeenth century fencing master Joseph Swetnam for a cut delivered from a molinello that changes inside and outside lines. ". . . bow thy Sword-elbow joynt, & with thy knuckles upward, and thy Sword hilt so high as your eare, and then by turning of your sword hand wrist, bend, or proffer the point of thy Sword with a blow towards your enemies Dagger eare, but presently turning your wrist, bringing the middest of your Sword close over the crowne of thy head, and with a compasse blow, striking it home to the Sword eare, or to the outside

of his legge."

COMPLEMENTARY FOOTWORK: Footwork in a fight that corresponds in measure to that of the opponent, keeping correct distance as they move across the floor.

COMPOSED ATTACK: See Compound Attack.

COMPOSITE EXERCISE: An acting exercise that combines the work on the Who, What, When, Where and Why of a fight. It takes the components of each of the given circumstances and brings them together into one improvisational exercise.

COMPOUND ATTACK: (also *Composed Attack*) a.) Any attack that requires the combined movements of at least one feint attack and a changement before the execution of the direct attack.

COMPOUND FOOTWORK: The execution of two or more simple elements of footwork as one complete action, such as the patinando (An advance followed immediately by a lunge).

COMPOUND-HILT: (also *Compound Guard* and *Complex Hilt*) - a term used to describe the various hilts of Renaissance and some late Medieval swords consisting of more than a simple cross guard, there were a great variety.

COMPOUND PRIS D'FER: An uninterrupted succession of blade taking actions.

COMPOUND RIPOSTE: A Riposte consisting of one or more feints.

CONFLICT: Battle; fight; combat.

CONNOTATION: The suggestion of a meaning to an action apart from any common significance the movement possesses.

CONSTRAINED: Said of any slow or controlled lowering to the floor that is executed in conjunction with a continual contact technique such as a choke hold or joint lock.

CONTACT: a.) To meet, come across, be brought into practical connection with. To touch.

CONTAINED MOVEMENT: Controlled or confined action, dictated by space, character or style.

CONTENT: The central concern or intent that guides the movement in a physical dialogue.

CONTENTION: A dispute, quarrel, fight; personal combat.

CONTINUE STEP: The second step of a Half Passe; starting with a Half Passe and continuing on with the same foot to finish in either a Passe, Thwart, Cross or Slip.

CONTRA CAVATIONE: (It.) (also *Contra Cavazione*) Fabris' term for the counter changement. "A contra cavatione is that which can be done, during the time that the enemy disengages, by disengaging yourself, so that he shall find himself situated as before. . . ." Of course today the action may as easily be a coupé as a disengage.

CONTRA GUARDIA: (It.) Giganti's term for a covered engagement of the blades.

CONTRA POSTURA: (It.) (also *Contra Guardia*) A placement of the body and weapon(s) that compliments or counters the guard assumed by the opponent. This idea, first presented by Fabris, is the beginning of the modern meaning of "guard." See also Postura and Proportion. "Wishing to form the `contra postura,'" says Fabris, "it is necessary so to place the body and the sword, that without touching the enemy's weapon one should be protected in the straight line which comes from the adversary's point towards the body, and that one should be thus in safety without making any movement whatsoever."

CONTRARISPOSTA: (It.) See *Counter Riposte.*

CONTRE TEMPS: (Fr.) See *Counter Time.*

CONTRE-PARADE: (Fr.) See *Counter Parry.*

CONTRETEMPS: (Fr.) See *Second Intention.*

CONTROLLING THE ATTACK: (also *Checking*) The process of curbing, or restraining the offending hand, arm or leg after a successful block. With pressure and force the defending hand or arm remains in contact with the opponent's (without gripping, locking or holding) in order to sense their movements,

feel or control the placement of the offending limb, and use that to both offensive and defensive advantage. The offending hand, arm or leg may be controlled in three ways; by *Bind, Envelopment,* or *Transport.* These actions command the opposing hand or arm and may retain it or remove it with the action of an *Expulsion.*

CONTROLLING THE POINT: A sixteenth century term for commanding or displacing the opponent's point.

CONTROTEMPO: (Ger.) See *Counter Time.*

CONTROTEMPO: (It.) See *Counter Time.*

COOP: Possibly a misspelling of the French *Coupé.*

COPERTINO: (It.) A false coupe, made without changing the line.

COQUILLE: (Fr.) The guard (shell) of the hilt, protecting the hand.

CORONA: ("Crown") See *Posta de Fronte.*

CORPS-À-CORPS: (also *Corps a Corps,* literally "body-to-body") a.) An action in which there is body contact or where the blades are locked together and distance is closed so that normal fencing action becomes impossible. b.) Applied to a clinch in swordplay, literally meaning "body-to-body." Describes the moment where distance is closed and there is body contact and/or the blades are locked together so that the weapons are immobilized.

CORRECT DISTANCE: The correct or prescribed measure the execution of a particular action, sequence or fighting style. See also *Distance, Correct.*

COULÉ: (Fr.) Literally "flowed." (also *Gissade* and *Glide*) A thrust in the line of engagement while keeping contact with the opponent's blade, gliding along its side.

COUNTER ATTACK: To take an action that will hit the opponent before the final movement of the opponent's attack is executed. See *Stop Hit, Time Hit* and *Stop Thrust.*

COUNTER CHANGEMENT: A changement executed in response to a changement executed by the opponent. The counter is executed during the opponent's changement, carrying their blade back to their point of origin. Such an action was taught by Fabris and is believed to be a common practice in the mid-seventeenth century, and possibly earlier.

COUNTER COUPÉ: One of the simple attacks, made in one motion, by executing a coupe as a deceive of the opponent's change of engagement.

COUNTER DISENGAGEMENT: a.) A simple offensive action that deceives a change of engagement or counter parry with a changement. b.) (also *Counter-Disengage*) One of the simple attacks, made in one motion, by executing a disengage as a deceive of the opponent's change of engagement. c.) (in French *Contre Degagemens*) (Small Sword) "A compound feint or movement performed instantaneously after, and somtimes contrarily to a simple disengagement.- This term is more particularly applied to the second disengagement made after you find that an adversary forms a low parade to your first.- There are various kinds of counter disengagements; such as the upper counter disengagements of carte and tierce, and the lower counter disengagements of semi-circle, octave, prime and seconde."

COUNTER GUARD: a.) Bars or rings placed on the inside of the hilt of sixteenth and seventeenth century rapiers to help protect the combatant's hand and wrist. b.) The practice of assuming various guards in response to the blade and body placement of the opponent. "for at some times, and for some purposes, one guard may better serve then another: for change of guards may crosse some mens play" See also *Contra Postura*. c.) (rare) See *Contra Postura*.

COUNTER OFFENSIVE ACTIONS: An attack into an attack. See Stop Hit, Stop Thrust, and Time Hit.

COUNTER PARRY: (also *Circular Parry*) a.) From the seventeenth century French *Contre-Parade*, meaning a counter or circular parry. b.) A parry that begins in one line, travels a full circle to meet the attacking blade in the original line.

COUNTER PRESS: A press attack offered in resistance to the opponent's initial press on the blade.

COUNTER RIPOSTE: The offensive action which follows the successful parry of a riposte.

COUNTER TIME: Initiating an action that provokes a stop hit or stop cut from one's opponent, parrying it and seizing time on the counter attack and landing with the second intention.

COUNTER: a.) A sixteenth and seventeenth century term for a simultaneous parry and riposte. The counter was an attack delivered into the attack of one's opponent that deflects the attacking weapon and hits the opponent. The stronger attack taking the advantage. Not to be confused with the *Counter Attack*. b.) A term commonly used for the riposte. c.) A term applied to all circular parries in which, while the hand retains the same position, the point is made to describe a circle. See *Circular Parry*.

COUNTERBLOW: (also *Counter Blow, Counter-Blow*) A blow delivered into an attack. See *Stop Cut*.

COUNTERPASSES: (also *Counter Passes, Counter-Passes*) The counter movements in footwork that maintain the distance between the combatants by either passing forward or back in response to the footwork initiated by one's opponent. See also *Complimentary Footwork*.

COUNTERPUNCH: (also *Counter Punch, Counter-Punch*) A punch thrown in response to one thrown by the opponent.

COUNTER–PUNCH: A punch thrown in response to one thrown by the opponent intended to land before the opponent's punch, thus stopping the attack. Such a punch leads to the term "beat to the punch."

COUP D'ARRÊT: (Fr.) See *Stop Thrust*.

COUP DE GRACE: (Fr.) Literally "the blow

of mercy" by which one would dispatch a mortally wounded foe – putting him out of misery. The term now means the finishing stroke, blow or thrust, which may or may not be merciful.

Coup de Jarnac: (also *Jarnac Stroke*) A cut below the belt delivered to the back of the knee or hamstring. Named after one Sieur de Jarnac in the mid sixteenth century. A duel between Jarnac and Chastaigneraie took place in France in 1547. Both men were favorites to the king. The duel turned into a route, however, because of a "dishonorable" blow to the back of the leg given by Jarnac, which felled Chastaigneraie. Jarnac then repeated the blow to the other leg, which sealed his opponent's fate. Since then, the "Coup de Jarnac" has been used to describe such a hit below the belt, and now is applied to any dishonorable stroke or blow.

Coup de Temps: (Fr.) A thrust in time.

Coup Double: (Fr.) See Double Touch.

Coup Droit: (Fr.) A straight thrust.

Coup Fourré: A simultaneous attack that results in a double touch.

Coup sec: A percussive engagement of the blades.

Coup: (Fr.) Derived from the Latin colpus, meaning a blow with the fist, a knockout blow. The French term came to represent the actual blow or hit delivered to one's opponent, and finally to the `touch' made in a fencing bout.

Coupé: (Fr., It. & Ger.) (also *Cut-Over*) a.) A changement associated with the French school executed from an engaged guard position and carrying the blade around the point of the opposing weapon. There are two different ways of executing a coupé. The standard coupé frees the point from the opposing blade and then performs a changement over the tip of the sword, the Engaged Coupé remains engaged as it travels up the blade. Both the coupé, and the engaged coupé must be executed from an engaged guard position and must travel

over the point of the opposing blade. b.) A movement that takes the blade around the partner's blade point. Usually carried out in the high line. Also see *Australian Coupé*. c.) A change of engagement executed from an engaged guard position that takes the blade around the point of the opposing blade. Sometimes called a cutover. Opposite of a *Disengage*. d.) One of the simplest, indirect, attacks, made with one motion by lifting the point over the opponent's point (in the high line) and extending the arm and weapon threatening the opponent's target.

Coupé-Coupé: (Fr.) A compound attack consisting of a feint of the cut-over, followed by a second cut-over.

Couple a gorge: An English malapropism for the French *coupe la gorge*, meaning "cut the throat."

Courageous Captain of Compliments: A reference to the mastery of the overly polite pretense of strict dueling *punctilio*.

Court Sword: a.) A somewhat impractical, practically useless imitation of the small sword, worn on rare occasions, by very few men, as an ornament with official court dress. b.) Often misapplied to the Small Sword.

Covered: (also *Closed*) Said of a line of engagement, when the defender's weapon prevents an attack to that line of engagement. Covering Up: A defensive maneuver in boxing in which a fighter uses both of his arms to close or protect the body and head. "This tactic is generally used when a fighter is in trouble and needs to last out a short time before the end of a round."

Coverta: ("Covering", meaning 'blanket') Fiore's term for the principle of covering a possible line or opening of attack by moving the body and weapon to close it. In Vadi the defensive controlling of the enemy's sword with your own or your hand. It consists of maintaining contact while entering close.

Covred: (also *Covering*) (Small Sword) "The act of securing yourself from an interchanged thrust from an adversary, at the time of longing, or executing an intended thrust.- When you justly oppose your adversay's blade in longing, and your arm does not deviate from the line of direction, it is then termed a well-covered thrust or longe-Time thrusts must not be attempted, unless you cover yourself minutely. See *Opposition*, and *Time Thrust*.

COWARD: The term is believed to have derived from the Latin cauda, meaning tail: a coward, like a puppy can sulk off with its tail between its legs or turn tail and run...

COWARD'S PARRY: (also *Ninth Parry*) With eight recognized parries in the French classical school of fencing, the ninth, or coward's parry was an ignoble term given to the avoidance of an attack by displacing the body, for the reason that fencing in that time was a skillful and dexterous display of blade play, and to retreat or displace the body was thought unstylish and cowardice.

CRACKER: A blusterer, swaggerer.

CRASH: (also *Crashing*) a.) Forcing measure. An aggressive close of measure, usually into a grapple or wrestling hold. b.) Unarmed block which involves moving inside the reach of the attack.

CRESCENT KICK: (MA) A large, arcing kick made with the entire leg traveling in a semi-circular path with the toes pointing upward. The curled inside edge of the foot is used to deflect to opponent's arm, or to strike to the face. The kick may be made from the inside *(Inside Crescent Kick)* or the outside *(Outside Crescent Kick)*.

CREST: a.) The helmet topping an armorial ensign. b.) Coat-armor. c.) A helmet.

CROISÉ: (Fr.) (also *Twist* or *Cut Down*) a.) A blade taking action that carries the opposing weapon from a high line to a low line, and vice versa, on the same side of the body as the engagement. The original object of this action was to displace the opponent's point, while keeping the blades engaged, to open a line of attack. To fling the blade aside would

deprive the aggressor of the definite information of the location of the opponent's blade. If, however, the opponent had a loose grip on their sword, the action could be executed with an Expulsion, quickly flinging off the blade with the intent to disarm, or thoroughly overwhelm the opponent for a moment. b.) Taking the partner's blade from a high line to a low line on the same side of the body. The Croise is a *prise-de-fer.* c.) An attack on the blade which carries the opposing weapon from a high line to a low line, or vice versa, but on the same side as the engagement, not diagonally across like a bind. d.) An attack on the blade made by engaging the blade and moving it vertically to the opposite line.

CROKED PACE: See *Slope Pace*.

CROSS BLOCK: a.) A defensive action executed by bringing the hand/arm across the body (rather than up/down or to the outside of the body). Used to stop or deflect an oncoming attack. b.) An inside or outside block made across the body.

CROSS BLOW: a.) A cut delivered across the body from the non sword-bearing side. b.) A term sometimes used by Saviolo in his description of a reverse cut or blow. [Saviolo]

CROSS BODY GUARDS: Guard positions that angle the blade of the weapon across the body, with the hand and hilt on one side and the point on the other. All rapier guards may be assumed across the body, either joined and engaged with the opponent's blade; or with the blades separated and free. Cross body guards are generally assumed in transitional rapier play. In Double Fence the rapier may be held in a cross body guard, but there are no such guards with the dagger.

CROSS FIVE: Sometimes applied to the double fence parry, *High Cross* or *Cross Parry One*, defending a descending vertical cutting attack to the head.

CROSS FOUR: (also *Cross Parry Four*) a.) See *Cross Left*. b.) (also *Cross Low Five*) A term sometimes applied to the last of four cross parries, protecting the crotch. The standard term for this parry is *Cross Two* or *Low Cross*.

CROSS LEFT: (also *Cross Parry Left Shoulder* and *Cross Parry Four*) The joined double weapon defense against attacks to the left shoulder or chest. This parry is generally made with the rapier hand above the dagger in a placement similar to rapier parry high one. The dagger hand is below that of the rapier, held in a fashion similar to the dagger parry of three. The cross may be made with either the dagger in front of or behind the rapier.

CROSS OF A WELSH HOOK: The point where the shaft of a halberd was crossed by the steel head which formed an ax on one side and a spike on the other.

CROSS ONE: (also *Cross Parry One* and *Cross Parry Five*) See *High Cross*.

CROSS PARRY: (also *Scissors Parry* and *X-Parry*) a.) A parry executed with two weapons, generally rapier and dagger, where the weapons are crossed at or near the forte, forming an "X" with the blades. The attacking weapon is blocked with the outer portion of the "X", away from the hands. A common parry in rapier and dagger play, the dagger is generally used to hold the attacking blade in check, or to remove it as an immediate threat while the rapier launches a counter attack. In rapier and dagger play there are two schools of numbering cross parries; the first school uses the standard numerical system defining targets in relation to the sword baring arm. The second style offers a separate numerical system, making cross parries separate from the standard numerical system. Both styles are in common practice and it is best for the combatant to confirm the target. b.) A parry using both rapier and dagger held forte to forte so that the blades cross, forming an open "V" to catch the attacking blade. c.) A parry executed with two weapons, generally rapier and dagger, where the weapons are

crossed at or near the forte, forming an "X" with the blades. The attacking weapon is blocked with the outer portion of the "X", away from the hands. d.) A joined parry in Elizabethan rapier and dagger play which although common, was advised against by many practitioners of the art. ". . . no man ought to accustome himslefe to defend blowes with the Rapier and Dagger both together, which manner of defending is now commonly used because men beleeve, that they stand more assuredly by that meanes. although in truth it is not so. For the Rapier and Dagger are so bound thereby, that they may not strike before they be recovered, and therein are spent two tymes. . ." e.) A parry executed across the body.

CROSS RIGHT: (also *Cross Parry Right Shoulder* and *Cross Parry Three*) The joined double fence parry against attacks to the right shoulder made with the rapier hand beneath the dagger in a placement similar to parry three and the dagger hand above that of the rapier, held in a fashion similar to the dagger parry of high one (made with either the dagger before or behind the rapier).

CROSS STEP: a.) A step that takes the body diagonally off-line to either the right or left, ending with the legs crossed.

CROSS TWO: a.) Common for the cross parry used to defending a rising vertical attack to the groin. See *Low Cross*. b.) (also *Cross Parry Two*) Sometimes used for the cross parry that protects the left shoulder. Generally referred to as *Cross Four*.

CROSS: (also *Crossing Punch*) A punch that travels across the victims jaw-line, from either the right to the left, or vice versa, delivered with the feet firmly planted and a rotation of the hips, waist and upper body in the direction the punch is delivered. A cross may be delivered from either the right or left. b.) Footwork [as in crossover step and sometimes the pass...] c.) A Posted, Passing Traverse on the Forward 45 degree line, taking the body Off-Line to either the right or left and ending with the legs crossed. d.) A term for the cross parry in rapier and dagger and other double weapon techniques. e.) A term for a block where both arms are used to deflect or catch the attack in the "X" or cross made by the arms. f.) A term for the parry as used by Elizabethan Fencing Masters such as George Silver. g.) Athwart, across.

CROSSBAR: a.) The protecting parts of the hilt of the Italian fencing foil, providing leverage to the grip. b.) See *Cross-Hilt*.

CROSS-BLOW: A term used by Vincentio Saviolo for the mandritta.

CROSS-BOW: A bow having the form of a cross.

CROSS-BUTTOCK: A peculiar throw over the hip made use of in wrestling and formerly in pugilism. "A cross-buttock in pugilism is, when the party, advancing his right leg and thigh, closes with his antagonist, and catching him with his right arm, or giving a round blow, throws him over his right hip, upon his head." See also Buttock.

CROSSE GUARD: A guard position in rapier and dagger play taught by seventeenth century fight master Joseph Swetnam where the rapier is carried low and across the body to the left and the dagger is held at waist level on the dagger bearing side of the body with its point directed straight up.

CROSSE STAFF: See Quarterstaff.

CROSS-GUARD: The very simple form of hilt, consisting of straight quil¬lons projecting at right angles from the weapon and so forming a cross with the blade and the grip.

CROSS-HILT: a.) (also *Cross-Guard* and *Cross-Bar*) A very simple form of sword guard, consisting of straight quillons set a right angles to the weapon, thus forming a cross with the handle and blade. b.) A term applied to a sword with a cross-hilt.

CROSSING: An eighteenth century term for the croisé. The technique was not popular with most fencing schools in this period, but was advocated quite strongly by Angelo.

CROSSOVER STEP: A double pass forward or back, that enables the combatant to gain or break ground quickly, ending with the same foot forward as when the action began.

CROSS-STEP: See *Pass*.

Crouch Style: A style of boxing frequently used by shorter fighters with a shorter reach than their opponent. The body is bent down, out of which the fighter can explode on to the offensive.

CROW HOP: A form of advance or forward movement in swordplay consisting of a jump forward pulling the back leg in.

CROWD: A tactic in armed and unarmed combat where one deliberately closes-quarters with an opponent in an effort to enable him from delivering effective or strong blows, then applying specific offensive pressure prepared for such in-fighting.

CROWN GUARD: A form of high center stance. Also *Frontale*.

CRUSH: (also *Crunch*) Violent compression or pressure applied by the hand or foot that bruises, breaks down, injures, or destroys. The term is generally applied to the action of compressing an object, such as the head, between the hands or between a foot and a fixed surface such as the floor.

CUDGEL: a.) A stick to strike with. b.) To beat with a stick.

CUDGELLED: (also *Cudgeled*) Having been struck with a cudgel; injury caused by a cudgel.

CUFF: A blow or strike with the fist or fists.

CUISSES: (also *Cushes*) Armor for the thighs.

CUP-HILT: a.) The cup or bell-shaped guard of the Spanish rapier; possibly deriving its name from not only its bell-like shape, but also the bell-like sound it emits upon being struck. The cup-hilt rapier offers the fencer almost complete protection of the sword hand. The guard assembly is still made up of the basic components, the quillons, pas d'âne and knuckle bow, but unlike the bars and rings of the two-ring and swept-hilted rapiers, there are no gaps or openings through which an offensive thrust can penetrate. The cup-hilt was devised by the Spanish, and was common among rapiers during the latter half of the sixteenth, and throughout the seventeenth and eight¬eenth centuries. In fact, the cup-hilt worked so effectively that it is the basis of the guard for the modern fencing foil and epée. b.) Often applied to the entire sword when fitted with a cup-hilt. The Cup-Hilt Rapier.

Curtle-Axe: (also *Curtleax* and *Curtaxe*) A perverted phonetic rendering for "cutlass" or the French "coutelas."

Cuscinetto: (It.) (Literally "little cushion") A small circular leather cushion placed on the inside of a cup-hilt to prevent the fingers from jamming against the guard.

Cut & Thrust: a.) Said of a weapon suitable for attacks both with the edge and point. b.) The action of using a weapon, attacking both with edge and point.

Cut Down: a) Kill. b) Sometimes used for a croisé executed from the high to low line.

Cut Over Your Adversary's Point: (Small Sword) "Is performed with a simple movement of the wrist upwards, by which your point is raised nearly perpendicular, and thereby disengaged from one side to the other,- The arm is not to deviate from the line of direction.- The cuts over the point answer the purposes of disengagements, when your adversary has his point too much elevated on guard." See also *Coupé*.

Cut to the Quick: a.) Quick originally had nothing to do with speed, but rather with living - the presence of life, hence, if someone has been cut to the quick, their living flesh has been cut and perhaps their life severed. b.) Edge blows, or cuts that land, or appear to land on the body. Such cuts can be drawn like a razor or sliced as with a knife.

Cut Up: Sometimes used for a croisé executed from the low to high line.

Cut: a.) A stroke, blow or attack made with the edge of the blade; distinguished from a thrust, made by pushing or driving the point forward. b.) A stroke, blow or attack made with the edge of a blade. c.) The theoretical offensive action of the edge of the saber blade. The cut may be executed as a drawing cut or a chop. The former specification of the use of the theoretical edge has been dropped and any part of the competitive saber blade is construed to inflict a valid offensive action. d.) To separate from the body... Cutlas: (also Cutlass) A short sword with a flat, wide and slightly curved blade, designed more for edge play than for point work.

Cutler: One whose occupation is to make knives. See also *Sword-Cutler*.

Cutover: (also *Cut-Over* and *Cut Over*) The English term for *Coupé*.

Cutting Edge: a.) The sharp, true or fore edge of any blade. b.) (also *True Edge*) That edge of the blade which, when the weapon is held correctly, is naturally directed towards one's opponent.

Cutting on the Circle: A drill in bladeplay that takes the combatants through a series of cuts, parries and ripostes while executing circular paces on the tracks of the imaginary circle.

Cutting Stroke: A blow or attack delivered with the edge of the blade. See *Cut*.

Cutting the Line: a.) Interrupting the opponent's feints with a sweeping action of the defending blade. b.) Circular parries made other than in the line of engagement. A combination of a Direct Parry and a Circular Parry. The action begins with the hand and blade moving from one position to another in either a horizontal or vertical plane; as the blade travels across the body, it also executes a Circular Parry for the line it is moving towards. Thus the action is a Circular Parry that cuts across the center-line of the body, starting on one side, ending on the other.

Cutting the Ring in Half: Containing an opponent by allowing him only half the

D

ring to move in. You slide from side to side, not allowing him access to the other side of the ring. Sluggers generally use this tactic against quick and nimble fighters.

CUTTING THROUGH STEEL: Used in modern sabre fencing when, due to the flexible fencing blades, an attack strikes the opponent around a successful parry.

CUTTLE: A swaggerer, bully.

DOUBLE-HAND TECHNIQUE: One or more actions executed with the sword grip being held in both hands. A technique often used in old swashbuckler films to imply desperation, power, exhaustion and so on.

DAGGER GRIP: a.) The method of holding the dagger. b.) The handle of a dagger.

DAGGER MEASURE: Measure is relative, determined by the length of the weapon being used. When working offensively with a dagger you must change your measure to suit the weapon. Correct distance is comparable to that of the rapier, being a distance of at least six to ten inches from the chest of one combatant to the furthest extension of the dagger at the completion of any aggressive action.

DAGGER PARRY: a.) A defensive action (generally a beat, detached or opposition parry) executed with the dagger. b.) Defensive actions for the left side of the body from knees up as assigned by most fencing masters of the Elizabethan period. The dagger was generally used to defend this area, leaving the lower legs and the right side of the body to the rapier. c.) A defensive action of the dagger as taught by seventeenth century English Fencing Master Joseph Swetnam. The dagger is held out, with a straight arm, its hilt at roughly cheek level and its point angled across the body towards the opponent's left shoulder.

DAGGER REINFORCEMENT PARRY: A defensive action of the rapier braced by the hilt or blade of the dagger being placed against the rapier's blade approximately one third of the way from the tip. These parries use the mechanics of several standard rapier parries, reinforced by the dagger. The placement and mechanics of the sword hand and sword do not change, the hilt or blade of the dagger is merely bolsters the sword blade, and then both hands push the parry out to meet the attack.

DAGGER: a.) A short stout weapon, like a little sword, with a blade designed for both cut and thrust; a poniard. b.) The defensive weapon used in the left hand, "main-gauche," along with the sword or rapier towards the end of the sixteenth century, taking the place of the buckler being both offensive and defensive.

DAMASK: a.) Damascus steel. Steel, or a combination of steel and iron manufacture at Damascus, or exhibiting a similar variegated surface. The wavy pattern of steel, or iron and steel when welded together and corroded with a weak acid, as in Damascus steel. b.) A mixture of red and white, like the wavy pattern created by Damascus steel.

DANCE FALL: Any action that quickly takes the individual to the floor in a manner that appears to be dance like, or as is taught and performed in dance.

DANCING RAPIER: An ornamental sword only worn in dancing.

DASH: a.) To smite, strike, to knock: with the idea of violence and rapidity. b.) To knock or smash out.

DEBATE: To combat about, to decide by combat.

DEBOLE: (It.) The section of the blade from mid-sword to the tip by which attacks should be made. See *Foible*.

DECEIVE OF THE BLADE: See *Deception of the Blade*.

DECEIVE OF THE PARRY: See *Deception of the Parry*.

DECEIVE: a.) Avoiding blade to blade contact with the opponent's weapon as they attempt to parry, engage, or attack your blade. See *Refusing the Blade*. b.) Any action which deliberately avoids contact with the opponent's blade.

DECEPTION OF PARRY: (also *Tromper*) a.) A form of refusing the blade where the aggressor avoids blade to blade contact with

the opponent's parry, or parries, during the final stage of a feint attack. If the blade deceives only one parry, the attack is a single feint attack while attacks which deceive two or more parries are double or multiple feint attacks. b.) The evasion of the defender's attempt to parry the attacker's blade.

DECEPTION OF THE BLADE: (also *Deceive of the Blade*) An action that con¬sists of removing one's blade from an opponent's attempt to make contact with it. See also *Refusing the Blade*.

DECEPTION: Originally from the Latin *capere*, meant to seize or take. Decipere meant `take away'; hence the deception in fencing takes the blade away from its original course - and with it, often too late, the defenders faith in the deceiver's attack.

DECISIVE PLAY: A fight with sharps.

DEFEND: a.) To be prepared against attack, to make armaments. b.) To protect from violence or injury. c.) To maintain by force or by argument, to secure.

DEFENSE: (UK *Defence*) a.) The action or position of keeping off or resisting an attack. To take action against attack, injury or threat; shielding; guarding; warding off; protecting. b.) The practice, art or "science" of defending oneself with or without weapons; self-defense. c.) Armament, preparation for war. d.) Arms, offensive as well as defensive. e.) Readiness for combat, means or practice of fighting.

DEFENSIVE BOX: An imaginary box that encloses the combatant (theoretically leaving no portion of the combatant unprotected), its walls being created by the placement of the blade when parrying. In theory a minimum of eight parries are needed to protect every portion of the combatant's body, creating a defensive box.

DEFIANCE: Challenge to fight.

DEFLECTED PARRY: See *Hanging Parry*

DÉGAGÉ: (Fr.) See *Disengagement*.

DEGAGE: Moving from the line of engagement by passing the point around the adversary's hand. May be to the same line or a different line.

DÉGAGEMENT: (Fr.) See *Disengagement*.

DEGEN: (Ger.) A German word from the 1400's generally meaning a sword, often slender, but also sometimes a Raufdegen or "brawling sword", or a broader Haudegen, though never a rapier. See *Epée*.

DEGENERATION: The process of declining to a lower or worse stage of being; playing the physical and mental impact of each blow received in a fight.

DELAYED: a.) Generally refers to a riposte that does not follow immediately after the parry. b.) Said of any action that is not executed at first opportunity.

DÉMARCHES: (Fr.) A sixteenth century term used by the French master Sainct-Didier to represent the gaining and surrendering of ground. These could be; advance and retreat or passing movements of footwork.

DEMI: (Fr.) Meaning partial or half.

DEMI-CIRCLE: Half circle. A Semi-Circular Parry.

DEMI-CONTRE PARRY: A half counter-parry, as may be executed in going from fourth to seventh, or sixth to eight lines.

DEMI-DISENGAGE: A half disengage, as may be executed in attacking from the high to low, or low to high lines.

DEMI-LUNGE: (also *Punta Sopramano*): A half, or short lunge developed by Angelo Viggiani around 1560, where the lead foot is extended slightly forward on the attack while the lag foot is held in place. This action suggested the first, clear development toward the "lunge" as practiced today. Viggiani's teachings show the development of a new school of thought in which "passing" tended to be replaced by the "lunge." Unfortunately, in his introduction of the punta sopramano, Viggiani was not bold enough to apply the execution of the "lunge" to all attacks.

DEMI-PLIÉ: A partial or half bending of the knees.

DEMI-VOLTE: (also *Circular Half Pace*) a.) A

method of removing the body from the line of attack by swinging the lag foot back, generally to the right, along the outer track of an imaginary circle, turning the body parallel to the line of attack. b.) (also *Slip*) A method of removing the body from the line of attack by swinging the lag foot back, generally to the right, turning the body so that the trunk is brought 90 degrees in relation to the attack. c.) (also *Demi Volte*) A method of effacing the target by moving the rear leg, so that the trunk is brought off-line. d.) A specific type of Slip to the 90 Right, removing the body from the Line of Engagement.

DEPTH PERCEPTION: The ability of the mind to refer its senses to the measurement in distance of an external object.

DÉROBEMENT: (Fr.) (also *Derobement*) a.) Blade movements executed with an extended arm, which evade the opponent's attempts to beat or take the blade. See also *Refusing the Blade*. b.) A deceive of the opponent's attempt to deflect the point in line. c.) The attacker's evasion of the defender's attempt to beat or take the blade whilst the attacker's arm is extended.

DÉSARMEMENT: (Fr.) Removing the opponent's weapon from his hand by either force or leverage. The Disarmament.

DESCENDENTE: (It. & Sp.) (Literally "descending" or "downward") a.) A cutting attack delivered from the high to the low line. b.) a cutting attack delivered from the high line, from either the right or left, downward on a diagonal to either the opponent's right or left shoulder. A *Squalembrato*.

DESCENDING BLOCK: A block delivered downward to defend against an ascending diagonal or vertical attack.

DESCENT: (Small Sword) "The act of the wrist's desending outwards in performing the parade of tierce, octave , and seconde.

DESTREZA: (Sp.) Literally "dexterity;" "skill." The name given to the extremely complex, mathematical and geometrical form of traditional sixteenth and seventeenth century

Spanish fencing. See *Verdadera Destreza*.

DESVO: (also *Desvio*) In later Spanish schools of fence, the technique of redirecting an attacking blow with a deflecting action rather than a solid block.

DETACHED PARRY: (also *Detachment*) A crisp defensive action of the blade (generally in the transitional style) that merely taps a thrusting attack to confirm the parry and then immediately leaves the parried blade to move on to the next action.

DETACHMENT: See *Detached Parry*.

DEUX TEMPS: (*En Deux Temps*, "in two actions") The practice of the late seventeenth century French school to separate the parry and riposte into two distinct and separate actions. Until then parries and ripostes were delivered simultaneously, as in the counter. See *Double Time*.

DEVELOPMENT: a.) The combined actions of the extension of the sword arm and the lunge. b.) The action of the simple thrust and lunge, executed as one movement.

DIAGONAL ATTACK: a.) Any armed or unarmed attack that travels from a high line to a low line, or vise-versa, at an angle of roughly forty-five degrees. b.) An offensive action that is directed at the opponent on the oblique, rather than on a straight line.

DIAGONAL AVOID: (also *Diagonal Evasion*) a.) An evasive step used against vertical and diagonal swipes, removing the body with a sloped pace or lunge onto either the NE, NW, SE or SW diagonal, roughly forty-five degrees off the standard north-south tracks of linear footwork. b.) An evasive action that removes the body from the plane of a diagonal attack by leaning or displacing the torso. See *Slip*.

DIAGONAL CUT WITH AVOIDANCE: An off line cut to either the inside or outside line. It may be a rising or falling cut. It is usually avoided by leaning to the side away from the cut.

DIAGONAL CUT: A rising or falling cut to the inside or outside line from the opposite line.

DIAGONAL PARRIES: (also Half Counter Parries) Any parry where the hand and blade travel diagonally across the body from the high to low line or vice versa and the parrying movement of the blade follows a semicircular path from one line to the other and from one side of the body to another.

DIAGONAL SLASH WITH AVOIDANCE: An off-line cut to either the inside or outside line. It may be a rising or falling cut. It is usually avoided by leaning to the side away from the cut (with or without footwork).

DIAMOND CROSS-SECTION: Said of the shape of a sword blade if viewed across the blade; a diamond section of a blade made by cutting transversely through the blade.

DIAMOND-GRIND SCHLAGER: A German fencing blade, diamond-shaped in cross-section.

DIG: A angular thrusting attack in epée fencing, generally delivered at the wrist and forearm from the extended arm position.

DIRECT ATTACK: An attack or riposte delivered in one blade movement without changing the relative positions of the blades.

DIRECT BEAT: (also Simple Beat) A beat attack delivered to the opponent's blade without changing their relative position.

DIRECT PARRY: (also Instinctive and Simple Parries) Defensive actions of the blade where both the hand and blade move from one position to another along the shortest possible route in either a horizontal or vertical plane; that is, remaining in the same line (High, Low, Inside or Outside) but moving to the opposite side.

DIRECT RIPOSTE: A riposte delivered as a direct attack.

DIRECT THRUST-CUTOVER ATTACK: A direct thrust is a feint delivered in the line of engagement, followed by the cutover as the final action of the attack.

DIRECT: An attack or riposte delivered in the line of engagement.

DIRECTION, LINE OF: (Small Sword) "Is, in a general sense, the posture of the feet, body and arms, kept invariably in a straight line on the proper side position of guard.– For it is evident that the approaches towards your adversary's body will be more sure and speedy on straight lines than on oblique ones.– It is sometimes applied to the direction of the arm and point in parrying and thrusting– If your form parades too wide, you deviate from the line of direction, and threreby leave some part of your body unguarded.– If you thrust at your adversary, without covering yourself by reshifting his blade, you also are said to deviate from the line of direction–Your point is also said to deviate from the line of direction, when it is not steadily directed to your adversary's body."

DIRTY: Said of fighting tactics that are considered dishonorable, sordid, base, mean, or corrupt; despicable. A style of fighting that stains the honor of the persons engaged. I.E. hitting below the belt, backstabbing, kicking someone when they are down, etc.

DISABLE: a.) To render one's opponent incapable or unable to use his weapon or continue in combat by disarmament, physical injury or bodily infirmity; to cripple. b.) A disarm.

DISADVANTAGE: Unfavorable state.

DISARM: a.) An action of the blade or body that forces the weapon from the hand of one's opponent in combat. The action is no longer valid in modern fencing, but it was taught by most of the old masters, and was a feature of swordplay until late into the eighteenth century. b.) The act of removing an adversary's weapon from their hand by force or threat. c.) An action of the blade or body that appears to force the weapon from the hand of one's partner.

DISARMAMENT: The action of disarming. See *Disarm.*

DISARMING: (Small Sword) "The act of depriving your adversary of his sword or foil.– The ancients used various modes of disarming, by feizing an adversary's wrist in different situations; but these are now exploded. The

methods now recommended are attended with no danger in serious affairs." See *Disarm.*

DISARMO SOPRANO: ("upper disarm") A technique of Fiore's for grabbing the opponent's wrist after closing and stifling their blade above their shoulders.

DISEDGE: To take the edge off; to deprive of its sharpness; to dull or blunt a weapon.

DISENGAGE: a.) A changement executed from an engaged guard position by passing the point either over or under the hilt of the opposing weapon. It is speculated that Agrippa developed the disengage in the mid-fifteen hundreds from studying cock-fighting. Whether this is true or not, it was not until Fabris that the action and all its intricacies were fully developed. He absolutely defined the rules and actions of engagement and disengagement. He developed a variety of disengages to fulfill the variables of point work and the ever changing contra postura that are still practiced today. b.) Passing the blade around the opposing weapon's guard, from an engaged position of the blade, and terminating on the side opposite to the original engagement. d.) A simple indirect attack made in one motion by passing the point into the line opposite to the engagement, under the opponent's blade in the high line, and over the opponent's blade in the low line.

DISENGAGEMENT: a.) The action of a disengage executed from a free (rather than engaged) guard position. See *Disengage* and *Change Under.* b.) A simple attack, or riposte, which consists of leaving the line of engagement to go into the opposite line by passing the point around the opponent's guard or sword-hand. c.) The act of removing the blade from contact with the adversary's blade. d.) (also *Disengaging*) (Small Sword) The act of changing the blade from one side of your adversary's to the other, performed by a dextrous motion of the wrist, without moving the arm. See *Caveating.* e.) The act of freeing or un-engaging previously joined blades. See *Free.*

DISH-HILT: A shallower "cup" in depth than that of a bell guard or cup hilt. The dish hilt, in varying forms and names was common among small swords and is still in use on the modern fencing foil.

DISPLACEMENT OF TARGET: A term in competitive fencing for the removal of valid target, generally by means of a low-line evasion. If, during an attack, another part of the fencer's body fills the space where the valid target was situated it may be hit and counted as a touch. See also *Substitution of Target*.

DISPLACEMENT: See *Evasion by Displacement*.

DISTANCE, CORRECT: a.) The specified distance for the safe execution of blade-play. The distance between two combatants engaged in armed combat, where, after the execution of any attack and/or footwork, the point of the weapon is six to ten inches, out of distance, from the opponent's chest. b.) In unarmed combat, correct distance is established by the length of the combatant's arms/ legs, technique being executed and the position of the audience/camera.

DISTANCE, IN: a.) Said of any combatant who can hit their opponent by merely fully extending the sword arm. b.) At a measure where the combatants can reach one another with their weapons without the aid of footwork. At Close Measure.

DISTANCE, OUT OF: a.) Being outside correct distance for any reason. b.) In unarmed combat; when a combatant cannot be hit or kicked without closing measure. c.) When a fencer cannot hit their opponent by means of a lunge alone, but must employ some additional footwork, such as an advance.

DISTANCE: a.) The Elizabethan term for remaining out of easy reach when on the defensive, and to be in reach while on the offensive. b.) The space between the combatants and their weapons that affords advantage to the one and disadvantage to the other. When one combatant's sword is closer to the opponent than the other, there they have the advantage and time to strike. c.) Proper space between combatants in the execution of swordplay.

DISTANCING: An evasive action that removes the body backward, out of the reach of the attack, while remaining in line with the attack.

DISTORTION: A change from the normal or average, whether by abruptness, complexity of movement or some other means. To alter the shape or style of movement without destroying continuity.

DIVE ROLL: (also Tiger Roll) A forward roll, executed from an airborne position, usually over some object or obstacle.

DODGE: To shift or move to and fro, backwards or forwards, to change or vary one's position or altering one's ground to elude a pursuer, an attack, a blow, or to get a sudden advantage on one's opponent by such an action. See *Avoid*.

DOIGTÉ: (also Doighté) a.) The technique of directing the sword's point in all sorts of movements, circular or lateral, without the stiffening of the arm's muscles. The point is directed by the manipulators (thumb and forefinger), with the other fingers giving the blade steadiness, power, and support in the various actions of blade-play. b.) (fencing) The proper use of the thumb and fingers in directing and controlling the energy and precision of the weapon. c.) The action of controlling the weapon by use of the fingers and the fine motor control achieved thereby.

DOMINANT: a.) A term for the lead foot or hand. b.) Said of a portion or side of the body that is more dexterous and better developed.

DOUBLÉ: (Fr.) (also *Douible Deception*) a.) A compound attack in any line which deceives a direct parry and a counter-parry. b.) A compound attack made in any line which deceives a direct parry and a counter-parry. c.) A compound attack in any line that consists of two deceptions of parry in the same line, deceiving both parries one after the other. d.) An attack formed of two disengages in the same line, deceiving a defense by counter-parry.

DOUBLE: a.) To redouble an attack. See also *Remise*.

DOUBLE BARREL ROLL: (also Joined Barrel Roll) A grappling technique where two combatants are holding one another (usually face to face) and rolling over each other in consecutive Barrel Rolls.

DOUBLE BEAT: Two beats delivered in quick succession on the same side of the opponent's blade.

DOUBLE CHANGE BEAT: A change beat being executed, the blade again changes its line of engagement and delivers a second beat from the original side.

DOUBLE CHANGEMENT: A Counter Changement executed against a counter changement allowing the combatant who initiated the action to continue with their original intent. This is done by making a second changement off of the opponent's counter changement. This action, like the counter disengage, is still used in competitive fencing but finds its roots in Seventeenth century rapier play. The action was originally called a ricavatione by Fabris, and was used then as it is today, as a second changement to deceive the counter disengage of the opponent.

DOUBLE FENCE: The practice of using an offensive and defensive weapon in both hands, (including but not limited to the sword and dagger, the rapier and dagger and the case of rapiers). Such a technique, where a dagger is used in conjunction with the sword was not developed until the Italian Renaissance. The addition of the dagger marked the transition from the old practice of sword and shield combat to the effective use of the sword as a weapon both offensive and defensive.

DOUBLE HAND CHOKE: (also *Two-Hand Choke*) A strangle hold executed facing the victim where both hands are placed around the neck with the thumbs wrenched in on the windpipe.

DOUBLE NELSON: (Wrestling) A strong hold in wrestling where one gets behind an opponent, place both arms under theirs, and then the hands are around the back of their neck, bending their head forward till their breastbone almost gives way. "Probably the most dangerous move in Lancashire and Cornwall and Devon wrestling . . . is what is called the 'Double Nelson'."

DOUBLE PARRY: (also *Parries Double*) A defensive action in double fence technique where both weapons are used together to defend against thrust or blow. This could be a cross parry, parallel parry, replacement parry or the like.

DOUBLE PASSE: (also *Double Pass*) The combination of two Passes, either both forward, or both back. See also *Crossover Step*.

DOUBLE PRIS D'FER: A succession of takings of the blade where contact is not lost between each one.

DOUBLE TIME: (also *Double-Time*) a.) A parry and riposte executed in two separate actions or "times." Not meaning twice as fast, but rather twice the time. See *Dui Tempi*. b.) Double the time specified or previously used. c.) Formerly, a pace of 150 steps in the minute, i.e. twice the number of those in slow time. According to the regulations in force c 1896 in the British Army it consisted of 165 steps of 33 inches (= 453 ¾ ft.) to the minute. In the U.S. Army, double time has superseded double-quick and is fixed at 180 steps of 36 inches a minute.

DOUBLE TOUCH: A term from modern fencing meaning both fencers have landed a hit within the same period of fencing time.

DOUBLE-CHANGE: Two changes of engagements made without lateral motion of the armed hand, returning to the original engagement.

DOUBLÉ-DE-DOUBLÉ: (Fr.) A compound attack consisting of the feint of a doublé followed by another doublé in opposite lines.

DOUBLÉ-DÉGAGÉ: (Fr.) A classic compound attack in fencing consisting of two feints; first a feint of the doublé followed by a disengagement that deceives the final simple parry.

DOUBLE-DISENGAGE: A composed attack formed of two disengages in the same line and a disengage to the opposite line, deceiving a counter-parry and a lateral parry.

DOUBLE-HAND HAMMER PUNCH: (also sometimes *Rabbit Punch*) a.) A large and violent punch made with the hands clasped one around the other, striking downward, in a vertical plane, with the little finger side of the fists like a large club or hammer. Often delivered to the spine or back of the neck. b.) A large and violent punch made with the hands clasped one around the other, striking downward with the little finger side of the fists.

DOUBLING: (Small Sword) "Is generally applied in performing a round parade twice, when your adversary doubles his feint upon you."

DOWN AND DIRTY: An ungentlemanly form of fighting.

DOWNRIGHT: A vertical blow or attack descending straight downwards.

DOWNWARD: Said of a descending blow or attack.

DRAG: a.) To pull the victim along the ground (or other surface where there is friction or resistance) with force, violence, or roughness. b.) See *Chape*

DRAW A BEAD (ON): The term comes from the American frontier, where, a bead was the front sight on a rifle (or pistol), and to draw a bead was to take aim at something, setting the weapons sights on it.

DRAW CUT: A cutting action made by a pulling or slicing action rather than chopping or hacking. Most of the treatises on the science of fence written during the sixteenth and early seventeenth century advocate that when a cut is used, it should be drawn. To be hit outright with the sword did not guarantee that the blade would cut. A pulling action after the blade landed better insured severing of the opponent.

DRAW: To remove or pull one's sword, or other weapon, from its scabbard or holster

for the purpose of either offense or defense.

DRAWING BACK ACTION: A term used by George Silver for the condition of activity, at work, in practical or effective operation of the body and weapon that is in a state of removal, detachment or extraction.

DRAWING DIAMONDS: A doigté exercise of point work that focuses on the diagonal rather than circular paths of the point by tracing the shape of a "diamond in the air with the point of the blade.

DRAWN: a.) Having one's weapon extracted or pulled from its sheath; naked steel. Said of a person with his sword drawn. b.) Said of a gun removed from its holster.

DRILLS: Specific choreographed routines in footwork and the positions and movements of the hands and/or blade, designed to educate combatants in style and form through repetition.

DRITTA: (It.) (also *Dritto*) Literally meaning "right." Generally referring to the right hand (the sword hand), the fencers sword arm or sword arm side.

DRITTO FILO: (It.) Right edge. The true, or fore-edge of the blade.

DROP CUT: A descending vertical cutting attack.

DROP PARRY EXERCISE: A technique exercise that focuses on the proper mechanics of the cutting attack. The combatants run the offensive/defensive blade-play drill and the combatant on the defense drops random parries during the routine. The offensive combatant does not know when their partner will not parry, thus they must focus on proper technique of the cutting attack.

DRUB: (also *Bastinado*) A stroke given in punishment or in fighting, esp. with a cudgel.

DRY-BEAT: a.) To inflict blows that do not draw blood (as a blow given with the fist or a stick, which merely causes a bruise). A blow, or a beating that inflicts injury but does not draw blood. b.) Probably to hit with the flat of the blade, or with the sword still in the scabbard.

Duck: a.) The instantaneous lowering of the head and torso vertically towards the floor to avoid an armed or unarmed attack attack at the head (cut, blow, punch or kick) that travels in a horizontal plane. There are basically two ways to avoid an attack by ducking; the first, the Squat Duck, is the most common; while the second, a low line evasion, is particular to modern fencers in conjunction with a stop thrust; see *Pasatta Sotto*. b.) Avoidance of an attack by bending the knees and allowing the attack to pass overhead. c.) The vertical lowering of the head and torso to avoid an attack at the head.

Dudgeon: (also *Dudgen*) a.) The handle of a dagger made of a cheap or low-grade wood of the same name. b.) A term for a dagger with a dudgeon wood handle, hence an inferior or unreliable weapon.

Due Spada: A fighting style simultaneously using two swords or later two rapiers, a "case of rapiers " or "brace" (sometimes now called "Florentine").

Duel of Chivalry: A meeting in single combat between two knights, generally on horseback and always with great public ceremony, to settle a difference of law, possession or honor. Knighthood was generally established in France, Spain, and England by the twelfth century, and the duel of chivalry with it.

Duel of Honor: An armed conflict fought for personal reasons. The cause of these encounters varied in both nature and seriousness. An insult or seduction of a wife, sister, daughter or female acquaint¬ance, a slap or blow, a slur on fame or reputation, and the gravest provocation being "giving the lie." In John Selden's, The Duello, or Single Combat (1610), he speaks of the rights of the wronged man. "truth, honor, freedome and curtesie being as incidents to perfit chivalry upon the lye given, fame impeached, body wronged, or curtesie taxed, a custom hath bin amoung the French, English, Burguignons, Italians, Almans and the Northern people to seek revenge of their wrongs on the body of their accuser and that by private combat seul à seul, without judicial lists appointed them." Although never legal in England, it was not viewed as murder by the participants. Those engaged in the duel felt they had just cause and confronted their wrongdoer face to face. Dueling continued up through the nineteenth century, but the sword was no longer the paramount weapon. The custom of wearing the small sword as part of everyday civilian attire started to fade toward the end of the eighteenth century and the duel with the pistol took precedence.

Duel: a.) A formal fight between two persons; a single combat. A private fight, prearranged and fought with deadly weapons, with the intent to wound or kill, usually in the presence of at least two witnesses, called seconds, having for its purpose to decide a personal quarrel or to settle a point of honor. b.) A trial by wager of battle; judicial single combat.

Dueling Punctilio: The strict rules that governed all aspects of a duel from the issuing of the challenge to the fight and or reconciliation. Dueling was an established institution, especially in Italy and France, and the rules governing it were generally understood and stringently enforced.

Duellist: (also *Duelist*) One who is an expert in the rules and practice of dueling.

Duello: The established code and convention of duelists.

Dui Tempi: (It.) To parry and riposte in two distinct actions. See *Double Time*.

Dull: To blunt.

Duration: The length of time which something is sustained.

Dust Back: a.) Clearing an opponent, or opponents, backward with a sweep or slash with the cloak. b.) Sometimes applied to any attack or blow that clears to opponent backward, whether made with the cloak, the unarmed hand or another weapon.

E

ECHAPPEMENT: See *Backward Lunge*.

ECUSSON: (also *Ecusson Block*) The metal center or bracket of the hilt's guard where the quillons join and on which the thumb and fingers are often placed when gripping (fingering).

EDGE FOCUS: a.) To place emphasis on cutting attacks and techniques made with the edge of a sword in drills and exercises. b.) To make a cutting attack directly out of a pressure glide or glissade.

EDGE PUNCH: (also *Edge Blow*) A strike or blow made with the edge or rim of a shield.

EDGE: a.) The thin sharpened side(s) of a cutting blade, opposed to the "flat" or broad side of the blade. See *Cutting Edge* b.) The sharpness given to a blade by whetting; to sharpen.

EDGELESS: Without an edge, blunt, unfit to cut.

EFFORT: a.) An attack on the opposing blade that travels from its foible to forte. See *Glisade*. b.) See *Froissement* and *Pressure Glide*.

EIGHT, PARRY OF: a.) The defensive position for a thrust or horizontal attack to the weapon bearing leg or thigh, closing the low outside lines. The hand is supinated with the point lower than the hand. b.) (also *Parry Octave*) Protecting the low outside line with the point down, the hand in supination. Usually used against a thrust.

EINLADUNG: (Ger.) See *Open Invitation*.

ELBOW ATTACK: (also *Elbow Strike*) An attack or blow delivered in close quarters with a bent arm, striking with the hard edge of the elbow.

ELBOW BLOCK: A defensive action made with the bony joint of the elbow, generally intended to protect the ribs, thorax and abdomen. The elbow is punched into the attack, generally striking the aggressor on the shin, wrist or tendons on the inside of the forearm.

ELZA: Vadi's term for "crosses" or the "cross-guard (what Fiore calls the *crucibus*).

EMBATTLE: (also Embattail) To array for battle.

EMPALE: See *Impale*.

ENARME: The strap by which a shield or buckler was held on the arm.

EN FINALE: (Fr.) Often applied to a parry deliberately executed at the last or "final" moment possible. By waiting as long as possible, the parry has the least chance of being deceived and allows for a quick execution of the riposte.

EN GARDE: (Fr.) The basic position assumed by a combatant when fencing. To come on guard.

EN GUARDE: (Fr.) a.) See *On Guard*. b.) The basic physical "ready" position of a combatant.

EN MARCHANT: a.) An attack on the march, extending of the sword arm while simultaneously passing forward. b.) Actions made while advancing:

ENCOUNTER: A hostile meeting; to fight; to assail; combat.

ENGAGE: a.) To cross swords; to join or interlock weapons. b.) To entangle, involve, commit or mix up in an undertaking, quarrel or fight.

ENGAGED COUPÉ: A changement executed over the point of the opposing weapon where contact of the blades is maintained until the blade clears the point of the opposing weapon, and then it is brought to rest at its intended target. The action is characterized by a sliding or scraping noise as the engaged blades quickly rub against one another. The engagement is only maintained until the blade clears the point of the opposing blade, and then it is brought to rest at its intended target.

ENGAGED: a.) Said of two crossed or joined weapons. b.) To be committed to, or locked in a fight.

ENGAGEMENT: a.) The crossing, joining or

touching of blades. The aim of joining the blades is to guard a specific line with the blade's placement, while slightly opening a line on the opponent by applying a little pressure on their blade. The touching of the blades also tells the combatant when the opponent's blade is at rest and when it is in motion. ". . . let each man use to oppose, one only weapon against the enimies sworde, keeping the other free, that he may be able to strike at his pleasure." [Di Grassi ff – 57] b.) The crossing, joining or touching of blades.

ENGLISH FIGHT: See *True English Fight*.

ENGLISH GUARD: (Rapier) Foreign fencing masters dominated the schools of rapier play in England, and an Englishman, depending on their taste and training, would assume either an Italian, Spanish, and sometimes even German guard; or an Anglicized version thereof.

ENGLISH MASTERS OF DEFENCE: A guild of professional swordsmen established in 1540, under a patent granted by Henry VIII. Members were trained and tested in many different weapons, advancing through the ranks of Scholar, Free Scholar, and Provost before being tested for the degree of Master. See *Master's Prize*.

ENGUARD: a.) To surround as with a guard, to arm. b.) See *On Guard*.

ENPIERCED: Pierced; wounded.

ENTER: (also *Entering* and *Close*) The technique of stepping inside measure, usually into an offensive action, to gain tactical advantage for both defensive and offensive actions.

ENTRENCH: To cut.

ENVELOPMENT: (also *Wrapping it Up*, or *The Wrap Up*) a.) An attack on the opponent's blade which, by describing a circle with both blades in contact, returns to the original line of engagement. The Envelopment can be executed both in a passive and active form. In both cases the foible of the opposing blade is captured by the forte and carried in a circular path by combined movement of the hand and wrist. The passive action is executed from the hand and wrist with the forte of the blade against the opposing blade's foible and describes a small circle with the tips of the blades. An active envelopment can use the whole arm, controlling the opposing blade with the forte or mid-blade and generally describes a large circle with the arm and blade. b.) Taking the adversary's blade and describing a small circle to return to the line of engagement without losing blade contact. An envelopment is a prise-de-fer. c.) A checking action in hand-to-hand and contemporary knife technique that is made on the opponent's hand, arm or leg, executed by blocking the attack and then by describing a circle with both arms in contact, bringing the opponent's arm back to the placement where the check began.

EPÉE BLADE: A triangular blade (fluted on three sides for lightness) approximately thirty-five inches in length, tapering evenly from forte to tip, generally provided with a button and narrow tang used in competitive fencing. The blade is extremely flexible at the foible with a forte and tang designed only for competitive fencing.

EPÉE DE COMBAT: (Fr.) (Literally "sword of combat") The formal sword for the Duel of Honor and predecessor of the modern fencing Epée. The Small Sword. See *Small Sword* and *Epée*.

EPÉE: (also *Epe*) a.) The modern "dueling sword," taken from the eighteenth century small sword, and evolved during the nineteenth century as a sport weapon designed to reproduce, as closely as possible, an actual small sword duel. The modern epée technique is very similar to that of the foil, only modified by the tactical considerations dictated by a longer fencing measure, unrestricted target and the absence of right of way. It is the heaviest of the modern sport weapons, and in many ways still resembles it ancestor, the Small Sword. b.) One of the three competitive fencing weapons. The epee is a thrusting weapon only, with a blade triangular in section. The target includes the entire body. c.) Applied to the blade of the modern fencing epée.

Errol Flynn Tah-Tahs: See *Baronial Hall*.

Erste Intention: (Ger.) See *First Intention*.

Escape: During the decline of the Roman Empire, when chaos and disorder ran rampant, the term *excappare* appears, its literal meaning is to slip out of one's cloak or cape. Robert Claiborne paints the image of "a traveler on a dark road, feeling the clutch of a robber on his shoulder, slipping out of his cloak and - escaping." The term is now applied to the process or procedure of gaining one's liberty by flight; to get free from detention or control, or from an oppressive or irksome condition.

Escrima: (Ph.) (also *Escrema, Kali* and *Arnis*) Similar to almost all nations, the Filipino's produced a method for utilizing sharp swords and daggers in combat. When swords were not available, fire-hardened sticks also served as weapons. These sticks were used in much the same style as swords and daggers. The Filipino's maintained and continued developed their use of the sword and dagger where Western nations discarded them for the gun. This intricate and highly sophisticated fighting style is what is now know as the martial discipline of Arnis or Escrima. See *Arnis*.

Escrime: (Fr.) The French word for fencing.

Esgrima: (Sp.) To skirmish, fight or fence. Fencing.

Esgrimador: (Sp.) A fencing master.

Eskrima: (Ind.) (also *Escrima* and *Escrema*) A martial art indigenous to the Philippines.

Eskrimador: (Ph.) A term used by Phillipino natives for a fighter or fencer.

Espada Ropera: (Sp.) Literally "dress sword". A civilian sword; a sword to be worn with common dress. See *Rapier*.

Espada y Daga: (Sp. & Ph.) Sword and dagger, or sword and knife fighting.

Espadon: Late Medieval Spanish cut & thrust sword.

Espée: (Fr.) The early spelling of Epée.

Esquire: a.) A chivalric term for a young man of gentle birth, who attended upon a knight, carrying his shield, and rendering other services to him, in hope of aspiring to knighthood. See *Squire*. b.) A title of dignity for a man ranking just below a knight in the higher order of English gentry.

Esquive: Any bodily action made to avoid being hit, such as ducking, side stepping, withdrawing, etc.

Esterna Linea: (It.) See *Outside Line*.

Estoc: (also *Tuck* or *Stocco*) Late Medieval edgeless, two handed, broad-bladed thrusting sword for piercing plate armor. Applied to various weapons at different times in history. Starting in the Victorian era the term became quite often misapplied to the rapier.

Estramacon: French term for the *Stromazone*, a tearing tip-cut to the face, used to harass or distract.

Evade Back: a.) Compound footwork that joins the action of a pass back with that of a backward lunge to avoid a horizontal attack across the chest or belly. b.) See *Jump Back*.

Evade: To escape or avoid a blow or attack by contrivance. See *Evasion*.

Evasion: a.) To escape or elude an attack by cleverness or stratagem. The action of avoiding or escaping a blow or attack by artifice or contrivance; dodging. In historical rapier play the idea was to avoid the oncoming attack while simultaneously extending the sword arm into the path of the assailant. This action was made in hopes that the opponent would impale themselves on the extended sword (See *Stop Hit, Stop Thrust* and *Stop Cut*). b.) A defensive action prescribed by Di Grassi and other sixteenth century fencing masters that employed a displacement of the body from the threat of attack.

Evasions by Displacement: The most common form of avoiding a thrust, by safely and effectively removing the target from the path of the intended attack. This may be a duck, jump, diagonal avoid, etc.

Evasive Body Techniques: Movements of

the body intended to remove or efface the target without changing placement on the ground.

EVASIVE FOOTWORK TECHNIQUES: Actions that move the combatant to and fro, backwards or forwards by changing or vary one's relative position or altering one's ground to elude a pursuer, an attack, a blow, or to get a sudden advantage on one's opponent by such an action. These actions can be accompanied by a blocking technique, but it is not essential to the technique.

EVASIVE TECHNIQUES: Any movement of the body and/or feet designed to escape or elude an attack by cleverness or stratagem. To avoid or escape a blow or attack by artifice or contrivance.

EXCHANGE PARRY: See *Transfer Parry.*

EXPLOIT: Combat, war.

EXPULSION: (also *Throw Off*) a.) Using the energy of a blade taking action (pris d'fer) to throw or fling the opposing blade aside. Opposite of *Command.* b.) A checking technique in hand-to-hand and contemporary knife technique that uses the energy and movement of a check to throw or fling the opposing arm aside. c.) Using the energy and movement of a check to throw or fling the opposing arm aside. d.) See *Froissement* or *Pressure Glide.*

EXTENDED PARRY: A parry executed with a fully extended arm. The action is generally used as part of a beat attack removing the point of the opposing weapon.

EXTENSION, POSITION OF: (Small Sword) The act of extending or stretching the left leg, right and left Arms, and projecting the right knee forward, while the point drops and is directed towards the object.

EXTENSION: a.) The reaching of the sword arm forward. b.) The position of the sword arm when straightened to its full length.

EYE POKE: Attack made usually with the finger(s) to one or both eyes.

EYES OF THE HILT: See *Pas d'ane.*

F

FACE: a.) To meet in front; to oppose. b.) To brave, to bully.

FAINT: a.) To pass out, lose consciousness and fall to the floor or into someone's arms, etc. b.) Any slow collapse to the floor (or other lower surface) that is instigated by lose of muscular control through lightheadedness and or blacking out. c.) Weak, feeble; sickly, out of condition. d.) To fall into a swoon.

FALCHION: (also *Faulchion*) A sword with a broad blade, curved on the convex side, more or less.

FALL AWAY SWIPE: A swipe delivered as the combatant falls backward, away from the opponent.

FALSE ART: "To overcome rather by disceit then true manhood." The Elizabethan practice of using tricks and misleading movements of the sword and body to dupe the opponent into unwittingly opening a line for attack. Although considered by many as an ungentlemanly or unsafe practice, the delivering of "false" attacks were a common practice in Elizabethan swordplay. The opposite of *True Art.*

FALSE ATTACK: An attack which is not intended to land, but is delivered to distract one's opponent, test their reaction, or to draw a parry and riposte, which would be parried and so allowing a counter riposte. The false attack could be considered the "first intention" of a "second intention" attack. See *Feint.*

FALSE BALESTRA: A form of balestra performed with the jump in place, gaining no ground, designed to draw an attack on the preparation from one's opponent so as to hit on the second intention.

FALSE COLORS: A trick used in naval warfare of old, where a ship would sail under another flag only to raise their true colors just prior to an attack. This was a legitimate practice, considered honorable as long as one's own flag was raised prior to any assault. The term is now applied to someone who appears what they are not, and by showing their true colors reveals themselves as they really are - usually an enemy.

FALSE CUT: See *Feint with the Edge*

FALSE EDGE: (also *Filo Falso*) The edge of the blade turned away from the knuckles of the sword hand. On the rapier, the back edge was generally sharp for at least the uppermost third of the blade, and would often be sharp from the point to forte like the true edge.

FALSE PLAY: See *False Art*.

FALSE THRUST: See *Feint with the Point*

FALSING: A blow or thrust delivered, not with the intent to hurt or hit home, but to cause the enemy to open a line of attack through their reaction, by means whereof the combatant may deliver a real attack to the discovered line. See also *Deception, False Art* and *Feint*.

FALSO DRITTO: (It.) A cutting attack from the right with the false, or back edge of the blade. See *Backswording*

FALSO FILIO: (It.) See *False Edge*.

FALSO MANCO: (It.) A backhanded cutting attack from the left with the false, or back edge of the blade. Sometimes referred to as *Backswording*.

FEATHER PARRY: (also *Feather Parade*) A term used by Angelo for a hanging parry designed to protect the high outside line. See *Hang Parry Left* and *Sword Arm Protect*.

FECHSTEELUNG: (Ger.) See *Guard*.

FEDER: (Ger.) A sixteenth century term for the rapier.

FEEBLE: See *Foible*.

FEINT: (also *Feint Attack*) a.) Any action (movements of the arm, body, legs, or various actions of the blade) susceptible to misinterpretation by the opponent as to the nature and sincerity of its intentions. Their intent is generally to provoke the opponent's reflex reactions in order to take advantage of

their responses. b.) A general term for actions which are not made with the intention associated typically with that action, but to influence the opponent. c.) (Small Sword) An offensive movement made to resemble an attack in order to draw a reaction from the adversary.

FEINT ATTACK: An attacking action made without intending to hit and designed to either probe the opponent's defensive reaction or to draw a reaction or a parry. See *Feint*.

FEINT DE COULE: (Fr.) See *Graze Feint*.

FEINT WITH THE EDGE: (also *Falsing the Cut, False Cut* and *Feint Cut*) Offensive movements made to resemble cutting attacks or the beginning of an attack with the edge.

FEINT WITH THE POINT: (also *Falsing the Thrust* and *False Thrust*) A feint of a thrusting attack where the arm commits to the action, but there is no footwork executed to land the point. When footwork accompanies this action, the arm is withdrawn prior to completing the attack.

FEINTE DE DEGAGEMENT: (Fr.) See *Circular Feint*

FEINTE: (Fr.) See *Feint*.

FELL: a.) To hew or cut down. To beat or outstrike an opponent until they fall to the ground injured or dead. b.) Having fallen.

FENCE: a.) The action, practice, art or science of offensive and defensive swordplay. Fencing. b.) The action of defending; warding; to defend. The attitude of self-defense.

FENCER: a.) A skilled swordsman or combatant. b.) One who fights with a sword or foil. c.) One who practices the modern sport of fencing; with a foil epée or sabre.

FENCING CONVENTION: The complex procedures derived from "gentlemanly" manners that have become the rules of modern sport fencing.

FENCING LANGUAGE: a.) The terms, expressions and phrases associated with and used within the sport of fencing. Generally based in the Terminology of the French school, although often Anglicized in pronunciation and spelling. b.) The official language of modern fencing is French. All international and other major competitions are refereed in French. All business of the Federation Internationale d'Escrime (F.I.E.) is conducted in French, including Congresses, correspondences, official notices, legislation, regulations, statutes, rules, and minutes of meetings. Many of the terms used in English pertaining to fencing are derived directly from an original French term. Nevertheless, there are a number of words which, because of their unique association with the Italian school, are universally understood in their original Italian form.

FENCING MASTER: A teacher or coach who has been accredited and licensed to instruct competitive fencing in three weapons - foil, epee, and sabre.

FENCING MEASURE: A distance in sport fencing where one competitor can touch the other with the extension of the arm and the execution of a lunge. See *Measure*.

FENCING STEP: See *Advance*.

FENCING TEMPO: See *Tempo*.

FENCING TIME: (also *Time*) The time required to perform one simple fencing action. There is no chronometric measurement of this time; it is subjectively determined by the referee of the bout.

FENCING: a.) The term derived from the practice of offensive and defensive swordplay. It now represents the action or art of using the sword scientifically as a weapon of offense or defense. b.) The practice or competition of all sword play with blunted and rebated weapons. c.) The action of protecting, or of setting up a defense against. A means of defense.

FENDENTE: (It.) (Literally "slash.") A cutting attack delivered down¬wards in a plane vertical to the floor.

FENTE: (Fr.) See *Grand Lunge*.

FERAILLEUR: (Fr.) A fencer whose tactics are based on brute force and erratic clumsy movement rather than a through understand-ing of strategic and precise swordplay.

FERITE: (It.) See *Offense*.

FERMA: (also *Punto Fermo*) a.) A strong or firm thrusting attack originally directed toward the opponent's torso or throat. b.) A pronated off-line thrust from Terza, at chest level, outside the opponents body to their right. In some schools the thrust is directed on-line, to the opponent's centerline at chest level. See *Stocatta*.

FIELD: See *Field of Honor*.

FIELD OF HONOR: a.) The established or set location for the duel of honor. Because the closed lists of the duel of chivalry was no longer either requested or granted, combatants no longer required a special enclosure in which to fight. Any flat space that was sufficiently large, open and free of obstacles became an appropriate arena in which to fight a duel. The only real condition defining it was the agreement of the two opponents who decided to meet there. b.) Sometimes applies to the lists of the judicial duel.

FIELD OF PLAY: The area in which the bout is contained. The boundaries can be determined by rules, regulations or the availability of space.

FIELDED: Said of combatants engaged in a fight on a battlefield or field of honor.

FIEND: a.) Originally from the Old English feond, meaning "enemy," then the common enemy of all men "Satan." The term has finally come to mean an enemy or foe. b.) A person of superhuman wickedness. (Now only with reference to cruelty or malignity.)

FIGHT: a.) To contend in arms; to combat; to battle. b.) Single combat. d.) A quarrel. e.) Cloth and canvas used to screen the combatants in ships.

FIGHT IT OUT, TO: (also *To Fight Out*) Not to cease fighting for a cause, until one combatant is victorious.

FIGHTER: a.) A combatant, a warrior. b.) A swordsman. One who fights duels. A duelist. c.) A pugilist, boxer, etc. One who fights.

FIGHTING MEN: Armed soldiers; combatants.

Figure-Eight Deception: A series of two or more deceptions of parries often used in double fence. The path of the offending blade draws a figure-eight in the air as it deceives the counter parry of the primary weapon and the counter parry of the secondary weapon.

Figure-Eight Drill: a.) A *doigté* exercise with the sword that has the combatant trace the pattern of a figure-eight in the air (horizontally or vertically) with the point of their weapon. b.) Sometimes applied to the *Wrapping the Eights* drill.

Filo Dritta: (It.) The true or fore-edge of a blade.

Filo Falso: (It.) The false or back or false edge of a blade.

Filo Finta: (Ger.) See *Graze Feint*.

Filo: (It. & Ger.) a.) The edge of the rapier's blade. See *Filo Dritta* and *Filo Falso*. b.) Sometimes used for the *Glissade*.

Filo: (It.) A Glide.

Finestra: ("Window" guard). See *Posta di Finestra*.

Finger Jab: a.) A forceful strike or blow made with the tips of the fingers (together or separately). Generally delivered to sensitive body targets such as the eyes, throat, sternum or groin. b.) See *Spear Hand*.

Finger Lock: A Joint Lock made by turning one or more fingers against their natural articulation.

Finger Loop: A small metal ring, found in some sixteenth century German weapons, through which a fencer could pass one finger of their sword hand. The loop was situated in the crook created where one of the quillons meets the blade.

Finger Play: A method of manipulating the sword with the fingers. See *Doigté*.

Finger Stomp: (also *Hand Stomp*) An crushing attack with the heel or flat of the foot made to the hand, specifically the finger(s).

Finger Waving: Exercises used to develop strength and agility in the base of the fingers, i.e. the palm. There are three Finger Waving exercises, the Flying Wing (where the motion of the hand and fingers looks like a bird waving its wing), the Finger Wave (where the motion of the fingers look like an ocean wave) and the Finger Roll (where the fingers roll in towards and out away from the palm).

Fingering: To wrap the lead (and sometime second finger and thumb) around the quillons and ricasso for superior tip control and grip. An innovative method of gripping known since ancient times, it found greatest use with Renaissance blades .

Finta: (It. & Ger.) (also *Finto*) See *Feint*.

Finta de Filo: (It.) See *Graze Feint*.

Finta di Cavazione: (It.) See *Circular Feint*.

Finta in Tempo: (It.) A composed stop thrust or cut, usually made against an attempted prise de fer or attack in countertime.

Fioretto: (It.) See *Foil*.

Firk: To beat; to drub.

First Blood: A duel that is fought only to the first sight of drawn blood as opposed to "to the death" or to the opponent yielding.

First Counter-Riposte: The initial riposte of the attacker.

First and Second Cause: The two predominant reasons for one to fight a duel. 1st: An unpardonable insult such as a slap or blow to one's person. 2nd: A verbal provocation of some sort, a lie or insult to reputation or honor.

Fist: a.) The hand clenched or closed tightly, with the fingers doubled into the palm; generally for the purpose of striking, hitting or punching. The area of the hand used in many punching techniques. There are many varieties of the fist, including front fist, back fist and hammer fist. b.) The clenched hand used for striking and punching.

Fisticuffs: (also *Fisty Cuffes*) Unarmed fighting, generally restricted to blows made with the fists. See *Pugilism* and *Boxing*.

Five, Parry of: (also *High Five*) a.) Defense for a vertical attack to the head with the blade held above the head, parallel to the floor, the hand and hilt on the weapon bearing side. The forte is in front of and above the center of the head. b.) A defensive position used by some instructors for a diagonal cutting attack to the right cheek or temple. The parry is similar to that of High 3. c.) (also *Parry Quinte*) Defense for a descending vertical or diagonal cut to the head with the blade held above the head, the hand and hilt on the weapon bearing side. d.) Broadsword defense against a Head Cut, made with the blade square across with the hands well to the outside to avoid being hit.

FIVE A, PARRY OF: (also Five Alternate and Window Parry) a.) A variation of the parry of high five placing the hilt and sword hand on the left side of the body, the point to the right and the blade parallel to the floor; above the head and in front of the body. b.) A defensive position used by some instructors for a diagonal cutting attack to the left cheek or temple. The parry is similar to that of High 4. c.) Defense for a descending vertical or diagonal cut to the head with the blade held above the head, the hand and hilt on the non-weapon bearing side. Sometimes referred to as Six in broadsword and sabre technique.

FLAIL: a.) (also *Morning-Star*) A military weapon resembling a threshing-flail (Flail c.) in construction, but usually of iron or strengthened with iron, and often having the striking part armed with spikes. b.) (also *Protestant Flail*) A weapon consisting of a short staff, loaded with lead, attached to the wrist by a strap; it is said to have been carried during the excitement of the "Popish Plot" by persons who professed to be in fear of murderous assaults by "Papists." c.) An instrument for threshing corn by hand, consisting of a wooden staff or handle, at the end of which a stouter and shorter pole or club, called a swingle or swipple, is so hung as to swing freely.

FLAMBERGE: (also *Flamberg*) a.) A "dish hilt" or "dueling hilt" style rapier, precursor to the later small sword. Starting only in the last century, these began to also be called "flambergs" by scholars. b.) A variant of waved rapier blade said to affect the feel of actions during parrying and once thought to make more brutal wounds, waved blades (such as on some two handers) are actually correctly known as "flambards" or "flammards".

FLANCONNADE: (Fr.) (also *Flanconade*) a.) Any attack to the flank (usually a thrust) preceded by a bind of the opposing blade. b.) An action directed against the flank of an opponent.

FLANK: a.) The muscle mass situated between the ribs and the hip. Often applied to a hip or waist cut. b.) The extreme left or right side of an army or body of soldiers in military formation.

FLANK CUT: A term used in sabre fencing, for a cutting attack made to the weapon bearing side of the body at roughly waist level. In a proper on guard stance the foot of the weapon bearing side is carried forward, turning the body and carrying that hip slightly forward and exposing the flank to the cut more than the non-weapon bearing hip. Opposite of a *Belly Cut*.

FLASH IN THE PAN: A term that comes from the use of match, and flintlock muskets and pistols. Each of these firearms was loaded through its muzzle with a charge of powder, wadding and a lead bullet. Once this was done, a small charge of powder was placed in the pan of the weapon, a concave piece of steel adjacent to a small hole at the butt end of the barrel. This priming charge was used to ignite the charge within the barrel (much like a fuse to a cannon). If all went well, when the piece was cocked and the trigger pulled, the match or flint would snap down (the flint striking a spark off of a steel plate above the pan) setting off the priming powder, which would then ignite the charge in the barrel of the gun. If all did not go well, and the priming charge failed to ignite the charge in the barrel, all that would happen is a useless flash in the pan.

FLASH: See *Flèche*.

FLAT FOOT: (also *Flat Footed*) Not toe/ball/heel - heel/ball/toe.

FLAT: The wide portion of the blade, in comparison to the edge.

FLATLONG: Not edgewise; but with the flat side downward.

FLÈCHE: (Fr.) (also *Fleche*, literally "arrow") a.) An offensive action in footwork that swiftly propels the combatant forward in a sprint or run. A form of running attack. b.) An attacking footwork formed by either leaping or running forward, with the rear foot crossing past the front foot.

FLEURET: (Fr.) A late seventeenth century term for the protective leather cap placed over the point of the foil blade. Referred to as a fleuret because of its resemblance to a flower bud; eventually representing the entire foil.

FLICK CUT: a.) The mechanics of the hand and wrist used in the execution of a wrist cut. The result of relaxation and tension of the fingers and hand during the thrusting of the blade forward. The wrist along with the manipulators steer the attack while the last three fingers or aids loosen and tighten on the grip of the sword, flicking the blade forward. The "flick" returns the blade to the placement of a standard cut as the thrust of the arm safely guides the blade past the opponent. See *Wrist Cut.* b.) A light wounding cut generally delivered with the foible of the blade to a major muscle group. Less brutal than ripping cuts, the draw cut can be used to startle or intimidate an opponent rather than cripple them. Because of the "delicate" nature of this cut, it is an action more often used in transitional rapier play.

FLIP: a.) Any fast or sharp action that uses leverage on the victim's joints or body to take them off center and bring them down from an erect position. b.) A throw that carries the victim over and around roughly 180 degrees. c.) (also *Throw*) An offensive movement which controls or appears to control the victim's center, giving the illusion of lift-ing them off their feet and returning them to the ground – usually into a break fall or roll. See *Throw.* d.) (also *Fillip*) A smart stroke or blow. e.) To move or throw about with a sudden jerk.

FLIP: See *Throw.*

FLOOR: a.) To knock one's opponent down; literally to knock them to the floor. b.) The fencing ground or strip.

FLORETT: (Ger.) From the French "fleuret;" a foil.

FLOURISH: a.) A showy brandishing or waving about of a weapon or anything else held in the hand; an ostentatious movement of the body or limbs. b.) A fast and graceful exchange of blade-play.

FLOURISH: a.) A showy brandishing of a weapon. b.) A fast and graceful display of movements with a sword.

FLOWING ATTACKS: Attacks on the blade that use a sliding or grazing action down the opposing blade in order to displace it. Flowing Attacks do not assault the opposing weapon. They use a gentle, but continuing amount of opposition to move the blade aside. The most common form of Flowing Attack is the *Glissade* or *Coulé.*

FLURRY: Rapid combination of attacks made in an apparently uncontrolled manner.

FLUTE: The groove, channel or furrow found in blades such as the small sword, and modern epee blade that removes precious ounces from the blades weight without jeopardizing its structural integrity.

FLUTED: Having, furnished, or ornamented with grooves, channels or furrows resembling the half of a flute split longitudinally, with the concave side outwards. See *Flute.*

FLY OFF THE HANDLE: A term now applied to a person or event that resembles the disastrous effect of an ax or mace-head that during combat or practice literally flies off its handle. This could injure friend or foe, and leave its wielder quite open for reproach.

FLYING KICK: Any type of kick where both feet clear the ground during execution and impact.

FLYING LUNGE: A jump forward that, instead of terminating in the on guard position, extends forward into a grand lunge.

FLYING MARE: A particular throw in wrestling where one combatant leaps at the other, turning themselves horizontal in the air and landing across the opponent's chest, taking them backwards to the floor.

FLYING PARRY-RIPOSTE: A parry and riposte made in one motion, usually as a coupé.

FLYING SNAP KICK: See *Scissors Kick.*

FOIBLE: (Fr.) (Seventeenth century French for "weak") a.) The uppermost, and weakest, third of the exposed blade closest to the tip. Modern fencing weapons; foil, epée, sabre, all have incredibly flexible foibles, designed to give, or bend, on a hit to avoid penetration. b.) The third of the blade nearest to the point, and normally used for offense. The weakest part of the blade. Seventeenth-Century French for faible; "Feeble."

FOIL: a.) The Elizabethan term for any rebated or blunted weapon, from the old French "fouler," "refouler," to turn back. The English word applied to all rebated, blunted or dulled weapons, weather a sword for practice, a lance, or any other weapon. b.) A light weapon used in modern fencing; a type of small sword with a blunt edge and a button on the point. Originally called the fleuret, the foil was the practice weapon for the small sword and is now the weapon of the modern sport of foil fencing, which unlike historical swordplay is limited by its strict rules and conventions. The modern fencing weapon is not now, nor was it ever, a real weapon. c.) One of the three competitive fencing weapons. The foil is a thrusting weapon only, with a quadrangular section blade. The target is restricted to the torso and bib. d.) A term in wrestling for a throw not resulting in a flat fall, hence; to throw, defeat (an antagonist); to overthrow, beat off, repulse. To defeat.

FOIN: (also *Foining*) A late sixteenth century English term for a thrusting attack. To make a thrust with a pointed weapon or the point of a weapon.

FOLLOW THROUGH: Commitment to an action from beginning to end. To continue the slap, kick, punch, stroke, or blow after the target has been struck, to the full extent of the blow.

FOOT AND HAND: To gain ground and attack simultaneously.

FOOT STOMP: a.) An aggressive thrust of the foot down onto the object being attacked, often the victim's foot. b.) Any slapping or striking of the foot to the floor.

FOOTSTAMP: Stamp attack made to the foot.

FOOT-TO-FOOT: Fighting in close combat with one's foot against the opponent's.

FOOTWORK: Work, activity or movement done with the feet. Such actions include Advance, Retreat, Passes, Slips, Voltes, Lunges, Traverses, etc.

FORCE PERFORCE: By force, by violence...

FORCE: (Small Sword) The act of advancing within measure, and delivering a thrust forcibly, so the adversary may not have sufficient power to throw it off. See also *Press* and *Pressure.*

FORE EDGE: (also *True Edge*) The edge presented towards one's opponent when the weapon is held correctly. On the rapier it was generally sharp from the tip to the forte.

FORE END: The leading end of the staff in the *En Garde* position.

FORE: Abbreviation for "forward," generally used in footwork as in a Reprise to the "Fore."

FOREARM BLOCK: One of the most common defensive actions for stopping a punch, kick or similar attack. It is made with either the hard edges of bone or the muscle groupings on the back or inside of the forearm.

FOREARM BLOW: (also *Forearm Punch* and *Forearm Smash*) A hard, flailing strike in which the lower arm is used like a bat or club, hitting the victim with the portion of arm between the elbow and hand.

FOREARM CHOKE: (also *Back Choke*) A

strangle hold made from behind that has the aggressor's arm wrapped about the victim's neck, using the forearm to crimp the windpipe.

Fore-Cut: A cutting attack with the fore or true edge of the blade.

Fore-Hand Guard: a.) A guard position in rapier and dagger play put forth by English Fight Master Joseph Swetnam. The blade placement is similar to Capo Ferro's *Quinta Guardia*, with the rapier held on the sword bearing side, the hand and hilt at roughly waist level, its point directed at the belly or mid-torso. The dagger is held above the rapier, the hand and hilt at mid-torso just to the left of the rapier, its point turned upward rather than across the rapier's blade in Capo Ferro's Quinta. See also *Quinta*. b.) A term applied to Swetnam's *Unicorne Guard* in backsword play. See *Unicorne Guard*.

Forehand Ward: A medium guard in Elizabethan swordplay.

Forehand: A term used to indicate an attack, usually with the edge, delivered from the right, much like a forehand swing in tennis.

Foreward: The vanguard.

Fork Cut: A rising attack delivered up and between the legs of the victim. A *Montanto*.

Form: A term for different styles or disciplines in martial arts.

Fort: a.) A fortified place; a position fortified for defensive or protective purposes, usually surrounded with a ditch, rampart, and parapet, and garrisoned with troops; a fortress. b.) Strong part or point. Now written "Forte". c.) See *Forte*.

Forte: (also sometimes *Shoulder* or *Strength*) a.) The widest, and strongest third of the exposed blade closest to the hilt. The portion of the weapon most often used by the combatant to block and parry attacks. b.) The third of the blade nearest to the hilt. The strongest part of the blade, and normally used for defense. c.) Someone's strong point or part; their strength.

Forte to Foible: The basic principal of defense in swordplay; the strongest section of the defending blade (*forte*) against the weakest point (*foible*) of the offending blade.

Forward 45: A specific line on an Imaginary Star that consists of 45 degree relationships to the primary North-South and East-West lines. The Forward 45 refers then to those lines of movement that would be to the North East and North West.

Forward 90: A specific line on an Imaginary Star that consists of 45 degree relationships to the primary North-South and East-West lines. The Forward 90 refers then to those lines of movement that would be to the North.

Forward Diagonal Avoid: An evasive action taken with a forward lunge or pass onto the NE or NW diagonal tracks of footwork. See *Diagonal Avoid*.

Forward Foot: See *Lead Foot*.

Forward Stance: (MA) A stance, generally in martial arts, where the hips are rotated forwards, the front leg is bent, with the knee directly above the instep. The rear leg is straight.

Founding Principals of Swordplay: Established in the dawn of history, are the two basic principles of swordplay; offense and defense. These categories are subdivided: the principles of offense, either by stabbing or crushing; and the principle of defense, either by interposing some object between the attacker's weapon and one's own body or by dodging the attacker's weapon. Both these ideas, with their subdivisions, are the basic foundation of the principles of the sword and run side by side through the history of swordplay.

Four Governors: One way of looking at the major factors in swordsmanship: perception, distance, timing, and technique.

Four, Parry of: a.) The defensive position for a thrust or horizontal attack to the non-weapon bearing shoulder, closing the high inside lines. The knuckles to the inside, palm facing back, away from the opponent. The blade is above the hand, its forte at the level of the muscular notch in the non-weapon bearing arm. b.) (also *Parry Quarte*) Protecting the high inside line with the point up, the hand in supination. c.) Broadsword defense against a Chest Cut, made with the point up, the hands a little higher than the waist and pushed out slightly away from the body, the blade points almost straight up, defending the inside high line.

FOUR-LEAF-CLOVERS: Exercises in point control or *doigté* that draw four circles in the air that make a patter similar to the leaves of a clover. This exercise not only focuses on the precise circular movement of the blade, but also of the specific starting point of the action. There are two patterns of drawing the clover, the first seems to be the more traditional pattern, the second being more a variation of the *Figure-Eight* drill than actually tracing the leaves of the clover.

FOUR-POINT STANCE: The fencing stance that places the feet equally apart in width and depth as if standing on two opposite corners of a square upon the floor. The stance provides a strong foundation that supports movement of the body in four directions, both from side to side and forward and back. This placement of the body also allows for the use of the left hand for defense, much like in modern boxing.

FOYNING: An Elizabethan term for puncture play. See *Foin*.

FRAY: a.) A fight; a battle. b.) A violent riot attended with bloodshed. c.) A single combat; whether armed or unarmed, verbal or physical.

FRECCIATA: (It.) See *Fleche*.

FREE: A common practice of Elizabethan rapier fence where the blade was kept from touching the opponent's weapon. Hence, said of blades that are not engaged or joined. When the blades are free, they can be in any guard placement, either cross body or standard, but the blades are not touching.

FROG: An attachment to the sword belt in which a sword or other weapon may be carried.

FROISSÉ: See *Pressure Glide*.

FROISSEMENT: a.) An attack on the opponent's blade that combines the action of a beat and press attack, accentuated by a quick glide along the blade to displace it. Generally used as a preparatory action to an attack. See *Pressure Glide*. b.) A preparation of attack made by deflecting the adversary's blade by a strong grazing action along it forwards and downwards. A type of graze, and therefore an attack on the blade.

FRONT: a.) To meet the enemy or opponent face to face. b.) To attack. c.) The lead of any army.

FULL BLOW: A cutting attack delivered from the shoulder with the full arm. The slowest, and most powerful of cutting attack made with the sword. See also *Shoulder Cut*.

FULL CUT: See *Shoulder Cut*.

FULL NELSON: Lock applied from behind in which the attacker's arms pass under the victim's armpits, in front of the arms and behind the neck where the fingers interlock.

FULL PASS: (also *Pass Forward-Lunge*) A compound action in footwork that combines a pass forward with the extended leg position of the lunge. Often completed with the upper torso extended beyond the lead leg with the non-weapon hand used for support.

FULL TILT: At full speed and with direct thrust (As in full gallop with lances lowered in jousting); with utmost adverse force or impetus.

FULL VOLTE: See *Grand Volte*.

FULLER: A groove, channel or furrow made in the flat of the blade, designed to lesson the weight of the blade without jeopardizing its structural integrity. See also *Fluting*.

G

GAFFLET: (also *Gaffle*) a.) A forked rest designed to support the barrel of a musket. See *Rest*. b.) A steel lever designed to draw back the bow of a cross-bow. c.) In early epée fencing, a tip threaded with a washer.

GAINING GROUND: Any step forward that purchases ground from your opponent.

GAINING: (also *Gaining on the Lunge*) a.) An alternative to the balestra where the lag foot is brought up against the lead foot with a half pass, just before the execution of a lunge. This action helps the combatant gain ground and increase the distance of the lunge. b.) A way of increasing the reach of the lunge by first moving up the rear foot near the front foot, prior to lunging. See also *Half Pass*.

GAINING THE MEASURE: (also *Finding the Measure*) Proceeding from out of to in range, or from the *misura larga* to *misura stretta*.

GALLOWGLASSES: Heavy-armed foot soldiers of Ireland and the western isles.

GARDANT FIGHT: A ward or fighting posture and technique taught by English Gentleman George Silver. In this ward the hand and hilt are held above the head on the sword bearing side, the blade and point angled down and to the non-weapon bearing side. The blade is not angled forward as in Prima Guardia, but is kept in close to the body with the point directed towards the inside knee. The body is carried upright, standing behind the ward of the blade. Silver instructs his reader not to lean forward in this guard, for danger of their life, but rather to hold the body "bolt upright" and to bear the head and body backward when being pressed in an encounter.

GARDE: (Fr.) See *Guard*.

GASH: A deep and wide wound.

GASHED: Cut deep and wide.

GAUCHE: (Fr.) a.) Literally meaning "left" such as for the left hand (*main gauche*). b.)

Due to the fact that at one time to be left handed was considered the mark of the devil, to be a lefty or "left" was to be wrong or off. Hence the term has come to mean something or someone wanting in tact or in ease and grace of manner, awkward or clumsy. Like the Italian word Sinister (sinistra, also meaning "left"), gauche is used today with little knowledge of its intended meaning; to slander the left hander.

GAUNTLET: a.) A glove worn as part of medieval armor, usually made of leather, covered with plates of steel or iron, intended to protect the weapon bearing hand(s). b.) To give a challenge, from the medieval custom of throwing down a glove or gauntlet to challenging an opponent. c.) To undertake the defense of a person or opinion. To accept a challenge.

GAUNTLET, THROW DOWN THE: If a knight wished to challenge another to single combat, he might throw one of his gauntlets at his opponent's feet; when the latter picked it up, the challenge was excepted. Throwing down the gauntlet still amounts to a challenge, as to a debate - though the results are seldom as bloody as in the good old medieval days. See *Gauntlet*.

GERADER STOSS: (Ger.) See *Straight Thrust*.

GERMAN GUARD: (Rapier) The on guard position in the German school of rapier play was based on, and thus resembled, that of the Italian school. See *Italian Guard*.

GETTING UNTRACKED: This is a term in boxing for the process of getting into your rhythm as a fighter.

GIANT EPÉE: (also *Musketeer Blade* and *Wide Epée*) A form of epée blade that has been widened severely at the forte and tapers to a much stiffer foible. As in the standard epée blade, the basic design is still for point work, being a triangular, fluted blade, and the tang has not been sufficiently enlarged to handle much edge-to-edge-play. This blade is quite popular, but still has the habit of breaking at the tang and foible. The "Musketeer blade" seems to work best on transitional rapiers, where there is much less edge-play.

Gioco Largo: ("far" or "large play" or "large game") Combat without body contact and at cutting or striking range in the Italian schools as opposed to seizing or grappling range.

Gioco Stretto: ("close playing or "close game") In the Italian schools a term for entering techniques used for body-contact fighting close-in at seizing and grappling range (in the later English systems of cut-and-thrust sword of the 1500's, these were known as "gryps" or "seizures"). All are based essentially on a handful of key actions: reaching out to grab the opponent's hilt or arm, striking with the pommel or guard, trapping their forearms with your second arm, slipping the blade against or between their forearms, using the second hand to hold the blade while binding/striking/slicing, and tripping and kicking. In the German schools close-in techniques for "wrestling at the sword" or *Ringen Am Schwert*, involved throws or grappling and disarming moves known as or *Schwertnemen* ("sword-taking") there was also ground-fighting (*Unterhalten*, "holding down").

Girata: Stepping out of line by either moving your leading right foot to the right or by crossing the left foot behind the right one.

Girdle: A belt drawn around the waist. Large belts were worn with the buckle before; but for wrestling the buckle was turned behind, to give the adversary a fairer grasp at the girdle. To turn the buckle behind, therefore, was a challenge.

Giving the Blade: An intentional threatening extension of the arm and weapon designed to provoke a response that can then be countered.

Giving the Lie: a.) The most severe of indignations in Elizabethan dueling *punctilio*. To be accused of lying was an open invitation to a quarrel. b.) Purposly offending the honor of another gentleman or his lady through insult, innuendo, or wit.

Gladiator: An armed combatant who entertained audiences in the Roman Republic and Roman Empire in violent confrontations with other gladiators, wild animals, and condemned criminals. Arising out of ancient Roman funeral rites, gladiators became popular public entertainers. Some gladiators were volunteers who risked their lives and their legal and social standing by appearing in the arena. Most were despised as slaves, schooled under harsh conditions, socially marginalized, and segregated even in death.

Gladius: (plural *Gladii*) A Latin word for sword and is used to represent the primary sword of Ancient Roman foot soldiers, most commonly referring to the Gladius Hispaniensis, or "Hispanic Sword." Varying between 20 and 33 inches long, with a blade 2 inches wide, Gladii were two-edged for cutting and had a tapered point for stabbing during thrusting.

Glasgow Handshake: Slang for the *Head Butt*.

Glide: (also *Graze*) a.) A thrust in the line of engagement that displaces the opponent's blade by maintaining contact and applying pressure while sliding down the blade. See also *Glissade*. b.) An attack on the opponent's blade executed by engaging the blade and sliding along the blade straight to the target.

Glissade Feint: A feint of a flowing attack on the blade meant to draw a parry against which an attack may be made with a redirection of the point.

Glissade: (also *Glizade, Glide* or *Coulé*) A flowing attack on the blade, executed from an engaged guard position, that displaces the opposing blade by gently sliding down the opposing weapon foible to forte. Excessive force is not needed in the Glissade because it is generally executed against an opponent whose guard insufficiently closes the line of attack. b.) [In French *coulé*, from the verb couler, to slip or glide along] (Small Sword) A flowing attack on the blade that displaces the opposing blade by gently sliding down the opposing weapon foible to forte. Excessive force is not needed because it is generally executed against a guard that insufficiently closes the line of attack.

GOLDEN AGE OF SWORDPLAY: The peak of the evolution and practice of the sword and swordplay spanning the sixteenth to eighteenth century, from the introduction of the rapier to the eventual retirement of the civilian sword.

GOLPE: (Span.) See *Hit*.

GOON: a.) Originally from the Arabic ghoum, meaning a fighter, thug. Now meaning a person hired to terrorize workers; a thug (especially by racketeers). b.) An amiable if not over-bright person, named after a creature that appeared in the comic strip "Popeye" with similar characteristics.

GORE: a.) To stab; to pierce. b.) Metaphorically, to wound, to hurt deeply.

GORGET: A piece of armor designed to protect the throat. From the French gorge, meaning neck or throat.

GOUGE: An digging or penetrating attack made with one or more fingers of the open hand, usually driving the finger(s) into sensitive body areas such as the eyes (*Eye Gouge*) to incur serious damage and/or dislodge them.

GRAB: (also *Grasp* or *Pull*) A quick, sudden, momentary clutch, grasp or seizure of any limb or part of the opponent.

GRACE: (Small Sword) After an adversary has parried your thrust of carte inside, the foil should fly off outwardly in an oblique direction, having only a slight hold of the grasp between the thumb and first and second fingers, in a similar manner to that of holding a pen; and the arm is not to deviate from the line of direction while performing the grace.- When your adversary has parried with tierce, your thrust of carte over the arm, the foil of course flies off obliquely inwards, whereby your adversary is seen through the angle formed by your foil and arm- As the

inward and outward oblique inclination of the blade are equal, therefore the angles made by these graces or covers are also equal to each other. To perform the graces well, distinguishes a nice susceptibility of the wrist to the resistance or oppostion of your adversary's parades; and your adhering to a good line of direction, distinguishes the justness of the longe and thrust."

GRAND BIND: See *Active Bind*.

GRAND CROISÉ: See *Active Croisé*.

GRAND ENVELOPMENT: a.) Taking the partners blade from the low line and describing a large three quarter circle above the head to the opposite low line without losing blade contact. An grand envelopment is a prise-defer. b.) See *Active Envelopment*.

GRAND LUNGE: a.) The classical movement which replaced passing as a means of reaching and attacking an opponent. From the on guard stance, the lead foot is raised (toes first) and propelled forward as far as the combatant can conveniently manage (about thirty inches). At the same time the lag leg is straightened pushing the entire body forward. The sword arm is thrust forward, the rear arm is snapped backward, and the trunk and the pelvis are turned slightly forward. b.) The Italian fencing masters Giganti (1606) and Capo Ferro (1610) defined the application and advantage of the "lunge." It was applied by both men to most common and practical attacks. The *Stocatta Lunga* ("Elongated Thrust") or *Botta Lunga* ("Elongated Blow"), respectively, were executed from the position of a bent arm. The arm extended and body traveled forward at the same instant concluding in a lunge. This seemingly simple move changed the execution and manner of swordplay. The old round circling style of footwork was slowly discarded and swordplay evolved to that of the direct linear style of today.

GRAND VOLTE: (also *Bum in the Face*) A large evasive step that removes the body from the line of attack by compassing the lag foot back and around the lead foot approximately one-hundred and eighty degrees. The scope of this evasion, basically turning the backside toward the opponent, has given it the nickname Bum in the Face or Bum in Your Face. The grand volte is more often executed to the right in order to maintain the sword arm as a threat to the opponent.

GRAND: (Fr.) Meaning deep, full or complete.

GRAPPLE: a.) To wrestle, to contend in close fight. b.) (Wrestling) A name given to various contrivances and implements for clutching and grasping. c.) To wrestling with, or fight in close quarters while grasping and holding one another. This may be executed standing, on the floor, or in any degree there between. Although the term implies grasps and holds, within the struggle there can be punching, kicking, tripping, biting, etc. See *Grappling*. d.) The securing of ships with hooks and rope and then pulling them together in battle.

GRAPPLING: a.) To endeavor to overpower or lay down another by seizing and holding their body and/or limbs in order to control, trip, overbalance or throw them. b.) The action of wrestling with, or fighting in close quarters with a partner. This action can either be in standing position, or on the floor, and can include punching, kicking, tripping, etc. The term grappling means that the partners do not let go of one another during the sequence.

GRASP: a.) (also *Gryps*) A sixteenth and seventeenth century term for closing measure and seizing and wrenching the opponent's hilt or arm in order to take their weapon or break their wrist in the attempt. The action may be executed from both offensive and defensive positions. b.) To use one or both hands for clutching or grasping the opponent with the intent to roughly pull or push them about. In grasping an opponent the hand can be used in three ways: 1 Standard: the hand being brought forward with the thumb up, like in a hand shake; 2 Flat: the hand being brought forward with the palm out, like in a game of "patty-cake;" 3 Reversed: the hand

being brought forward with the palm down and thumb trailing. c.) A term in wrestling for coming to close quarters; body to body. To come to the grasp; to grapple. d.) See *Grip*

GRASPING THE BLADE: A seizure, or disarm of the opponent's weapon by grabbing the blade rather than the hilt. Historically the action was considered, even with a naked hand, because the risk of injuring the hand was taken to avoid more serious injury.

GRASSING: Old wrestling slang for laying out or *Flooring* one's opponent.

GRAVES: Ancient spelling of greaves, an armor for the legs.

GRAZE: a.) A Glide, forcefully executed. b.) A preparation of attack made by sliding on the adversary's blade. An attack on the blade. see *Glissade*.

GRAZE FEINT: A glide executed only with the extension of the arm (no attack or lunge). This action is meant to draw a parry with which a hit may be made upon its deception.

GRIP: a.) The manner in which the weapon is held, which can vary depending on the weapon, school, period and personal preference. b.) The part of the sword situated between the guard and the pommel. Also referred to as the handle. c.) The part of the handle normally held by the hand. Also the manner in which a weapon is held. d.) See *Grype*.

GRIPES: (also *Grappling*) The techniques of swordplay that favor the locks, holds, grips and throws of wrestling. This practice is mentioned in disfavor by Di Grassi and Saviolo, yet both Masters point out that it is a common practice in rapier-play.

GROIN CUT: a.) A rising cut delivered upward to the crotch. See *Montanto*. b.) See *Low Inside Cut*.

GRYPE: (also *Gripe* and *Grip*) a.) To wrestle or grapple at close quarters. b.) The seizing of the opponent's sword-hilt with the unarmed hand.

GRYPES: A sixteenth and seventeenth century technique of seizing and wrenching the opponent's hilt or arm in order to take their weapon or break their wrist in the attempt.

GUANTO DA PRESA: A gauntlet or glove specially made with a mail palm section, specifically designed for grasping and seizing the opponent's blade. "The 'grype' is the seizing of the sword-hilt with the left hand, - for this purpose a "guanto da presa," or gripping gauntlet with the palm protected with fine mail, was sometimes used.

GUARD (ON): One of the two fencing postures, characterized by offering the option of either attacking or defending. See *On Guard*.

GUARD: a.) (UA) A posture of defense; a placement of the body, arms and hands that closes the upper lines of attack and allows the fighter to deliver every possible attack and safely execute defensive maneuvers while expending the least possible amount of energy. b.) (Swordplay) Originally a position from which to initiate an offensive or defensive action. Nowadays, however, a posture of defense; a placement of the blade that closes one or more lines and allows a fencer to deliver every possible attack and come to every possible parry while expending the least possible amount of energy. c.) Often applied to the hilt of the sword. d.) Sometimes used as a loose synonym for "on guard," or the on guard stance. e.) The portion of the hilt between the blade and the grip which protects the hand.

GUARDE: (Fr.) See *Guard*.

GUARDIA: (It.) The fencing position that allowed for the best offensive move in relation to whatever guardia was assumed by one's opponent.

GUARDIA ALTA: Alferi's term for *Prima Guardia*.

GUARDIA DI BECHA POSSA: Marozzo's term for *Prima Guardia*.

GUARDS: (Small Sword) Particular postures, adapted either for defending from the attempts of an adversary, or from whence one may execute any offensive movements.

GUIDING HAND: a.) An exercise designed to break the habit of bending forward at the waist during blade-play by placing a fencing glove upon the combatant's head. The glove is used as a sensory guide, telling the combatant when they bend or reach forward during the exercises. A slight bend causes the glove to shift. A dramatic lean in the torso will cause the glove to fall. b.) A variation on the original exercise that places focus on the activity of the arm during various forms of cutting attacks. For Shoulder Cuts the unarmed hand actually lightly pushes the upper arm to emphasize the full arm activity of the attack. For Elbow Cuts a fencing glove is placed upon the combatant's upper arm to focus the attack to that of the elbow and wrist. On Wrist Cuts, the glove is placed on the attacking arm's forearm. The glove is used as a sensory guide, telling the combatant when they use a part of the attacking arm not necessary for the attack being practiced. Movement of the upper arm or forearm causes the glove to shift, while active involvement will cause the glove to fall.

GUN: An instrument from which shot is discharged by fire; a canon; a musket...

GUNNER: A cannoneer.

GUN-STONES: Cannon-balls of stone, used for shot in the Middle Ages.

H

HALBERD: (also *Habred, Halbert, Halbard*) A military weapon, especial¬ly in use during the fifteenth and sixteenth century; a kind of combina¬tion between a spear and a battle-ax, consisting of a sharp edged blade ending in a point, and a spear head mounted on a haft five to seven feet in length.

HALF BLOWS: As taught by Giovanni Dell'Agochie in 1572, a form of parry, also a strike not meant to reach the opponent but deflect their sword by counter-cutting.

HALF CIRCLE: See *Semi-Circular Parry*.

HALF COUNTER PARRY: A parry that travels diagonally across the body from a high to a low line and vice versa. IE: from 3 to 7 & 7 to 3; 3 to 1 & 1 to 3; 4 to 2 & 2 to 4; 4 to 8 & 8 to 4; etc. See *Diagonal Parry*.

HALF DISENGAGE: (also *Meggia Cavatione*) A form of changement executed to the same side of the body as that of the engagement. If the opposing guard closes the high inside line, the changement lowers the point to the low inside line, and vice versa.

HALF NELSON: (Wrestling) a.) A hold in which one arm is thrust under the corresponding arm of the opponent and the hand placed on the back of their neck. b.) An arm-lock applied from behind in which the arm is held at the wrist and twisted up the victim's back.

HALF PACE: See *Half Pass*.

HALF PASS BACK: (also *Half Passe Back*) The action of bringing the forward foot back to the rear foot in preparation to take a second step. The second step can be executed as: 1.) Change - Starting with a Half Passe, the feet change so that the rear foot kicks out, remains behind, or performs a Thwart, Cross or Slip. 2.) Continue - Starting with a Half Passe and continuing on with the same foot to finish in a Passe, Thwart, Cross or Slip. 3.) Re-turn - The back foot returns to the original En Garde. The action of all Half-Passes and second steps are performed in two counts; one-Half Passe, two-Continue, Change or Return.

HALF PASS FORWARD: (also *Half Passe Forward*) The action of bringing the back foot up to the front foot in preparation to take a second step. The second step can be either: 1.) Change - Starting with a Half Passe, the feet change so that the forward foot kicks out, remains forward, and steps to either a linear step, Thwart, Cross or Slip. 2.) Continue - Starting with a Half Passe and continuing on with the same foot to finish in either a Passe, Thwart, Cross or Slip. 3.) Return - The back foot returns to the original En Garde. The action of all Half-Passes and second steps are performed in 2 counts; one-Half Passe, two-Continue, Change or Return.

HALF PASS: (also sometimes *Cheat Step* or *Paused Step*) a.) A simple form of footwork that carries the foot forward/backward in the same manner as a pass, only bringing the foot to rest parallel to the opposing foot rather than one foot length passed it; generally executed in conjunction with a similar action of the foot that completes the pass. The first step to parallel is the half pass, and at this point an offensive or defensive action can be executed without committing the body forward or changing measure. Once the action is complete, the body can be carried forward on an attack. The pause between the first and second action of the feet is quite short, and is followed immediately by another action forward. b.) An off-line action of footwork where the moving foot is placed alongside the stationary foot in preparation for a 2nd step. The step may continue (same foot) or change (other foot then moves).

HALF PRONATION: (also *Middle* or *Vertical Position*) The placement of the weapon bearing hand where the thumb is held at roughly twelve o'clock or six o'clock.

HALF STANCE: (also *Two-Point Stance*) An on

guard position, suggested by the early twentieth century fencing master, Professor Leon Bertrand, in which the body was turned so as to expose as little of the chest as possible.

HALF SWORD: (also *Half-Sword*) a.) The term "half-sword" is a literal translation of the German "halb Schwert." The name comes from the method of holding the sword: the right hand upon the grip, while the left hand holds the middle of the blade, dividing it in half. Held in this manner, the long sword was wielded like a short spear. The advantage of this technique is that it allows the swordsman to use their sword effectively at a very close range - especially when opposed by a swordsman who holds their sword with both hands on the grip. The half-sword grip also allows the swordsman to make forceful, accurate thrusts at the gaps in his opponent's armor. See also *Shortening the Sword*.

HALF-COCKED: The flintlock musket or pistol, after being loaded and primed, had to be manually "cocked." This was done by drawing back the hammer portion of the lock until it was caught by the trigger mechanism. It was released for firing by pulling the trigger. Some models had a safety feature that pulled the hammer back about half way, keeping the flint from resting on the pan, and locking the trigger so that the gun can not be fired. To go off half-cocked was to inadequately prepare one's firearm pulling the hammer to the half-cocked position and attempting to shoot. The trigger is of course locked and the gun will not fire, hence the phrase now means to start something without adequate preparation.

HALFE PACE: A simple form of footwork that carries the foot forward/backward in the same manner as a pass, only bringing the foot to rest parallel to the opposing foot rather than one foot length passed it; generally executed in conjunction with a similar action of the foot that completes the pass.

HALF-STAFF: a.) To be at close quarters with staffs; fighting at half the length of a staff. b.) Half the length of a staff.

HALF-SWORD: a.) (also *Close* and *In-Fighting*) Being in close quarters; fighting inside measure where the blades cross at their middle, at half the swords length. "at the halfe of the enimies sword" b.) A small-sized sword; a sword roughly twice the length of its counterpart; a dagger. c.) See *Half Sword*.

HALF-TIME: The execution of two actions, a parry and a riposte, in the time it would have taken to complete the initial attack. Two complete actions in the time of one.

HAMMER BLOCK: A defensive action made with the base of the fist, striking into the aggressor's attack with a hammer punch. The base of the hand is swung into the attack, generally striking the aggressor on the wrist or tendons on the inside of the forearm.

HAMMER BLOW: An unarmed attack which hits with the little finger side of the fist.

HAMMER FIST: (also *Hammer Punch*) a.) The use of the hand, little finger down and thumb up, to strike like club or hammer. This may be delivered with one or two hands. b.) Punch delivered with the "pinkie finger" edge of the fist .

HAMMER PUNCH: (also *Hammer Fist, Hammer Blow* and *Jackhammer Punch*) a.) An unarmed attack made with a closed hand which hits with the little finger down and thumb up, striking downward, in a vertical plane, like swinging a club or hammer. This may be delivered with one or both hands (see *Double-Hand Hammer Punch*). b.) An descending, vertical attack made with a closed hand which hits with the little finger down and thumb up, to strike like club or hammer.

HAMMER-LOCK: (Wrestling) A position in which a wrestler is held with one arm bent behind his back.

HAND PARRY: a.) A defensive move where the hand (usually gloved) is used to deflect, block, or seize an attack. b.) A method of defense where the unarmed hand (usually gloved) is used to deflect, block, or seize the opposing blade. Generally used against thrusting attacks. c.) A method of defense with the unarmed hand that beats or swats the opposing blade aside. Such actions are only used against thrusting attacks.

HAND TO HAND: (also *Empty Hand Combat, Hand-to-Hand, Hand to Hand Combat, Hand unto Hand* and *Unarmed Combat*) a.) Fighting at close quarters where the only weapons are the combatants' hands, feet, etc. b.) Any form of fighting that uses the "natural weapons" of the human body: fists, feet, elbows, knees, etc. rather than weapons. It may also include techniques of falling, rolling, and wrestling or martial arts type throws. It can be used as an addition to weaponry, or against someone with weaponry.

HAND-AND-A-HALF SWORD: (also *Bastard Sword*) A sword with a broad (roughly 2 inches at the forte), straight, double edged blade from 33-40 inches in length, a simple Cross-Guard and a handle about seven inches long that could be used in one or both hands. The weapon was bigger than the single-handed sword of the infantry, but smaller than the Great Sword- neither one or the other, but rather a "bastardized" version of both. This sword was popular in the 15th and sixteenth century.

HANDLE: See *Grip*

HAND-PLAY: A Old English term for the interchange of blows in a hand to hand encounter, revived by some modern fight masters.

HANG FIRE: A term used to describe the sputtering of the primer of a flintlock musket or pistol, which does not immediately ignite the load in the chamber, but could set it off at any moment. As long as there is fire in the hole the gun was dangerous and if improperly handled could easily go off in one's face. The term is now generally a metaphor applied to anything that may or may not "go off."

HANG LEFT: (also *Hanging Five*) The hanging parry for the left shoulder. The hand over the head, the blade below the hand, sloping down with the tip at roughly eight o' clock.

The middle of the blade in front of and above the notch in the left shoulder.

HANG PARRY FIVE: (also *Hanging Five*) See *Hang Left*.

HANG PARRY NINE: (also *Hanging Nine*) See *Hang Right* and *Sword Arm Protect*.

HANG RIGHT: (also *Hanging Five - A*) The hanging parry for the right shoulder. The hand and hilt over the head on the left, the blade below the hand, sloped down and to the right with the middle of the blade in front of and above the notch in the right shoulder.

HANGER: (also *Hangers*) a.) An often richly ornamented loop or strap on a sword belt from which the sword was hung. See *Sword Hanger*. b.) A kind of short sword, originally hung from the belt. c.) A *Hanging Parry*.

HANGING FIVE: A defensive action made against a Cheek Cut, where a standard head parry is angulated, the point being dropped toward the ground on the inside. See also *Hang Left*.

HANGING FIVE-A: (also *Hang Parry Five-A*) See *Hang Right*.

HANGING GUARD: A guard taken with the short sword and dagger where the sword hand and arm are held out and forward, the hilt held at head level (or higher), the blade angled downwards and across the body to the non-sword bearing side. The rise of the sword arm and the slope of the blade present a vantage for the combatant to look through towards their opponent. The dagger hangs at the side, as if it were not to be used.

HANGING NINE: A defensive action made against a Cheek Cut, where a standard head parry is angulated, the point being dropped toward the ground on the outside. See also *Hang Right*.

HANGING PARRY: (also *Sloped Parry* or *Waterfall Parry* and *Hanger*) A defensive action against a diagonal or vertical swipe that presents a sloped or angled blade that meets the attack and causes it to sheer or ricochet off to the side, deflecting rather than blocking or intercepting the offending blade. Unlike other parries the opposing blade meets the middle of the defending blade, not the forte. Vertical swipes meet the blade and skid down the remaining two-thirds. The sliding down the blade is characterized by a fast scraping noise. Diagonal swipes ricochet off the defending blade rather than slide down the parry. The angle of the attack allows the blades to meet, and then avert the attacking blade off to the side. In this type of parry the blades still meet edge to edge, but at a more drastic angle than standard parries. b.) A parry protecting a high line with the hilt high and the point down. c.) A parry protecting the high lines with the hilt high and the point down, such as a high parry of one.

HARNESS: a.) A collective term for the body armor of a man-at-arm or foot- soldier; all the defensive equipment of an armed horseman, for both man and horse. Military accouterments and equipment. b.) The possible derivative term for the Phillapino martial art Arnis.

HARNESSED: Furnished, equipped, mounted, armed, in armor.

HATCHETTE: (also *Hatchet*) A short handled ax furnished with a smaller or lighter head; adapted for use with one hand.

HAUKES/HALF HAUKES: ("hawk") A term from the 15th century English text by J. Ledall (Harliean Manuscript BL MS. 3542), that refers to "downright blows", likely a downward cut, as if striking down like a bird or prey. Forms include hauke, half hauke, broken hauke, broken half hauke, contrary hauke, and double hauke. Perhaps related to the Italian "Falcon" guard (*Posta di Falcone*).

HAVE-AT-HIM: (also *Heave at him*) a.) An official call to begin a trial by combat or contest at arms. b.) The action of attack. A thrust or stroke.

HAVOC: The cry of "Havoc!" is an archaic military command that was given upon the capture or sacking of a town, which, approximately meant a soldier could stop fighting and start looting. The term is now applied to a disaster or catastrophe that resembles the absolute ruin the cry of havoc most surely issued.

HAY: a.) The exclamation of the crowd when a gladiator was wounded in the Roman games; hence an exclamation upon hitting ones opponent; the thrust home, the killing thrust. b.) Possibly an appel, of the Italian school, which is a striking of the ground with the lead foot, during or immediately before, the execution of an attack; often accompanied by a loud shout - "hay." c.) An Elizabethan country dance having a winding or serpentine movement, or being of the nature of a reel. d.) A Medieval term for a net used in the catching of wild animals, especially rabbits, being stretched in front of their holes, or round their haunts.

HAYMAKER: (also *Hay-Maker* and *Roundhouse*) An overlarge hooking punch. This punch would be a "10", on a scale of 1 to 10. It is delivered either right or left handed, usually to the head. Uppercut haymakers are also used, either right or left handed. The reaction, and knap are appropriately large. As this punch is so big, care must be taken to miss the target by several inches. See *Round House*.

HEAD BUTT: a.) A forceful thrust with the top of the head into the face or body of another. b.) A deliberate strike using the head as a weapon (in reality uses the hardest bones of the skull against the softest bones of the face); it is usually produced while both partners are standing face to face. This action has gained in popularity recently, and is now seen as something of a "clever" move, whereas before it was considered somewhat low class and crude, which was perhaps a holdover from its almost legendary use by hooligans and ruffians in the British Isles, where it is sometimes affectionately referred to as either a *Glasgow Handshake* or *Liverpool Kiss*.

HEAD CRUSH: (also Head Crunch) The action of compressing the head between the hands or between a foot and a fixed surface such as the floor.

HEAD LOCK: a.) A hold in which the wrestler encircles the opponent's head with one or both arms. See also *Double Nelson* and *Half Nelson*. b.) A grappling or wrestling hold on the head designed to prevent movement.

HEAD RAM: a.) "Running" the top of the victim's head into an obstacle. b.) A strike using the top of the head.

HEAD SLAM: A grasp with one or both hands in which the victim's head and hair is clasped in the fist of the aggressor and then the head is forcibly pushed or pulled into hard contact with a stationary object such as a wall, table or floor.

HEAD SMASH: "Driving" opponent's face/head into an object or an object into opponent's face/head.

HEAD THROW: The use of the head or neck as the fulcrum for a throw in wrestling or judo. To throw (an adversary) by a maneuver in which the head or neck is used. See also *Head Lock*.

HEAD-HUNTER: A slang term for a boxer or combatant who tries only for a good blow to the opponent's head, disdaining the rest of the body.

HEADLOCK: Any grappling or wrestling hold on the head that effectively prevents movement of the victim. There are many types of headlocks, some from the front, others from the back or side which use one or both hands and arms. All trap or hold the head and neck and apply pressure that causes pain to the victim if they were to move or struggle further.

HEAD-PIECE: Armor for the head; a helmet.

HEAVY HANDED: Slang for hard or powerful contact blows or continual contact techniques.

HEAVY PARRY: (also *Bind Down*) An offensive action made from a successful high line parry which closes measure and carries the opposing blade to the floor in an action similar to the *croisé*.

HEEL HOOK: See *Roundhouse Kick*.

HEEL KICK: Any kick that uses the heel as the impact area. See *Heel Thrust*.

HEEL THRUST: A straight attack with the foot delivered from a chambered or bent leg position by punching the foot directly toward the target, striking with the heel, ball, flat or outside edge of the foot. The foot is then quickly snapped back to its point of origin.

HELM: That part of the armor that covers and protects the head; a helmet.

HELMET: a.) A defensive cover for the head; a piece of armor, usually made of, or strengthened with, metal, which covers the head wholly or in part. The helmet has varied greatly in form, shape and material, and is still used as the term for head protection by men at arms today. b.) A term given to the modern fencing mask.

HIGH CROSS LEFT: A defensive action in double fence for a diagonal cutting attack to the left shoulder. Generally made with the rapier hand above the dagger in a placement similar to rapier parry high one. The dagger hand is below that of the rapier, held in a fashion similar to the dagger parry of three (either before or behind the rapier).

HIGH CROSS RIGHT: A defensive action in double fence for a diagonal attack to the right shoulder. Generally made with the rapier hand below the dagger in a placement similar to parry three. The dagger hand is above that of the rapier, held in a fashion similar to the dagger parry of high one (either before or behind the rapier).

HIGH CROSS: a.) (also *Cross Parry Head, Cross Parry of One* and sometimes *Cross Five*) A double fence defensive action against a vertical cut to the head. The cross may be made either with the dagger before or behind the rapier.

HIGH EIGHT: (also sometimes *Hanging Parry*) A supinated parry used to defend the sword bearing hip or shoulder. The point is down with the blade roughly perpandicular with the floor.

HIGH FOUR, PARRY OF: The parry of four

executed in such a manner as to defend the non-weapon bearing shoulder from a descending diagonal cutting attack. Hilt just below the elbow, knuckles to the outside, blade angled at roughly forty-five degrees, tip up and above the head.

HIGH GUARD: A guard in rapier and dagger taught by the seventeenth century English Fight Master Joseph Swetnam assumed with an opposition grip upon the rapier, the arm lifted and bent at the elbow, its hilt held at cheek level, the blade angled down and to the inside (in the manner of Prima Guardia). The dagger held at waist level with a straight arm, its point turned up and towards the right, outside that of the rapier. The body was carried upright, with a narrow stance, the feet being held close together. This guard (similar to the double fence guard of Prima) was said to be "a great enemie" to all other guards.

HIGH HORSE, ON ONE'S: During the middle ages great horses or war horses were specially bread and trained to carry the weight of a man in armor. These horses were then only ridden by knights or other people of high rank and were obvious symbols of status to any observer. The term has come to mean to assume, with no good reason, the air of some exalted personage.

HIGH LINE: a.) The area of attack and defense located above the sword hand in a neutral guard, roughly waist level and up. b.) The lines or parry positions protecting the combatant from the waist up.

HIGH LINES: The parts of the target above the waist.

HIGH ONE, PARRY OF: (also *Watch Parry* and sometimes *Hanging One*) a.) The standard parry of one raised to defend the non-weapon bearing shoulder. The hand and hilt are on the non-weapon bearing side of the body at roughly neck level, the blade is below the hand, its forte at the level of the notch in the non-weapon bearing arm where the deltoid meets the biceps. b.) (also *High Prime*) Protecting the high inside line with the point down, the palm turned out.

HIGH SECONDA: (also *Low Prima*) The single rapier guard assumed with the arm extended forward, the hand and hilt at approximate ear level. The hand is pronated, the quillons are horizontal with the floor, the tip lowered to the level of the opponent's chest. The guard may be formed either Standard or Across.

HIGH THREE, PARRY OF: Defense for an descending diagonal attack to the weapon bearing shoulder. The parry of three executed with the hilt just below elbow level, knuckles to the outside, blade angled at forty-five degrees, tip up and above the head.

HIGH TWO: Defense against an attack to the weapon bearing shoulder. The arm is angled up, elbow at roughly ear level, the hand just above shoulder level, the blade is below the hand, its forte at armpit level. Because of the need to push the blade out through the center at shoulder level, High 2 is most commonly executed as a diagonal or circular parry.

HIGH WARD: The single rapier guard taught by seventeenth century fencing master Di Grassi, assumed after drawing the sword from its sheath by carrying the hand and hilt above the head while keeping the point angled down and across the body.

HIGH-LINE BLOCK: (also *Rising Block*) A block delivered upward to defend against a descending diagonal or vertical attack.

HIGH-LOW ATTACK: A compound attack where the first action is a feint in the high line to draw a parry. The second action deceives the parry and moves the blade into the low line to complete the attack.

HILT: (also *Guard*) a.) A portion of the weapon comprised of three parts: the guard, the grip, and the pommel. (also *Handle*) b.) Strictly, collective term for parts of the sword above the ricasso including guard, quillons, grip (and pommel). The term, however, is loosely applied to the guard itself in cup-hilt and cross-hilt. c.) The haft or handle portion of any weapon.

Hilt, To the: a.) A thrusting attack that is delivered and lands in one's opponent and, is further, driven into the victim's body all the way up to its hilt. b.) A metaphor, derived from the old meaning, for going all the way or all out.

Hip Throw: a.) A judo technique that combines upper body manipulation with leverage from the hip to take the opponent off balance and bring them to the floor. b.) A throw in which the victim is taken over the hips of the thrower and delivered to the ground on their back at the thrower's feet.

Hip: A target in swordplay that generally refers to the muscle mass located on either side of the body, above the waist and below the rib cage. See *Flank*.

Hit: a.) A clear and distinct contact to the opponent that would have drawn blood either by penetration or by cutting if sharps were being used. b.) To strike with aim or intent; to get at or reach with a blow; to deliver a blow to, either with the hands or with a weapon. c.) To strike or touch after taking aim; not to miss. d.) To kill.

Hold: (also *Grasp*) To use one or both hands for clutching or grasping the opponent.

Hole in the Parry: Slang for an inco¬rect or unsuccessful parry through which a hit is made.

Home: a.) The intended target or mark. b.) To strike or hit the intended target. See *Thrust Home*.

Hoodlum: A young ruffian, thug, footpad; one who commits acts of violence. The term `hoodlum' was first recorded in San Francisco in the early 1870's, it has no traceable origin, but, its definition is such that it is easily applicable to `one who hoodwinks' and may well have derived from such a practice.

Hood-Wink: (also *Hoodwink* and *Hoodwinke*) Originally an Elizabethan rendition of blindmanbluf, in which one player is blindfolded and must grope about trying to tag the other players. The term was then applied to a form of surprise attack delivered by footpads,

assassins and other ruffians, where a lantern is held in the unarmed hand – its hood being winked open to blind the victim while a sword was placed at their throat. The practice was so common in Naples in the seventeenth and eighteenth century, that assaults of this kind were made a capitol offense. The modern term `hoodwink' (to deceive by false appearance: impose upon - Webster's New College Dictionary) derives from this practice, and it is supposed the term `hoodlum' and `hood' may also have come from hoodwinking.

Hook: a.) A punch delivered from the side at close range that crosses the plane of the face (or body) from one side to the other, with the arm curving through the air in a tight hooking motion; often made in an ascending trajectory. Starting in the basic guard stance, the combatant leans forward and slightly to the side from which they are punching. Keeping the elbow tight to the body, they turn their hip and shoulder as they bring the hook around with the fist turned inward toward them. The hook may be delivered from either the right or left, in boxing, however, the left hook is the most common. b.) A lateral punch made in a circular motion.

Hoplite: A heavy-armed foot-soldier of ancient Greece.

Hoplology: a.) The science of weapons or armor. A term derived from the hoplite of ancient Greece. b.) A term used for the combat techniques and ethos of the combative arts.

Horde: a.) A tribe or troop of Tartar or kindred Asiatic nomads, dwelling in tents or wagons, and migrating from place to place for pasturage, or for war or plunder. The term derives originally from the Mongolian word ordu, meaning "encampment." The term was transformed into the Polish horda, which eventually came to mean not the encampment but the Mongolian army encamped there. These "hordes" were actually small in number, but moved quickly and struck hard and fast, seeming to be able to attack several places at once. This gave the impression of enormous bodies of men, hence, the modern meaning. b.) A great company, esp. of the savage, uncivilized, or uncultivated; a gang, troop, crew.

HORIZONTAL ATTACK: Any cutting attack that travels in a plane parallel to the floor.

HORIZONTAL KNEE STRIKE: An attack with the bent leg that travels in a horizontal plane, intending to strike with the point of the knee. Often delivered to the recipient's midsection. See also *Knee Strike* and *Roundhouse Knee*.

HOX: To hough, to hamstring.

HUSSAR: a.) One of a body of light horsemen organized in Hungary in the time of King Matthias Hunyady, in the second half of the 15th century. b.) The name of light cavalry regiments formed in imitation of Hungarian cavalry, which were subsequently introduced, and still exist, in most European armies. The dress of the Hungarian force set the type for that of the hussars of other nations, these being distinguished by uniforms of brilliant colors and elaborate ornament, two special characteristics being the dolman and busby.

HYPEREXTEND: To go beyond the natural range of motion for a joint or part of the body moving about a joint. To extend in the sense opposite to flex, so as to attain an abnormally great angle.

I

ICE-BROOK'S TEMPER: The allusion is to the ancient Spanish custom of hardening steel by plunging it red-hot in the rivulet Salo near Bilbilis.

ICE-PICK GRIP: (also *Ice Pick Grip*) A term for holding a weapon, usually a knife or dagger, blade down in the manner of an ice-pick. See *Underhand Grip*.

ILL-SHEATHED: a.) Poorly sheathed. b.) Put or housed in a damaged sheath or scabbard.

IMAGINARY CIRCLE: (also *Mysterious Circle*) The seventeenth century Spanish school's *Lines Infintas*. The geometrical basis from which all footwork and distance was to be calculated and executed in Spanish rapier play.

IMAGINARY STAR: (also *Star*) The hypothetical directions of movement that radiate out from a central apex like the points of a compass or lines of an astrex. The points of the star indicate the variable planes of movement on the floor that a combatant can take.

IMBRACCIATURA: (It.) A long shield used for defense in duel during the early part of the sixteenth century, eventually replaced by the parrying dagger or main-gauche as the rapier came into more popular use.

IMBRCATA: George Silver's spelling of the Italian *Imbrocata*.

IMBROCCARE: (It.) To hit.

IMBROCCATA: (It. & Ger.) a.) A downward thrust, generally delivered from the right with the hand pronated, over one's opponents sword arm. b.) (also *Imbrcata*) Said by sixteenth century gentleman George Silver to be a guard or wardant posture assumed with the sword or rapier in the manner of Capo Ferro's *Prima Guardia*, Di Grassi's *High Ward*, and Swetnam's *High Guard*, the hilt carried higher than the head, the knuckles turned upward and the blade angled down with its point toward the opponent's face or chest. c.) (also *Imbrokata*) A falsing thrust, taught by seventeenth century English Fight Master Joseph Swetnam, where a feint attack is delivered from a High Guard as if it were directed to the lower body at roughly knee level and then with a turn of the hand, in the manner of a Punto Reverso, redirect the point into a thrust to the dagger shoulder or arm. Such a thrust seems deadliest when the rapier is held in his Stokata Fashion. d.) A time thrust in the outside line.

IMBROKATA: Joseph Swetnam's spelling of the Italian *Imbrocata*.

IMMEDIATE: Generally refers to a riposte that follows a parry without a pause in the action.

IMMORTAL PASSADO: (also "the immortal passado") a.) An English spelling of either the Spanish *passada* or the Italian *passata* – both of which are the chief means of gaining and breaking ground in fencing. Both schools generally executed a thrust on the "passado." "if your adversarie being furious, should passe on you in the same time, he might put your life in jeopardie." b.) A term mistakenly applied to the *Passato Sotto* by C. Turner and T. Soper in their book Methods and Practice of Elizabethan Swordplay. No evidence is provided to support their claim and existing primary source material stands strongly against their claim.

IMPACT: The act of impinging; the striking of one body against another; collision.

IMPETINATA: (It.) See *Appel*.

IMPRESSION: A tactical use of fencing movement to mislead an opponent as to the fencer's true intention.

IMPUGNATTURA: (It.) See *Hilt*.

IN DISTANCE: See *Distance, In*.

IN FIGHTING: (also *In-Fighting, Infighting* and *Inside Fighting*) a.) When two combatants have closed distance and are inside normal measure, but without the blades being locked as in a corps-a-corps, and any normal swordplay is impossible. See *Close Measure* and *Closes*. b.) The practice of moving inside fighting measure, getting up close to one's opponent to deliver a blow with the hand or hilt of a weapon. c.) Fighting or boxing at close quarters, hand to hand.

IN LINE: a.) (also *On-Line* and *On Point*) Having the sword arm extended straight forward, with the point threatening the opponent. b.) See *On-Line*. c.) See *Point In Line*.

IN-THE-ROUND: A modern term to describe historical sword fighting that is 360 degrees, not linear as with the smallsword or modern sport fencing, but uses sidesteps and diagonal movements (voids and traverses).

INCLINATION OF A BLADE: (Small Sword) "The degrees that the blade may incline, either one way or other, from a horizontal position. It is more particularly applied to the angles formed by the blade in the different parades."

INCONTRO: (It. & Ger.) See *Double Touch*.

INCROSADA: ("crossing the swords") Fiore Dei Liberi's term for the action of blade contacting against blade ("crossings of the blade" or "tied up") just before any action is made. Possibly equivalent to *Anbinden* in the German schools, the engaged position with weapons crossed in which the weapons collide together in their moment of contact.

INCURSION: Hostile encounter, a going to meet the enemy.

INDIRECT ATTACK: An aggressive action that in its execution does not immediately threaten the body, but is directed towards the opponent's blade (such as beats, pressures or *pris d'fer*), not the opponent.

INDIRECT: a.) An attack not delivered in the line of engagement. b.) An action directed into a line other than the original. See also *Indirect Attack*. d.) George Silver's term for the manipulation, maneuvering or forcing of the opponent from the shortest and most direct line of attack.

INDUCTION: The tactical process of evoking a desired fencing action from the opponent.

INERTIA: Tendency to remain at rest or in motion unless some outside force intervenes.

INFIGHTING: The practice of getting close up to an opponent during a fight or boxing match. See *In Fighting*.

INQUARTA: (It.) (also *Inquartata* and *Inquarto*) See *Demi-Volte*.

INQUARTATA: (It.) An evasive maneuver executed by pivoting on the front foot and making a demi-volte to the outside line, often accompanied by a stop thrust.

INSIDE BLOCK: a.) A defensive action made with the hand or arm executed across the body, generally made on the inside or inner part of the defending hand, arm or leg. b.) A block made on the inside or inner part of the attacking hand, arm or leg.

INSIDE CRESCENT KICK: A large, arcing kick (similar to the dancer's "fan kick") where the foot is carried across the body and up towards the opponent's face, and then swung out across the face, returning to the floor. The foot travels in a semicircular path, taking the outside edge of the foot across the recipient's face.

INSIDE LINE: a.) The area of attack and defense on a combatant, delineated by their vertical center line, which is furthest from their weapon bearing side. Opposite of *Outside Line*. b.) The lines or parry positions protecting the side of the body farthest from the sword-arm.

INSIDE LINES: The side of the body farthest from the sword-arm.

INSIDE MEASURE: See *Close Measure* and *Closes*.

INSIDE MOULINET: (also *Inside Mollinello*) A moulinet executed on the inside (non-weapon bearing side) of the body.

INSIDIOUS: From the Latin insultare, meaning "ambush."

INSISTENCE: The continuation of an attack in the same line after being successfully parried. See *Remise*.

INSISTENCIA: (Sp.) See *Remise*.

INSISTENCIA DE CORTE: (Sp.) A remise with a cutting attack.

INSISTENCIA DE PUNTA: (Sp.) A remise with a thrusting attack.

INSTABILE: Fiore describes his posta/stances as being either stable or unstable, or rather being active or reactive. His unstable guards are the Window, Longa, Two-Horn, and Front/Crown. These stances are "unstable" positions in that they are intended to react to attacks. *Stabile* (stable) positions are ones that move to receive. *Pulsatina* positions are those that provoke or offend.

INSTANCE: The term used by the seventeenth century Spanish master Narvaez for the corresponding footwork of two combatants traversing the imaginary circle; maintaining their relative position to one another. See *Complimentary Footwork*.

INSTINCTIVE PARRY: See *Simple Parry* or *Direct Parry*.

INSULT: a.) To beset with offensive, dishonoring or contemptuous speech or actions. To treat with scornful abuse or offensive disrespect. b.) To exult, to triumph as a victorious enemy.

INTENSITY: Presence of a greater or lesser degree of energy; relative level of energy concentration.

INTENTION, FIRST: See *First Intention*.

INTENTION, SECOND: See *Second Intention*.

INTENTION: What the character wants from his opponent within any given phrase or beat of a fight. I.E. to escape, to crush, to immobilize, to subdue, to pummel, etc.

INTERCEPTING THE BIND: (also *Stealing the Bind*) A form of *pris d'fer*, executed against a pris d'fer in double fence techniques where the victim of a bind uses their second weapon (usually the dagger) to catch the opponent's blade and bind it back to its point of origin.

INTERCHANCED THRUSTS: [in French *coup-fourré*] (Small Sword) A thrust exchanged between two adversaries at the same moment.

INTERNA LINEA: (It.) See *Inside Line*.

INTRENCHANT: (also *Entrenchant*) Not to be cut, indivisible, invulnerable.

INTRENCHED: (also *Entrenched*) Fortified with a ditch and parapet.

INVITATION OUVERTURE: (Fr.) see *Opening*.

INVITATION: a.) Any movement of the blade/ arm intended to tempt the oppo¬nent into an attack. b.) Opening a line to offer the adversary the chance to make an offensive movement. C.) Any movement of the weapon or body designed to lure the other combatant into an attack. d.) An action made to provoke the opponent to attack. See also *Open Invitation*.

INVITO: (It.) The placement of the blade so that it is not in line or threatening one's opponent. See *Open Invitation*.

INVITO APERTO: (It.) See *Absence of Blade*.

INVOLUNTARY SOUNDS: Reactive sounds, springing from accident or impulse rather than a conscious exercise of the will. Natural sounds of the working body including grunts, groans, sighs and other unintentional phonations on the exhalation.

IRISH WHIP: a.) A fast or sharp wrestling grasp or hold that uses the victim's wrist as a hand hold for leverage that can be used to whirl the body around like a lash or whip. The leverage on the arm can be used to take the victim off center, flipping them, or to swing them about until enough momentum has been achieved to throw them across the room. b.) Throw which works by clasping opponent's wrist, raising their arm and passing under their armpit. On completion of a 180 turn on the part of the thrower, the throwee flips forwards onto their back and the thrower follows through.

IRON: The most abundant and useful metal; among its many other applications iron is used for tools, swords and armor; hence, a nonspecific term used to refer to armor, swords and weapon both offensive and defensive.

IRON DOOR GUARD: A type of low guard. See *Porta di Ferro*.

ISOLATION: The ability to move or maneuver a specific part or parts of the body independent of the others.

ITALIAN GUARD: a.) The two-ring and swept-hilt rapier guard common in Italian design. b.) (Rapier) The on guard positions for the sixteenth and seventeenth century Italian school are that of Terza, low Terza and Seconda (high, low and proper). Capo Ferro, however, advised the use of Terza proper.

ITALIAN SCHOOL: a.) The practice and philosophy of swordplay, and in particular rapier play that is characterized by the introduction of double fence (rapier & dagger play), the superiority of the point and the introduction of linear patterns of footwork. This type of blade-play is introduced with the work of Marozzo (1517) and reaches its zenith with the works of Capo Ferro (1610). b.) Used to describe the style and practice of competitive fencing used by the Italians.

J

JAB: a.) A straight punch, generally made to the face, delivered from the leading or dominant shoulder and foot. The left jab (for the right hander) and right jab (for the left hander) are the beginning point of most boxing attacks. The combatant delivers the jab by extending the arm straight from the leading shoulder (thumb up), and twisting the hand (thumb to the inside) on impact. Generally the combatant steps into the attack by taking a short step with the leading foot as they deliver the punch. The arm is then quickly snapped back to the beginning position to protect the face and body. Opposite of a *Straight Punch*. b.) A straight, in-and-out punch delivered from the leading shoulder and foot.

JACKHAMMER PUNCH: (also *Hammer Punch*) A strike with the base of the fist much like hitting with a hammer.

JACK-SLAVE: A mean fellow.

JAM PARRY: (also *Stop Parry*) a.) A blocking parry thrust forward (often inside measure) towards the middle or forte of the offending blade, taken on the guard or hilt of the parrying weapon. b.) A head parry in broadsword play where the defender closes measure while pushing their sword up and forward (either to the right or the left), bringing the attacking blade to rest on the hilt of the defending blade. The blades meet true edge to true edge; forte to forte.

JAR: a.) A dissension, dispute, quarrel. Now used chiefly of petty (esp. domestic) altercations. b.) To clash, to quarrel.

JARNAC STROKE: See *Coup de Jarnac*.

JAVELIN: a.) A light spear thrown with the hand, with or without the help of a thong; a dart. b.) A weapon designed for thrusting; consisting of a long shaft and a pointed head. A form of spear.

JEU DE SOLDAT: (Fr.) A fencer whose tactics are based on brute force and erratic clumsy movement rather than a through understanding of strategic and precise swordplay.

JOIN: To meet or come together in combat; to engage in a fight, conflict, combat.

JOINING: a.) The action of meeting in combat. Engaging in a fight or conflict. b.) To engage weapons. See *Engagement* and *Sentiment De Fer*. c.) See *Disarmament*.

JOINING BLADES: To engage weapons. Practiced early in the development of swordplay, it was not a common practice until the mid-seventeenth century. See *Engagement* and *Sentiment De Fer*.

JOINT LOCK: A grasp or hold associated with martial arts executed with one or both hands, applied to the joints in the wrist, arm, leg, etc. to immobilize one's opponent, or to be used as a lever for further techniques such as a throw.

JOOK: (also *Juke*) To bend or turn the body with a quick adroit movement downward or to one side, in order to avoid a missile or blow; to dodge; to duck.

JOSTLE: a.) To come into collision in the tournament; to just or tilt. b.) A just or joust; a struggle, tussle. c.) A shock or encounter, a collision; a push or thrust that shakes; the action of a pushing or elbowing crowd.

JOUR: (Fr.) See *Opening*.

JOUST: (also *Just*) a.) A trial of skill in which two horsemen charge each other with leveled lances from either sides of the lists, each attempting to unhorse the other. b.) To engage in such a tournament; to tilt.

JUDGMENT: (also Judgement) The first governor of George Silver's principals of defense. To know when your opponent can reach you, and when they cannot; as well as knowing when you can reach them, how they stand in their guard and from that posture knowing what action are available to them and how they may be performed.

JUDO CHOP: (also *Karate Chop*) A slang term for a *Knife Hand Strike*. See also *Chop*.

Jug, String & Stick: A hand a wrist strengthening exercise that uses an empty milk jug fastened to the middle of a rod by a piece of string. The jug is then partially filled with water and the combatant then repeatedly winds and unwinds the string around the rod.

Jump: A footwork action, either forward or backward, where both feet leave the ground simultaneously (as in the first part of a balestra).

Jump Backward: (also *Active Retreat*) An evasive action, removing the body backward with an exaggerated retreat where the lag leg is kicked backward two or three times that of a standard retreat.

Jump Forward: a.) (also *Active Advance*) A forceful hop or glide forward made with an exaggerated advance where the feet travel forward two or three times that of a standard advance. The action is executed quickly, remaining close to the ground. b.) Any leap or hop that carries the combatant forward.

Jump Up: (also *Jump*) The classic cliché move where the dashing swordsman leaps over an adversary's attack at the feet. A leap over a horizontal attack to the feet.

Just: A "Joust," tilt or tournament.

Justle: (also *Jostle*) a.) A just or joust; a struggle, tussle. b.) To wrestle, to fight. c.) A shock or encounter, a collision; a push or thrust that shakes; the action of a pushing or elbowing crowd.

K

Kali: (Ind.) (also *Arnis* and *Escrima*) Indonesian fencing. Developed over 500 years ago, tjakalele or Indonesian fencing was one of the earliest known forms of the martial art now known as Arnis. The term Kali, derived from tjakalele, is another name familiar to stick fighters around the world today. The term refers to blades in general, and although among purists a dis¬tinction is made between the art of kali and that of escrima and arnis de mano, the terms escrima and arnis are commonly used to mean all Philippine martial arts taught in the West today. See *Arnis*.

Karate Chop: A type of blow delivered with the edge of the hand, supposedly with devastating results. This blow is aimed to major muscle groups such as the stomach, the "lats" or the shoulder muscles. It is either a contact, or non–contact blow, with the hand of the attacker "chopping" forward, and snapping back with great speed. The partner receiving the blow reacts violently as if struck in a vital nerve center.

Keen-Edged: Having a sharp or razor-like edge.

Keep Your Shirt On!: An expression derived from the custom of stripping to the waist before engaging in a fight or pugilistic match, hence, the modern meaning to keep calm and to refrain from swinging the proverbial fists.

Keeping Proportion: See *Proportion*.

Keeping the Beat: A concentration exercise where a routine is set at a specific rhythm and tempo, and a metronome or drum is then used to establish contradictory rhythm. The combatants must focus on the rhythm of the fight and try to avoid adopting the dominant external rhythm.

Kerne: a.) A light-armed Irish foot-soldier

(c. 1600); one of the poorer class among the "wild Irish," from whom such soldiers were drawn. Stanyhurst divides the followers of an Irish chief into five classes; daltins or boys, grooms, kerns, gallowglasses, and horsemen. b.) Sometimes applied to Scottish Highlanders.

KICK BLOCK: a.) A defensive action made with the foot, using a kicking action to oppose, displace, beat or strike into the aggressor's attack. b.) Any defensive action used against a kicking attack.

KICK: a.) The use of the leg and foot in striking techniques. To strike with the foot. b.) A driving attack made with the foot, other than a stamp.

KILL: a.) To deprive of life, to put to death by some means or action. b.) The finishing stroke or blow.

KISSING–THE–BUTTON: Derogatory Spanish term for harassing rapier thrusts aimed at the mouth.

KISSING STEEL: Describing the gentle and controlled meeting of blades during offensive/defensive blade-play. The blades meet without excessive force, and then part immediately much like a friendly kiss.

KNEE ATTACK: Any attack with the knee giving the illusion of contact.

KNEE BLOCK: a.) A defensive action made with the bonny joint of the knee. The knee is thrust into the attack, generally striking the aggressor on the shin, wrist or tendons on the inside of the forearm. b.) Any defensive action made against a knee attack.

KNEE DROP: a.) Any trip, stumble, feint, fall, collapse, drop or throw that takes an individual to one or both knees. b.) A technique of quickly descending onto a fallen victim with one or both legs bent, landing with the point of the knee, or knees, being driven into the victim.

KNEE STRIKE: (also *Knee Attack, Knee Blow* and *Knee*) An attack, or attempt thereof, executed with the bent leg, intending to strike with the hard bone at the point of the knee (patella). A knee strike is generally used as an infighting technique and can be delivered three ways: 1 *Horizontal Knee Strike:* An attack with the bent leg that travels in a horizontal plane, intending to strike with the point of the knee. Often delivered to the recipient's midsection; 2 *Roundhouse Knee:* A rising diagonal attack with the bent leg, usually made to the stomach; 3 *Vertical Knee Strike:* An attack with the bent leg that travels upward in a vertical plane, intending to strike with the point of the knee. Often delivered to the recipient's groin, extended arm, and face.

KNEE TO THE FACE: A Knee Strike executed to the recipient's face.

KNIFE HAND BLOCK: An open-handed block, associated with martial arts, using the outside edge (little finger side) of the hand to strike into the aggressor's attack. The "cutting edge" of the hand is snapped into the attack, generally striking the aggressor on the wrist or tendons on the inside of the forearm.

KNIFE HAND: (also *Chop, Judo Chop, Karate Chop* and *Shuto*) a.) An open-handed strike, associated with martial arts, using the outside edge (little finger side) of the hand, with the fingers tensed. A cliché move from action movies from the 1960's & 70's. b.) (also Karate Chop) Attack made with the edge (the 'pinkie' side) of the open hand.

KNIFE: a.) A bladed, hand-held weapon and tool ranging in length from a couple inches to sixteen inches in blade length. The blade may be used for cut, thrust or both. A dagger. b.) An offensive and defensive weapon consisting of a blade with a sharpened longitudinal edge fixed in a handle, either rigidly or with a joint (such as in a pocketknife) or clasp-knife. The blade is generally of steel, but sometimes of other material, as in the silver fish- and fruit-knives, the (blunt-edged) paperknife of ivory, wood, etc., and the flint knives of early man. c.) To knife someone. To cut, stab or slash with a knife.

KNIGHT: *(noun)* a.) A military servant or follower (of a king or some other specified superior); later, one devoted to the service of a lady as her attendant, or her champion in war or the tournament. This is logically the direct predecessor of sense b, the 'king's knight' having become the 'knight' par excellence, and a lady's knight being usually one of knightly rank. b.) Name of an order or rank. The distinctive title of a knight (medieval or modern) is Sir prefixed to the name, as 'Sir John Falstaff': Knight (also abbrev. Knt. or Kt.) may be added. In point of rank the medieval knight was inferior to earl and baron, and the dignity is not hereditary. In early use, the knight, as the type of the military profession, was frequently contrasted with clerk, merchant, etc., and, in point of rank, with king. The characteristic qualities expected in a knight, as bravery, courtesy, and chivalrous conduct, are frequently alluded to, and the name (esp. with adjectives, as a good knight) often implied these qualities as well as the mere rank. 1.) In the Middle Ages: Originally a military servant of the king or other person of rank; a feudal tenant holding land from a superior on condition of serving in the field as a mounted and well-armed man. 2.) In the fully-developed feudal system: One raised to honorable military rank by the king or other qualified person, the distinction being usually conferred only upon one of noble birth who had served a regular apprenticeship (as page and squire) to the profession of arms, and thus being a regular step in this even for those of the highest rank. 3.) From the 16th century: One upon whom a certain rank, regarded as corresponding to that of the medieval knight, is conferred by the sovereign in recognition of personal merit, or as a reward for services rendered to the crown or country. c.) A member of an order of chivalry. d.) Applied to females belonging to Diana's order of chastity.

KNIGHT: *(verb)* To make or dub one a knight.

KNIGHTHOOD: a.) The rank and dignity of a knight. b.) Chivalry. c.) Being one of an order of chivalry.

KNIGHTLY: In the manner of a knight.

KNITTING NEEDLES: A slang term for the sound produced from two swords engaged in a long and fast sequence of attack, riposte and counter ripostes. The sound and movement of the play is said to resemble that of knitting.

KNOCK ABOUT: (also *Knock-About* and *Knockabout*) To strike hither and thither by a succession of blows; hence, to treat roughly and without respect.

KNOCK: a.) A blow, a cuff. b.) To dash, to drive.

KNOCKDOWN: (also *Knock-Down*) The result of an armed or unarmed blow that lands on one's opponent and physically fells him to the floor; flooring an opponent.

KNOCK-DOWN-AND-DRAG-OUT: (also *Knockdown-Dragout*) A free-for-all, a rough-and-tumble fight, a brawl.

KNOCKOUT: a.) To render someone unconscious with a stroke or blow. b.) A term in boxing applied to a knockdown in which the floored fighter is unable to get up within ten seconds. This is one way of winning a boxing match.

KNUCKLE BOW: A quillon or branch of the sword guard that sweeps from the hilt to the pommel in a bow shape offering protection to the sword-hand.

KNUCKLE-GUARD: (also *Knuckle-Bar*) - a protective bar on the forward quillon sometimes extending to the pommel.

KNUCKLE SANDWICH: Slang for a punch in the mouth.

L

La Cane: (Fr.) A modern martial art based on French fencing and swordplay that uses a stick or cane for offensive and defensive interplay.

Lag Foot: The foot in the rear or back position at any time during footwork.

Lama: (It.) See *Blade*.

Lamp Hand: The belief that the elevated unarmed hand in competitive foil (and epee) fencing is reminiscent of the need to hold a lantern while fighting at night with the sword. There is no truth in the story (although sword and lantern was a style of fencing) as plates from historical fencing manuals depict the lamp hand in a quite different position than that of the curved arm and raised hand of the modern competitive fencer.

Lance: (also rarely *Launch*) a.) A weapon consisting of a long wooden shaft with an iron or steel head, used by knights, or men at arms on horseback, in a charge at full tilt, sustained originally by a rest, now by a strap through which the arm is passed. Often referring to a spear. b.) To pierce or thrust through with, or as if by, a lance.

Lash: a.) To strike with a whip, to scourge. b.) To strike out as if with a whip; a whipping blow. c.) The thong or cord of a whip.

Last Ditch: A strategy of warfare, from at least the sixteenth century, where an army besieging a fortress or walled town would dig a line of trenches or ditches around it, to protect themselves and their cannon from enemy artillery. If all went well, a second and then a third line would be dug, each closer to the walls; eventually, the besiegers' cannon could be brought close enough to smash a breach in the walls, through which the town could then be taken by storm. If the besieged forces were strong enough, however, they would mount a sortie against the besiegers,

forcing them out of one line of trenches after another until they were defending the last ditch. If they failed, the siege was broken.

Last Fingers: See *Aids*.

Lateral Parry: See *Simple Parry* or *Direct Parry*.

Latten Bilbo: A derogatory term implying a weapon made of a form of brass (Latten: a mixed metal of copper and zinc alloy, yellow in color, which was used as a decorative element in armor) which was yellow, and to soft and weak to function properly as a blade.

Launce: (also *Launch*) See *Lance*.

Laurels: During the Olympic, and similar, games of ancient Greece, a wreath of laurel leaves (also known as bay leaves) was placed on the head of the victor. Since the sixteenth century the English term "laurels" has meant victory or victor. The terms `to rest on one's laurels' and `to look to one's laurels' are both reminiscent of the sixteenth century term: to rest on one's laurels is to quite while ahead, while looking to one's laurels means to keep a sharp eye on one's competition.

Lay On: a.) To hit hard. b.) A call or command to begin a combat or fencing contest. An official command, allowing weapons to be laid upon the opponent.

Layout: Knocked down and out into a prone position. See *Knockout*.

Lead Foot: The foot in the forward position at any time during footwork.

Lead: Slang for bullets or shot; derived from the most common substance for bullets or shot - lead.

Leading: a.) To have the weapon bearing hand and/or foot forward. See also *Dominant*. b.) (also *Showing Point*) The extension of the swordarm towards the target, leading the body in the attack. c.) A beat, feint or attack accompanied by a step forward.

Left Cross: (also *Left Hook*) The most common punch, it begins by drawing back over the attacker's left shoulder, then follows a horizontal arc toward its' target's the right cheek.

LEFT DOMINANT: Leading with the left side of the body, usually implying a left lead foot.

LEFT FOOT STANCE: An En Garde that places the left foot on Forward 45 left and back foot on Back 45 left of the Imaginary Star, the upper body to facing the Line of Engagement.

LEFT HOOK: Even more than with the right cross, delivering the left hook properly depends on how well the whole action is coordinated. Start in the basic position and lean forward and to the left slightly. Keeping your elbow tight to your body, turn your left hip and shoulder to the right as you bring your left around with your fist turned inward toward you. Step forward with your left foot, shifting your weight from your right to left foot. Bring the punch straight across if it is a body blow, or bring it slightly upwards if it is aimed at the head. The left hook should be delivered in a whipping fashion. It should be delivered in as small as arc as possible. A wide looping left hook is easy to block or avoid and leaves you wide open for a counter-punch from your opponent. Delivered in crisp, quick, compact fashion, the left hook can be a devastating punch.

LEFTY: A slang term for a left handed fencer or fighter. See *South-Paw*.

LEG ROLL: (also *Leg Throw*) a.) A wrestling or grappling technique that uses the aggressor's leg as a fulcrum for leverage against the victim's center in order to take them off balance and bring them down from an erect or standing position.

LEGAMENTO: (It.) a.) The crossing of the swords. See *Engagement*. b.) More recently meaning the bind.

LENGTH: Extent from end to end, contrary to breadth. The size and reach of a sword or weapon.

LIE, GIVING THE: A proscribed retort in the code Duello leading up to the accepting of a duel. See *Giving the Lie*.

LIE: To be in a posture of defense.

LIÉMENT: (Fr.) (also Liement) See *Bind*.

LINAS INFINITAS: (Sp.) (Literally "Infinite" or "Never-ending" Lines) The imaginary lines on the floor that join the combatants' feet in Spanish rapier play. The patterns of stepping on this imaginary circle (Circle Steps) have offensive and defensive purposes in both directions. See *Imaginary Circle*.

LINE OF ENGAGEMENT: a.) The area in which the point or blade is threatening. See *Line*. b.) The specific line (high, low, inside, outside) in which two combatants blades are engages. See also *Lines, Engagement,* and *Joined*. c.) An imaginary line that represents the shortest distance between two combatants. d.) The imaginary line on the Star consisting of the Forward 90 and Back 90 that connects two combatants when in an *En Garde* position.

LINE OF GRAVITY: An imaginary vertical line that can be visualized joining the ears, shoulders, arms, ribs, hips, knees, and instep in correct relative position to one another.

LINE: a.) The specific area of the body to be defended or attacked. See *Lines of Attack*. b.) Referring to the imaginary planes that bisect the body, one vertical (delineating Inside and Outside) and one horizontal (delineating High and Low), dividing the body into four equal sections: High Inside, High outside, Low Inside, and Low Outside. c.) The lateral designation of the target areas, as: high-outside, low-outside, high-inside and low-inside. The line may be open or closed, according to the relationship of the attacking blade, the target, and the defending blade.

LINEA: (It.) The lines of engagement; alta (high), bassa (low), esterna (outside), interna (inside).

LINEAR FOOTWORK: The practice of moving or working the actions of the feet in straight lines rather than in circular planes. Such actions of the feet introduced the development of the *Advance*, *Retreat* and eventually the *Lunge*.

LINES OF ATTACK OR DEFENSE: Referring to the imaginary planes that bisect the body into four equal sections, one vertical (delineating

Inside and Outside) and one horizontal (delineating High and Low). The line may be open or closed, according to the relationship of the attacking blade, the target, and the defending blade.

LINES OF ATTACK: The areas of offense and defense determined by placing the armed hand in a Central Guard (Neutral Guard). An attack coming above the hand is in the High Line; below, in the Low Line; on the weapon bearing side, in the Outside Line; on the non-weapon bearing side, in the Inside Line. Lines of attack were first introduced in 1570 by celebrated Italian Master Giacomo di Grassi. See also *Line*.

LINSTOCK: A stick to hold the gunner's match.

LIST: (also Lists, Listes) a.) The limit, bound or boundaries enclosing a space set apart for tilting; the enclosed space where tilting matches or tournaments were held. c.) The physical barrier that marks the grounds for a Trial by Combat.

LIVERPOOL KISS: Slang for the *Head Butt*.

LOCK, STOCK AND BARREL: The three essential parts to a functioning muzzle loading firearm were its lock, (match-lock, flintlock, wheel-lock) the firing mechanism; the stock, the wooden portion or framework of the firearm; and barrel, the discharging tube of the firearm, hence, the term has come to mean the whole thing, the works, everything.

LOCK: (also Joint Lock) A grasp or hold executed with a weapon or one or both hands, applied to the joints in the wrist, arm, leg, etc. to immobilize one's opponent, or to be used as a lever for further techniques such as a throw.

LOCKS: Moves which immobilizes specific parts of the body.

LONG FORM: a.) Hand positions for quarterstaff utilizing the full length of the staff for attack or defense. b.) The hand placement for quarterstaff that utilizes the full length of the staff for attack and defense.

LONG GUARD: See *Posta Longa*.

LONGE: [From the French verb *alonger*, to extend or stretch out] (Small Sword) The act of extending yourself on the line of direction the full distance of your stride, in order to make your approaches to an adversary's body in delivering a thrust. See also *Lunge*.

LONG-STAFF: A pole-arm averaging roughly eight to fourteen feet in length. See also *Quarter-Staff*.

LONG-SWORD: A sword with a simple cross-hilt and a long cutting blade. In the Renaissance, a term used for a Medieval-style hand-and-a-half or "bastard" sword.

LOOPHOLE: An aperture in the wall of a fortification.

LOOPS: (also Looping) A slang term used to describe the circular actions of changements, disengages and coupés.

LOOSE PLAY: (Small Sword) Synonymous with assault; where one practices with foils, performing all the variations of small sword play, offensive or defensive.

LOOSE: The discharge of an arrow.

LOP: To cut or strike off limbs, as branches from a tree.

LOW BLOW: A term in boxing for a punch delivered below the belt line. Such a blow is a foul in boxing and wrestling.

LOW CROSS LEFT: (also *Cross Parry Left Hip*) The joined double fence defense for an attack to the left hip made with the rapier and dagger crossed. (The dagger is usually placed behind, so the rapier is not trapped between the dagger and the body). The left leg is generally removed away from the attack for this parry.

LOW CROSS RIGHT: (also *Cross Parry Right Hip*) The joined double weapon defense for an attack to the right hip made with the rapier and dagger crossed. (The dagger is usually placed behind, so the rapier is not trapped between the dagger and the body). The right leg is generally removed away from the attack for this parry.

LOW CROSS: (also *Cross Parry Two* and sometimes *Cross Low Five*) The joined double fence defense for either a montante or a thrust to the low mid torso. The parry is usually executed with the dagger behind, so the rapier is not trapped between the dagger and the body.

LOW FIVE, PARRY OF: a.) The single weapon defensive position for an ascending vertical attack to the groin (Montant) made with the hand and hilt outside the weapon bearing leg, the blade parallel to the floor at about knee level with the forte protecting the groin. b.) Sometimes applied to the *Low Cross* in double fence.

LOW GUARD: A defensive position with the blade pointing downward.

LOW INSIDE CUT: (also *Groin Cut*) A cutting attack made to the non-weapon bearing side of the body to the inside of the forward thigh. In a proper on guard stance the foot of the weapon bearing side is carried forward, exposing the groin and inner thigh of the lead leg to an attack.

LOW LINE EVASION: A form of "duck" that lowers the torso to avoid a horizontal attack or high line thrust by propelling the lag foot backward, lowering the torso forward and placing the non weapon hand on the floor for support. This action should end in a lunge like position with the lag leg straight and the lead leg bent with the knee over the instep of its foot, but with the torso leaning forward. See also *Passata Sotto*.

LOW LINE: a.) The area of attack and defense located below the sword hand in a neutral guard position (at roughly waist level). See *Lines* and *Lines of Attack*. b.) The lines or parry positions protecting the combatant from the waist down. c.) The area of attack and defense located below waist level. Opposite of *High Line*.

LOW LINES: The parts of the target below the waist.

LOW QUARTA: (also *Quarta Guardia Bassa*) The single weapon guard (rapier or dagger) guard assumed with the hand supinated, knuckles towards the inside, quillons hori-

zontal to the floor, the arm in front of the body (about three inches away from the belly). Formed either *Standard* or *Across*.

LOW SECONDA: (also *Seconda Guardia Bassa*) The single weapon guard (rapier or dagger) assumed with the arm hori¬zontal to the floor, fully extended from the shoulder, the hand supinated, with the tip of the blade lowered to the level of the opponent's waist. Formed either *Standard* or *Across*.

LOW TERZA: (also *Terza Guardia Bassa*) The single weapon guard (rapier or dagger) assumed with the hand just above the waist with the elbow outside the body (roughly three inches forward) and bent at roughly ninety degrees with at least a four inch gap between elbow and flank. Formed either *Standard* or *Across*, held in pronation, supination, or vertical/middle position.

LOW TWO; PARRY OF: Defense for an attack to the weapon bearing thigh made with the hand and hilt just below waist level, blade is below the hand, its forte at the level of the weapon bearing leg's quadriceps, just above the knee.

LOWER CARTE THRUST: (Small Sword) One of the low thrusts naturally corresponding to the parade of semi-circle; hence this thrust is by some masters called semi-circle thrust.

LOWER PARADES: (Small Sword) Parries made in the Low Lines.

LOWER SIDE-RING: (also *Lower Port*) The larger of the two side-rings found on two-ring and swept-hilt rapier hilts, situated the closest to the weapon's pommel. See *Side-Ring* and also *Upper Side-Ring*.

LOW-HIGH ATTACK: The first action is a feint into the low line to draw a parry. The second action is avoiding the parry and moving the blade into the high line and completing the attack.

LOW-LINE BLOCK: A block made below the waist or belt-line.

LUNGA: (It.) (Literally "elongated") See *Lunge*.

LUNGE: a.) A forward movement executed by

advancing the leading foot toward the opponent while the rear foot remains stationary (usually following the extension of the weapon arm). See also *Longe*. b.) A forward movement of the body toward the opponent that elongates the combatant's reach without advancing the lag foot. c.) The "extended" leg position used as a method to 'reach' the partner on an attack. The front leg extends forward in a long step, while the back leg straightens and the back foot stays in place. d.) The "extended" leg position used as a method of reaching the other combatant on an attack. To lunge, the leading leg extends forward in a long step, while the trailing leg stays in place. e.) A thrust with a rapier, epee, foil, or any other weapon. f.) A blow or punch delivered straight forward with an unarmed hand; a Jab.

LYING SPENT ACTION: A term used by George Silver for the condition of activity, at work, in practical or effective operation of the body and weapon that deprived of force or strength, a relaxed or recumbent movement. See also *Action*.

M

MACE: a.) A club of wood and metal used to crush or crack the opponent's armor. b.) A club of metal used as an ensign of authority carried by an officer of justice.

MAESTRO: (It.) a.) An eminent master in the art. See *Master*. b.) Old Italian for "Teacher".

MAGIC CIRCLE: See *Mysterious Circle*.

MAIL: A piece or suite of armor composed of interlaced rings, chain-work, or of overlapping plates fastened upon a groundwork, generally of heavy cloth or hide. (Chain-Mail, Plate-Mail, Ring-Mail)

MAILED: To be armored; covered, protected, wearing or consisting of mail armor.

MAIN GAUCHE: (Fr.) (also *Main Gauche Dagger*) Literally "left hand." A name for the parrying dagger used in the left hand, in conjunction with the rapier. Now applied to the dagger, whether used in the left or right hand.

MAKING GROUND: To move forward. See *Gaining Ground*.

MAN DRITTO SQUALEMBRATO: (It) A descending diagonal cutting attack delivered from the weapon bearing side.

MAN DRITTO: (It.) (also *Mandritto* or *Mandritta*) (Man = "hand;" Dritto = Right) Literally meaning "right handed" or "forehand." Said of a cut or thrust delivered from the right side of the body. Generally refers to any supinated cutting attack delivered from one's right to the opponent's left in rapier play. See *Man Dritto Tondo*.

MAN DRITTO TONDO: (It) A supinated horizontal cutting attack delivered from the sword bearing side. *Man Dritto Tondo Alto* is directed to the opponent's shoulder, *Mezzo* to the hip and *Basso* to the thigh.

MANAGE: To handle; to wield a sword.

MANCIO: (It.) See *Grip*

MANDABALO: (It.) An upward cutting attack

with the false edge.

MANDOBLE: A light slash of the point delivered by a flick of the wrist.

MANDRITTI: An attack cutting from the right to the left.

MANHANDLE: To handle roughly; to pull or push about.

MANIPULATORS: The index finger and thumb of the hand that holds and 'manipulates' the movements of blade and point of the weapon.

MANREVERSO: Vadi's left side horizontal cut.

MARK: Target, aim, goal.

MARK–MAN: (also *Marks-man*) One skillful in shooting.

MARSHAL: The chief officer of arms, who regulates combats in the lists and establishes rank and order at royal feasts and processions.

MARTIAL: a.) (from Mars, god of war) Pertaining to war, opposed to civil. b.) warlike, becoming or like a true warrior. c.) See *Martial Arts*.

MARTIAL ARTS: a.) Sports, exercises, techniques, etc., that serve as training for warfare or self defense. b.) Any of various fighting sports or skills mainly of Asian origin, such as judo, karate, and kendo.

MARTINGALE: In non–electric fencing, a short strap around the handle and grip intended to restrain the weapon from being lost and to keep it in a safe position.

MASTER: A celebrated *maestro* of the old science and school of fence. Previous to the sixteenth century there were no established "masters" of fence. The skill one developed in the handling of the sword came from personal experience and those that taught any tricks of combat generally had no schools, were regarded as rogues and only taught a few moves that seemed to serve them well in a rough and tumble style of swordplay. The instructors of arms in England were originally classified along with vagabonds, gypsies, actors and the owners of performing bears. Edward I forbade the teaching of fencing within the city limits of London, being of the opinion that to allow groups of armed and trained men to assemble in one spot was unwise. In 1540 under a patent granted by Henry VIII, the corporation of "Masters of Defence" was established. Organized much like a guild, its members were trained and tested in many different weapons, advancing through the ranks of Scholar, Free Scholar, and Provost before being tested for the degree of Master. It was the Italian masters of fence, appearing in England in the later half of the sixteenth century, however, that gave the title of "master" the social dignity associated with it today. Being gentlemen of noble birth (in Italy only those of gentle birth were allowed the privilege to teach fencing) the Italians believed themselves above their English counterparts, both in birth and in skill. They catered to the court and had elaborate "colleges" where the gentlemen of England could work in elegance and style. In 1624 the English corporation of "Masters of Defence" was abolished and the Italian school of rapier play was replaced by the French science of fence and the practice of the small sword. In 1656, Louis XIV of France provided letters of patent, granting the status of nobility to the six senior masters of the Paris Academy of fence. The French school, becoming the predominant school of fence in the eighteenth and nineteenth centuries, established the codes of honor and punctilio in all matters of fence. Noblemen and gentlemen looked to their "Master" for the finer points of decorum in the art, and were regarded as their equal. This establishing forever the honored and revered position of a true "Master" of fence; an expert in his craft, being professional in every positive sense of the word. A swordsman respected as an instructor, knowledgeable and skilled in the science of fence.

MASTERS–PRIZE: See *Prize*.

MAT: A piece of padded material, canvas, vinyl, etc., used as a floor covering in gymnastics, wrestling, etc.

MATCH: a.) A meeting of two individuals

in personal combat. b.) To cope, to meet in combat.

Maul: a.) A mace, hammer or heavy wooden club. b.) A heavy blow or blows, as with a mace or hammer.

Measure: a.) The distance between combatants when on guard, determined by the length or reach of the fencers lunge or thrust. b.) (Small Sword) The distance or space between two adversaries, when they have joined blades for an assult.

Media Proporcional: In the later Spanish schools, the key concept of achieving and maintaining proper distance of weapon and body to the opponent's weapon and body.

Mediatajo: Cuts made from the elbow. Faster than from the shoulder, but not as strong.

Medium: (Small Sword) The middle part between two extremes, applied to that part of a blade between the forte and the foible. It is also applied to a position of the wrist on either guards, by keeping it in a middle way and having two sides on guard to defend, in place of one when completely covered. See also *Middle*.

Meet Parry: A defensive action accompanied with a displacement of target that meets the opposing weapon, intercepting it and knocking it past the target, rather than stopping it or displacing it from its intended path. Opposite of *Follow Parry*.

Meeting Angle: The opposing planes of swords that allow the blades to be joined. These planes must cross forming an "X", "T" or open "V" with blades or they cannot be engaged.

Meggia Cavatione: Fabris' term for the *Half-Disengage*, where the sword does not complete its passage from one side to another, but remains under the opponent's blade. The action may now be made from the high to low line or vice versa. The term *mezza cavazione*, however, is still used by the Italian school of fencing for an attack on a half disengagement from a high to a low line on the same side of the opponent's body. See *Half-*

Disengage.

Mensur: (Ger.) a.) A German fencing duel between students fought with partially blunted Schlagers. b.) See *Measure*.

Mercenary: A soldier working merely for the sake of monetary or other reward; actuated by considerations of self-interest. Hence of motives, dispositions, etc.

Mesure: (Fr.) See *Measure*.

Metal: (also *Mettle*) a.) The material of which arms and armor are made, hence, the slang term nonspecifically referring to "sword." b.) The quality of disposition, temperament, spirit or characteristics of metal. The "stuff" of which a man is made. c.) A fiery temper, ardor, spirit, enterprise, high courage.

Meter: A systematically arranged and measured rhythm for movement.

Mezza Cavazione: (It.) An attack on a half disengagement from a high to a low line on the same side of the opponent's body. See *Half-Disengage*.

Mezza Cerchio: (It.) a.) A semi-circular parry of seven, made from the high to low line. b.) The first foil parry of the Italian school, executed as a half circle movement of the blade upward in the inside high line (*Septieme haut*).

Mezza Spada: ("Half-Sword") Equivalent to the German "Halb-Schwert". Special techniques of grabbing the sword's blade by the second hand (or both even hands) and thrusting, deflecting, or striking. Often used in combat against heavy armor. Fiore lists 6 Mezza Spada: *Posta Serpentino, Posta Serpentino Superiore, Posta Sagittarria, Posta Vera Croce,* and *Posta Croce Bastarda.* Vadi used *Mezza Mela* ("half-blade") for Halb-Schwert and *Mezza Spada* for *Incrosar a Mezzo Spada* (perhaps a result of the universal linguistic tendency to shorten lengthy phrases).

Mezzane: Fiore's horizontal cut, as in *Dritto Mezzane* and *Reverso Mezzane. Dritto* cuts right to left with true edge, *Reverso* cuts left to right with false edge.

Mezzo: (It.) Literally "middle." Generally

used in reference to the target at the middle of the opponent's body; at the hip or waist-line.

Mezzocerchio: (It.) A parry from the neutral guard upward to the inside high line (Italian: 1st, French: *Septime Haute*)

Mezzo-Dritto: (It.) A cutting attack to the inside of the opponent's wrist delivered from the right.

Mezzo-Tempo: (It.) Literally meaning "half-time," the mezzo-tempo is two actions, a parry and a riposte, executed in the time it would have taken to complete the initial attack.

Middle: a.) (also *Center of Percussion*) The name given by most schools for the portion of the blade that links the weaker foible to the stronger forte. As the Center of Percussion it is the mediator between the percussive attacks of the foible and percussive blocks of the forte. b.) The placement of the sword-hand between Supination and Pronation. c.) The center third of a quarterstaff when held in Short Form.

Mill, Like a: The water mill, used for grinding grain, was the world's first machine employing non-human, non-animal power on land. Its historic importance is shown by the fact that we now use "mill" as almost a generic term for powered machinery, as well as for places where it is used (sawmill, rolling mill, paper mill, steel mill). The mill's grinding action inspired the nineteenth century sportsman's "mill" (prizefight), in which one or both contestants would be "ground up"; the circular motion of the mill-wheel inspired the fencing terms mollinello and moulinet; meaning "little windmill," as well as the milling around of a crowd of people.

Mis-Sheath: (also *missheathed*) A euphemism for a thrusting or stabbing wound; the weapon being sheathed in the body, not the scabbard.

Misura Larga: (It.) Fencing measure at which one can only hit his opponent with accompanied footwork such as a pass, advance or lunge.

Misura Stretta: (It.) Fencing measure at which one may hit his opponent by simply extending the sword arm.

Misura: (It.) See *Measure*.

Mixing it Up: a.) A phrase used to denote action in the ring. b.) A term used to describe any exchange of blows, weather armed or unarmed.

Mollinello: (also *Moulinet*) Literally "like a little windmill." The action of pivoting the blade (from the shoulder, elbow or wrist) in a circle, like a windmill, in either a clockwise or counter-clockwise direction, over the head or on either the inside or outside lines.

Montant: (Fr.) Literally meaning "rising." Cutting attacks generally delivered upward to the groin or under the arms. In Elizabethan English the term was applied to an upward cutting attack. "an upright blow or thrust"

Montante Sotto Mano: (It.) A cutting attack, with the false edge of the blade, from a low to high line.

Montante: (It.) Literally "rising," "mounting"; an "uppercut." A rising vertical cutting attack to the groin. The montante can be executed from either the right side of the body (Man dritto) or from the left (*Riverso*).

Montanto: (also Mountanto) A name give to the character Benedick, by Beatrice, in Shakespeare's Much Ado About Nothing, implying him to be a great fencer and bully.

Morris-Pike: (also *Moris Pike & Mores Pyke*) A frightful pole-arm, believed to be of Moorish origin.

Mortar: A short piece of ordnance with a large bore and with trunnions on its breech for throwing shells at high angles.

Moulinet: (Fr.) (also *Molinello*) a.) Derived from the word moulin, meaning "windmill" (et meaning "little"), hence, moulinet, "like a little windmill," applied to the circular swinging of a sword, like the blades of a windmill. See *Mollinello*. b.) [BASSC] (also *Molinello*) Means 'little windmill' and describes the action of pivoting the blade in a circle in a diagonal, vertical, or horizontal plane. c.) The term is also applied to a portable apparatus carried by cross bow-men for winding up their bows.

MULTIPLE FEINTS: A combination of two or more single feint attacks. There are an infinite number of feints that may be executed together, but each feint must deceive its intended parry. Once an attack is parried, the series of feints is ended.

MURDERING-PIECE: A piece of ordnance charged with grapeshot.

MUSKET: a.) A muzzle loading hand gun of the kind with which the infantry soldiers were armed. Originally applied to the matchlock, and in the 18th c. still sometimes distinguished from the Firelock or Fusee. (From early examples it appears that arrows as well as bullets were discharged from muskets.) Subsequently it became the general name for the infantry gun, whatever its construction. b.) Any obsolete form of long barreled firearm.

MUSKETEER BLADE: A nickname for the theatrical epée blade. See *Giant Epée.*

MUSKETEER: a.) An infantry soldier armed with a musket. b.) The romantic guardsmen of King Louis XIII as depicted in the novels of Edmund Rostrand (The Three Musketeers, etc.).

MUSTACHIO: A technique in sword & buckler and rapier & buckler play where in close combat the spiked shield boss of the buckler can be used as an offensive weapon being punched into the adversaries face.

MYSTERIOUS CIRCLE: (also *Magic Circle*) The Spanish *Lines Infinta.* The infinite circle that joined the combatants at the feet and formed the basis of all footwork and distance in the complex geometrical style of sixteenth and seventeenth century Spanish swordplay. The circle, and the lines, angles and tangents thereof, was centered on the Renaissance concept of symmetry in all things. See also *Circle Steps.*

N

NAKED: a.) A term for a sword or other weapon not covered by a sheath; unsheathed, drawn. b.) Unarmed, without weapon, armor, shield or protection; defenseless.

NARROW STANCE: A right foot forward stance that places the feet straddling the Line of Engagement and the 90 right and left lines of the Imaginary Star, keeping the feet almost heel to heel (much like ballet's First Position) and allowing the upper body to either face the line of engagement, or turn away.

NARVAEZ, DON LUIS PACHECO DE: A student of Carranza who became the master of the Spanish school in the later part of the sixteenth and early seventeenth century. He offered his own reproduction of Carranza's work, where he verbosely expounded the dignified, but unrealistic principles of the Spanish school, basing his system on the imaginary circle.

NECK THROW: Throw made from in front of the victim with the attacker's back to them. The thrower's inside arm reaches around the front of the neck , the other arm reaches over the back of the neck and the throwee is thrown over the attacker's shoulder as the thrower drops to the inside knee.

NELSON: (Wrestling) The name of a class of wrestling holds in which one or both arms are passed under the opponent's from behind and the hand(s) applied to their neck; often with words prefixed to indicate the precise form of the hold. These are: 1) Half Nelson: a wrestling hold where one gets behind an opponent and passes one arm under theirs (right to right or left to left), and then the hand is brought up and around to the back of their neck, applying pressure to bend their head forward and immobilize them; 2) Three-Quarter Nelson: ; and 3) Full Nelson: (also *Double Nelson*) the strongest and most dangerous nelson, where one gets behind an opponent, place both arms under theirs, and then the hands are brought up and around the back of their neck, bending their head forward till their breast-bone almost gives way.

Neutral Guard: See *Central Guard.*

Neutral: The position of the sword hand with the thumb on top, and the palm turned toward the inside (left); halfway between supination and pronation.

Night-Brawler: One who raises brawls at night…

Nine, Parry of: a.) An alternate defensive action for the head, made with the blade square across, its point directed outside and the hands well inside. b.) See *Coward's Parry.* c.) See also *Hang Parry Nine.*

Nip: A small, sharp cut.

No Man's Land: A term used to describe the unnecessary space between the foible of the attacking blade and the forte of the defending blade on a missed or deceived parry. If a parry is deceived, the offending blade must be within measure to potentially meet the parry, if it is outside of measure the blade are said to be in no man's land.

O

Octave: (also *Eight*) The guard and parry used in small sword, and modern fencing, that closes (protects) the low outside line. The hand is supinated, with the point lower than the hand.

Octave Parade: (Small Sword) A lower parade and the opposite to semicircle. Octave is one of the most useful lower parades, being the most favorable for making straight returned thrusts.

Octave Thrust: (Small Sword) The natural thrust corresponding to the parade of that name. A lower thrust.

Off Line: See *Off-Line.*

Offense: (also *Offence*) To be on the attack or assault.

Offensive/Defensive Footwork Drill: An exercise of complementary footwork that may be repeated without having to readjust position or stance. The pattern of this drill compliments the Offensive/Defensive drill of blade-play.

Offensive-Defense: In the sixteenth and seventeenth century it was the theory that the best defense was a good offense, the offensive-defense is a term for the counter attack by means such as a *Stop Thrust* or *Stop Cut.*

Off-Line: (also *Off Line*) a.) Any attack which is directed to a target away from the body. b.) A footwork position in which both feet are off the center line. c.) To be off or outside the imaginary line that connects two combatants when in an En Garde position.

Off-Line Footwork: The "extended" leg position used as a method to 'reach' the partner on an attack. The moving leg extends in a long step, while the back leg straightens and the back foot stays in place. All off-line footwork may be performed in any direction. (An offensive action). Please see *Star System.*

See also *Advance, Cross Step, Half Pass, Pass Step, Pivot, Retreat, Slip Step, Thwart,* and *Traverse.*

OFF-LINE STEP: Any movement that takes the body away from the Line of Engagement. See also *Traverse.*

OFF-SET: (also *Offset*) Where the centerline of two combatants facing one another do not line up. One combatant is cheated to one side or the other. See also *Off-Line.*

ON GUARD: a.) The fundamental position of the combatant preparatory to actions of an offensive or defensive nature. Most commonly the guard of *Terza.* b.) (Rapier, Rapier & Dagger) The ready position, stance and posture where the feet are shoulder width apart, right foot one foot length forward, left foot angled slightly out, the knees in a slight demi-plie, center of gravity carried between the legs, the head, shoulder, ribs, and pelvis in correct placement with the line of gravity, left hand in a defensive position in front of the chest, the right hand generally in *Terza* (but also may be held in any other guard). c.) Being consciously aware and prepared for any event or happening. d.) See *En Guarde.*

ON LINE: a.) Any attack which is aimed directly to the combatant's body. b.) A footwork position in which both feet are on the center line. c.) The relationship of combatants' bodies when both partners' vertical center lines are lined up, either face to face, back to back, or front to back.

ON THE EXCHANGE: A series of attacks, parries, ripostes, parries, counter ripostes, etc. Exchanging offensive and defensive actions between combatants.

ONE, PARRY OF: a.) The defensive action for a thrust or horizontal attack to the non-weapon bearing hip, the hand at roughly waist level, knuckles to the inside, blade below the hand closing the low inside lines. b.) (also *Parry Prime*) Protecting the low inside line with the point down, the hand in half pronation with the thumb down. Sometimes referred to as the "watch parry" because the wrist position is similar to looking at a wristwatch.

c.) Broadsword defense against a Belly Cut, made with the point down, crossguard just below breast level as if looking at a watch on the weapon hand. The parry of one may also be lifted to protect against a cut to the chest (Hight One) or lowered to protect the groin or legs (Low One). d.) A high line parry derived from drawing the sword from the scabbard. See *High One, Parry of* and *Prima.*

ONE-HALF PRONE: (also *Middle* or *Vertical Position*) The placement of the weapon bearing hand where the thumb is at roughly twelve o'clock and the palm is towards the inside. Sometimes jokingly called "goofination."

ONE-HALF TIME: See *Half Time.*

ONE-QUARTER TIME: (also *Quarters, Quadruples* or *"Quads"*) Literally meaning four actions executed in the time of one. One quarter-time is four actions, a parry, a riposte, a counter parry and a counter riposte all executed in the time it would have taken to complete the initial attack. Needless to say one quarter-time can only be executed with point work in rapier and dagger.

ONE-THIRD TIME: (also *Thirds* and *Triples*) Literally meaning three actions in the time of one. One-third time is three actions, a parry, a riposte and a counter parry, executed in the time it would have taken to complete the initial attack.

ONE-TIME: See *Whole Time.*

ONE-TWO ATTACK: a.) A compound attack consisting of a disengage designed to draw a direct (lateral) parry, and a second changement, deceiving the intended parry. b.) See also *One-Two*

ONE-TWO: a.) (also *The Old One-Two*) A combination attacking in boxing consisting of a left jab followed by a right cross. b.) (also *One-Two Attack*) An attack formed of two disengages in laterally opposite lines.

ONE-TWO-THREE: An attack formed of three disengages in laterally opposite lines.

ON-LINE STEP: Any step that either moves forward or backward along the Line of Engagement.

ON-LINE: (also *On Line*) a.) On target, inside the body. Opposite of *Off-Line*. See *On-Line Fencing.* b.) To be on or inside the imaginary line that connects two combatants when in an *En Garde* position.. See also *Line of Engagement.*

OPEN HAND BLOCK: (also *Soft Hand Block*) A defensive action made with an open, unarmed hand. In defense of both armed and unarmed attacks, the open hand is brought against the muscle grouping on the attacking limb. Generally this is the inside or base of the aggressor's forearm, but may also include the muscles on the upper arm, the upper leg, shin or calf. To avoid jamming or breaking the thumb, the defensive hand is open with its thumb against the hand in line with the fingers. The unarmed hand is extended into the attack, meeting the aggressor outside and in front of the body.

OPEN INVITATION: A deliberate placement of the blade, which exposes the entire body, intended to draw an offensive reaction from the opponent. This would be met by a counter attack or parry and immediate riposte.

OPEN LINE(S): Area(s), position(s) or parts of the body unprotected. When a line is open voluntarily, the action becomes an invitation to an attack.

OPEN-HAND TECHNIQUES: Offensive and defensive techniques with the hand(s) that are executed with the hand open. Opposite of *Closed-Hand Techniques.*

OPENING: The area on one's opponent that is unprotected. See *Open Line(s).*

OPPOSE: To be set against, to be an adversary to, to face, to confront.

OPPOSITION: a.) A movement of engaging and not releasing the opponent's blade. b.) The art of closing the line of engagement to the opponent's blade while attacking, preventing them from striking with a stop thrust or other counter attack. c.) A blade action against an opponent's weapon, wherein the fencer deviates the opponent's blade by

keeping contact with it and pushing it aside (covering). d.) The action of setting oneself opposite or against another; offering oneself for combat. e.) See *Opposition Parry.*

OPPOSITION BLOCK: A defensive action where the hand or arm is brought up as a solid wall or shield against the attack.

OPPOSITION GRIP: a.) Holding a sword or dagger with the pad of the thumb placed in line with the false, or back edge of the blade (or on the back edge of the ricasso), in opposition to the grip of the index finger and the true or fore edge of the blade. The last three fingers lightly grip the handle, bringing it to bare against the palm of the hand, and very nearly at a right angle to the arm. b.) A quarter-staff or pole-arm hold where the hands grasp the haft of the weapon with the right hand supinated (underhand) and the left pronated (overhand) with both thumbs directed to the fore end of the weapon.

OPPOSITION PARRY: (also *Parry With Opposition*) See *Standard Parry* or *Blocking Parry.*

OUT OF DISTANCE: See *Distance, Out of.*

OUT OF MEASURE: (Small Sword) When you are so far from your adversary that is not possible for the extent of your longe to touch him.

OUTSIDE BLOCK: a.) A block made on the outside or backside of the attacking hand, arm or leg. b.) A defensive action made on the same side of the body, generally made on the outside or backside of the defending hand, arm or leg.

OUTSIDE CRESCENT KICK: A large, arcing kick made with the entire leg traveling up and across the recipient's face in a semicircular path, striking with the inside edge of the foot.

OUTSIDE LINE: The lines or parry positions protecting the side of the body nearest to the sword-arm. The weapon-bearing half of the body. Opposite of *Inside Line.*

OUTSIDE LINES: The side of the body on the side nearest to the sword-arm.

OUTSIDE MOLLINELLO: (also *Outside Mouli-*

net) A moulinello executed on the weapon bearing side (outside) of the body.

OUTSIDE MOULINET: (also *Outside Mollinello*) A moulinet executed on the outside (weapon bearing side) of the body.

OUTSTRIKE: To deliver blows faster and harder than one's opponent.

OVERHAND GRIP: a.) Holding a sword or dagger with the point above the hand. Opposite of *Underhand Grip*. b.) A quarter-staff or pole-arm hold where the hands grasp the haft of the weapon with the palms pronated (overhand) with the thumbs directed to the middle of the weapon.

P

PRESS: A term in gymnastics for a raising or lifting of the body by continuous muscular effort.

PACE: a.) An early 14th-15th century spelling for *Pass*. A pass or walking step. See *Pass*. b.) A measure of two and one half feet. c.) A definite but varying measure of length or distance; sometimes reckoned as the distance from where one foot is set down to where the other is set down (about 2 ½ feet), as the military pace; sometimes as that between successive stationary positions of the same foot (about 5 feet), as the geometrical pace.

PAD: a.) Something soft, of the nature of a cushion, serving to protect from or diminish jarring, friction, or pressure. b.) A guard or protection used in many sports for parts of the body, such as the leg or shins.

PALISADOES: Stakes set in the ground by way of defense.

PALM HEEL: The lower part of the palm, next to the wrist, used to deliver open hand punches in unarmed combat techniques. Generally associated with the Martial Arts.

PALM STRIKE: a.) Any attack delivered with the palm heel. b.) A forceful thrust with the open palm associated with Martial Arts.

PAPPENHEIMER: A rapier hilt of pierced shell guard style named after a military leader Gottfried Heinrich Graf zu Pappenheim, field marshal of the Holy Roman Empire in the Thirty Years' War.

PARADE CIRCULAIRE: (Fr.) See *Circular Parry*.

PARADE DE TAC: (Fr.) See *Beat Parry*.

PARADE: (Fr. & Ger.) (also *Parry* or *Parrying*) a.) (Small Sword) The act of defending against a particular thrust of an adversary, by the turn of your wrist and the forte of your blade in opposition. b.) See *Parry*.

PARALLEL BLOCK: (also *Double Block*) A block made with the defending arms placed one beside the other for greater defense. The arms are not crossed.

PARALLEL PARRY: a.) A Double Fence parry executed with the blades placed side by side rather than crossed. b.) A parry made with two weapons (sword & dagger, sword & buckler, Case of Rapiers, Sword & Cloak, etc.) where they are placed one beside the other for greater defense. Example: (Cloak & Rapier)

PARALLEL: Said of two or more lines (imaginary or tangible), surfaces, weapons, or other concrete things lying or extending alongside of one another always remaining at the same distance apart; continuously equidistant.

PARATA DI CONTRO: (It.) See *Circular Parry*.

PARATA DI PICCO: (It.) See *Beat Parry*.

PARATA: (It.) See *Parry*.

PARRIER-DOLCH: German term for using the dagger's quillons to trap a sword blade.

PARRY: a.) A defensive action of a bladed weapon where the forte opposes the foible of the attacking weapon stopping the attacking blade at its weakest point with the strongest point of the defending blade. b.) The defensive action of deflecting or blocking an attacking weapon. c.) A defensive action (made by a sword, dagger, shield, hand, etc.) which blocks or deflects an attack. When executed with a blade, the parry is generally made edge to edge, its forte against the opposing blade's foible. d.) A defensive action of the blade and guard of the weapon, deflecting an attacking blade. Parries may be executed either by opposition, percussion, or shielding. e.) To ward off or turn aside an offensive blow or weapon by opposing one's own weapon, hand or other means of defense. To take such an action.

PARRY BY DISTANCE: An evasive action that removes the body backward, out of the reach of the attack, while remaining in line with the attack.

PARRY DOUBLE: See *Double Parry*.

PARRY OCTAVE/8: a.) Protecting the low outside line with the hand in supination. b.) See *Eight, Parry of*.

PARRY PRIME/1: a.) The hand is in half pronation with the point down. Although this parry is intended to protect the inside line of the body anywhere from the shoulders to the ankle, it is usually used against attacks from the waist down. When used to protect the low line it is sometimes referred to as the "watch parry" because the wrist position is similar to looking at a wrist watch. b.) See *One, Parry of*.

PARRY QUARTE/4: a.) Hand is in supination with the point up protecting the high inside line (waist to head). b.) See *Four, Parry of*.

PARRY QUINTE/5: a.) The hand is in pronation protecting the head from a downward vertical cut. The hilt is toward the outside line of the body, the point toward the inside. b.) See *Five, Parry of*.

PARRY SECONDE/2: a.) The hand is in pronation with the point down protecting the low outside line. b.) See *Two, Parry of*.

PARRY SEPTIME/7: a.) Protecting the low inside line with the hand in supination. b.) See *Seven, Parry of*.

PARRY SESTA/5A: a.) Protecting against a vertical cut to the head. The hilt is toward the inside line of the body, the point toward the outside. b.) See *Five A, Parry of*.

PARRY SIXTE/6: a.) Protecting the same area as a parry Tierce or 3, except the hand is held in supination. Usually used against a thrust. b.) See *Six, Parry of*.

PARRY TIERCE/3: a.) The hand is in pronation with the point up protecting the high outside line (waist to head). b.) See *Three, Parry of*.

PARTIZAN: (also *Partisan*) A 16th and 17th c. pole-arm consisting of a long-handled spear, the blade having one or more lateral cutting projections of various shapes, generally carried by foot-soldiers although some forms were also used in boar-hunting.

PAS D'ÂNE: (Fr) (also *Arms of the Hilt*) a.) Literally "donkey step" or "mule foot." The two protective half rings branching up from the cross guard to protect the index finger of the sword hand. The common practice of placing one or two fingers over the cross guard of the sword, for better management of the blade, led to the introduction of these arms of the hilt in the early fifteenth century. Once adopted they became part of the foundation from which the most complicated, and eventually the simplest, sword guard was constructed. b.) According to Tarassuk, the term was used in seventeenth century to describe one of the oval shells that formed the swords guard and not the arms of the hilt.

Pass: a.) (also *Pace* and *Passata*) The chief means of gaining and breaking ground prior to the seventeenth century. This form of footwork made up the greater part of offensive and defensive movement before the introduction of the lunge and was most likely the original form of footwork in armed encounters. The pass consists of passing one foot by the other changing the placement of the lead and lag foot. See *Passing*. b.) A round, bout or tournament of swordplay. A course of fencing, until one of the combatants is hit. c.) A thrust or lunge with the rapier. To make a push in fencing.

Pass Back: a.) (also *Pass Backward* and *Walking Step Backward*) A simple action of footwork that moves a combatant backward by passing their lead foot to the rear beyond their lag foot into a new lag position. Opposite of the *Pass Forward*. b.) The placing of the front foot in back of the rear. c.) Used by some to represent the *Crossover Step Backward*.

Pass Backward: a.) A linear step backward made by passing the lead foot to the rear. Opposite of the *Pass Forward*. b.) See *Pass Back*.

Pass Backward–Demi-Volte / Grand Volte: A compound step that allows the lead foot to shift backward and into a demi or grand volte.

Pass Forward: a.) (also *Walking Step Forward*) A simple action of footwork that carries a combatant forward by passing their lag foot to the fore, past their lead foot into a new lead position. Opposite of *Pass Back*. b.)

A linear step forward made by passing the lag foot to the front. Opposite of *Pass Backward*. c.) Used by some for the *Crossover Step Forward*.

Pass Forward–Circle Left: A compound circle step that allows the right foot, when in the lag position, to shift to the lead position both forward and to the left on the inner ring of the imaginary circle.

Pass Forward–Circle Right: A compound step that allows the right foot, when in the lag position, to shift to the lead position both forward and to the right on the inner ring of the imaginary circle.

Pass Step: An off-line action of footwork where the moving foot is placed ahead or to the rear of the stationary foot without crossing the centerline (a walking step).

Pass to the Fore: See *Pass Forward*.

Pass to the Rear: See *Pass Back*.

Pass Traverse: Passing steps executed to the combatant's immediate right or left. See *Traverse* and *Ten Directions of Footwork*.

Passada: (Sp.) A passing step traveling approximately two feet.

Passada Doble: (Sp.) Two passes, one after another. See *Crossover Step*.

Passada Simple: (Sp.) A passing step of 30 inches in length.

Passade: (Fr.) See *Pass*

Passado: An English spelling of either the Spanish *Passada* or the Italian *Passata*, which came to represent a forward thrust with the rapier, accompanied with a pass (which was not always the case with the actual passada and passata).

Passata Sotto: (It.) (Literally "pass beneath") a.) A low line evasion that vertically removes the body from the plane of attack by expanding the base and lowering the physical center. Executed in two ways, the *Passata Sotto to the Side* and the *Passata Sotto to the Rear*. b.) An evasive action by a defending fencer executed by placing the unarmed hand on the floor and, at the same time, ducking into a rear-lunge position. c.) An action mistakenly associated to the "imortal passado" of Shakespeare's Romeo & Juliet by T. Soper and C. Turner in their book Methods and Practice of Elizabethan Swordplay. There is no proof of this association and most research disproves their hypotheses.

PASSATA SOTTO TO THE REAR: A low line evasion that vertically removes the body from the plane of attack by propelling the lag leg straight backward, bending the lead leg's knee (as if in a deep lunge), angling the pelvis and trunk directly forward in line with the extended lag leg, and placing the left hand on the floor (for stability).

PASSATA SOTTO TO THE SIDE: A low line evasion that vertically removes the body from the plane of attack by extending the lag foot backward and across the path of the lead foot (traversing East, to the right), bending the lead leg's knee, angling the pelvis and trunk forward and to the left in line with the extended lag leg, and placing the left hand on the floor (for stability).

PASSATA: (It.) See *Pass.*

PASSEMENT: See *Beat.*

PASSING JUMP BACK: A compound action of footwork initiated with the action of a pass back and propelled backward with the completing action of a jump back.

PASSING THE POINT: The movement of the tip of the weapon from one line of engagement to another executed either under (Change Under) or over (Change Over) the opposing weapon. See *Changement.*

PASSING: The chief means of gaining and breaking ground in fencing, facilitating the greater part of footwork before the introduction of the lunge (1606-1610) by simply passing one leg by the other.

PASSIVE DEFENSE: a.) To run away; to remove one's body from the line of attack, or threat of attack, without execution of any offensive action. Defensive actions that protect the body without any harming or endangering the aggressor. b.) See *Parry by Distance.*

PASSIVE FOOTWORK: (also *Standard Footwork*) Standard footwork that when executed carries the combatant roughly the length of one foot in their intended direction. The size and scope of this step is not an arbitrary decision, but is indicated in the fencing manuals of the Elizabethan period. Opposite of *Active Footwork.*

PASSO OBLIQUO: (It.) A sloped pace back on the diagonal away from the line of attack. See *Ten Directions of Footwork* and *Sloped Pace.*

PASSO RECTO: (It.) A pass forward closing measure.

PATIENTE: (It.) See *Defense.*

PATINANDO: (It.) (also *Advance-Lunge*) A compound piece of footwork involving a quick succession from an advance to the grand lunge. Generally ending with an attack.

PATROL: A term derived from the French patrouiller, meaning to paddle with the feet in the mud. The Anglicized term became the soldier's slang for the infantryman's interminable marching or tramping around a garrison, camp, post, etc. for the purpose of watching, guarding, and checking irregularity or disorder.

PAUNCH: An Elizabethan slang term for a stab, cut or wound to the belly.

PEEK-A-BOO STYLE: A boxing style in which the fighter puts up both gloves around the sides of his head and "peeks" out to see his opponent. This is a variation of the crouch style made famous by boxer Floyd Patterson.

PELL-MELL: (also *Pell-meal*) With confused violence, as in a scuffle where strokes are dealt at random.

PELT: A vigorous blow or stroke, as with a pellet or other missile.

PERCEPTION: A conscious awareness of seeing, hearing, smelling, touching, moving, or kinesthetic feeling.

PERCUSSION: The sharp impact of one object with or against another, rendering on contact a perceivable shock or sound.

PERFORCE: By force, by violence.

PESO: (Span. & It.) The balancing point of a

sword; a term believed to have derived from the Spanish peson which was a weight used in the balancing of scales. See *Point of Balance*.

PETAR: A case filled with explosive materials.

PETITE BIND: See *Passive Bind*.

PETITE CROISÉ: See *Passive Croisé*.

PETITE ENVELOPMENT: See *Passive Envelopment*.

PHILIPPAN: "Sword Philippan." The sword that triumphed over Brutus and Cassius at Phillippi. Some believe it is actually the proper name for the sword.

PHRASE D'ARMES: An uninterrupted series of fencing exchanges (such as an attack, riposte, and counter-riposte).

PHYSICAL INVENTORY: a.) The process of trusting the body instead of the eyes to correct technique. To look internally and feel what is right and what is wrong with specific techniques or placement. Taking physical inventory informs the combatant where their weight is, whether they are centered, what foot is where, and so on. b.) To check the body for points of tension, stress or strain and to effectively identify those areas so as to avoid accident or injury.

PHYSICAL LIMITATIONS: The fixed points between which the possible or permitted extent, amount, duration, range of action, or movement of the body is confined; a bound which should not be passed, or beyond which pain or physical injury occurs.

PIATTO: (It.) The "side" of the sword, i.e. the flat part of the blade on either side, between the two edges. This part of the sword has no active role in traditional Italian rapier play, as no offensive or defensive action involve it directly.

PICK: To prick, to stick, to strike with a pointed instrument.

PICKING OFF PUNCHES: A boxing term used to describe a technique for blocking or redirecting punches before they land by catching them on a glove.

PICKING: A quick succession of digs, with a small sword or epée, at the opponent's forearm or wrist.

PIED FERME: An action performed from a stable position of the feet.

PIKE: a.) A common weapon for a large part of the infantry consisting of a long, sturdy wooden shaft with a pointed head of either iron or steel, eventually replaced in the eighteenth century by the bayonet. b.) A sharp point or spike; as the pointed metal tip of an arrow, spear, or the spike found on some bucklers, located in the center of the shield boss. (i.e. central spikes used sometimes in the center of a buckler or target were affixed by means of a screw) c.) A wooden stake, about 1.75 meters in length, sharpened at both ends and bound with iron, which is driven into the ground as a defense in front of archers. d.) A staff furnished with an iron pike-head; a pike staff. e). The position of the body when bent straight from the waist, with the legs, and the body is in an "L" shape.

PIKE HEAD: The metal head of a pike.

PIKE & MUSKET: The term used today to refer to the Renaissance's newer methods of mass warfare that replaced those of the Middle Ages which emphasized heavy cavalry and archery.

PILCHER: A contemptuous term for a scabbard.

PILE DRIVER: a.) A very strong or powerful hit, stroke, kick, or blow; something of great strength or power. b.) A descending diagonal punch delivered to an opponent who is doubled over, in a crouch position or on one knee, generally executed downward to the head (or the back of the head) much like how a mallet strikes a pile to drive it into the earth.

PINION: The term is originally applied to a bird's wing and then to the human arm. Hence, the grabbing and holding of the elbows behind the victim's body, rendering them defenseless.

PIROUETTE: (Fr.) The act of spinning round, generally on one foot (or on the point of the toe), as performed by ballet-dancers. See

Spin.

PISTE: The strip used in modern fencing.

PISTOL: a.) A small firearm, with a more or less curved stock, adapted to be held in, and fired by, one hand. b.) To shoot a pistol. c.) Quibbling.

PISTOL GRIP: a.) Any number of molded handles used in foil an Epée. b.) A grip on a competitive fencing foil or epée which fits the hand in a similar fashion to that of the handle of a pistol.

PISTOL WHIP: To strike or beat someone with the grip of a pistol.

PISTOL-PROOF: Impenetrable to a pistol-shot.

PIVOT: a.) An off-line action of footwork where the hips, feet and body adjust to face a new direction. b.) A 180° turn executed in place, often turning on the balls of the feet.

PLANCHE: The modern fencing strip or piste.

PLANE: A perfectly straight, imaginary line that an action (offensive or defensive, armed or unarmed, footwork or body motion) can travel upon, from any one point to another, at any angle (horizontal, vertical, diagonal).

PLANES OF MOVEMENT: a.) The path in which any action can be made to travel (including horizontal, vertical, diagonal and circular planes). b.) Specific directions that an action (offensive or defensive, armed or unarmed, footwork or body motion) can travel, from any one point to another, at any angle (horizontal, vertical, diagonal).

PLASTRON: (Fr.) a.) A steel breast-plate formerly worn beneath the Hauberk. b.) A form of shield or pad, often leather-covered, worn by professional fencers over the breast as a protection against bruising. c.) An auxiliary protector used by coaches to absorb the impact of hits during the lesson. d.) See also *Plastroon*.

PLASTROON: (Small Sword) a). The breast-piece of an armour, or a leather cover for the stomach. b). A fencing scholar, whose breast is covered with a leather cushion to protect him from his students. See also *Plastron*.

PLAYING THE PRIZE: The public testing of a student for advancement in the English schools of Defence. See *Prize*.

PLIÉ: (Fr.) The bending movement in the knees required for almost all footwork in swordplay. A shallow or half-bend is called a Demi-Plié, a deep bend, a Grand Plié.

PLUMMET: See *Pommel*.

POINT: The sharp end of a spear, sword, knife, dagger or other such implement.

POINT CONTROL: a.) The ability to regulate the movements of the point accurately and aim it at the exact part of the target desired. b.) In modern fencing, by keeping the point on-line to threaten the opponent's target.

POINT D'ARRET: An attachment to the tip of the competitive fencing blade (Foil and Epee) to aid in registering hits (either electrical or non-electrical).

POINT FOCUS: a.) To place emphasis on thrusting attacks and techniques made with the tip of a sword in drills and exercises. b.) To make a thrusting attack directly out of a pressure glide or glissade.

POINT IN LINE: A position by a defending fencer holding their arm straight from the shoulder and presenting the defending point directly at an attacker, offering to impale them. The point in line is a "defensive threat" and has the right of way until deflected.

POINT OF BALANCE: a.) The point on a sword, located on the forte of the blade about two to three inches from the hilt, that will maintain its equilibrium when balanced on a finger. b.) Rudolfo Capo Ferro da Calgi in his Gram simulacro dell'arte e dell'uso della scherma (1610) indicated that, for a rapier to be well balanced, the point of balance had to be 3.1 inches (8 cm.) down the blade from the ricasso. c.) The apex from which an actor/combatant transfers from a centered, equalized stance or placement to a state of toppling or falling. d.) Any stance or placement of the body that has the actor/combatant in a state of equilibrium.

POINT-BLANK: With a certain aim, so as not

to miss.

POLE: a.) A long, slender piece of wood... b.) See *Quarter-Staff.*

POLE-AXE: (also *Poleaxe, Poll-ax, Pollax & Polacks*) A kind of ax formerly used as a weapon of war, a battle-ax. A short-handled weapon with a broad sharp ax-head and usually a cutting edge or point on the side opposite the broad face. The savageness of the weapon caused it to be forbidden in the lists and trials by combat. Chaucer makes reference to this fact in his Knight's Tale: "No man ther fore vp peyne of los of lyf No maner shot polax ne shorte knyf In to the lystes sende ne thider brynge Ne short swerd for to stoke with poynt bitynge." (c. 1386) The pole-ax stayed in use (in various forms) till the end of the eighteenth century. At that time it was mainly used in naval warfare for boarding, resisting boarders, cutting ropes, etc.

POLICE CHOKE HOLD: A suppression choke hold associated with police close quarter tactics that has the aggressor's arm wrapped about the victim's neck from behind, using pressure from the upper and lower arm to crimp the windpipe.

POMMEL: (also *Pummel*) (Fr.- meaning "little apple") a.) The metal fixture that locks together the different parts of the weapon and acts as a counter weight to the blade. On historical weapons, the tang is fed through a hole in the pommel, heated, and riveted over the end of the pommel permanently securing the parts of the sword together. The pommel of most modern weapons is threaded like a large nut and screwed onto a threaded tang. b.) The metal cap, in the old days often ornamental, which screws onto and locks in place the 'tang' of the blade, where the latter passes through and projects just beyond the top of the handle. The pommel, by its not inconsiderable weight, also serves to balance the blade. c.) To strike, beat or attack with the pommel of a weapon instead of with its blade. d.) To beat or strike repeatedly with the hands or fists as with the pommel; to bruise.

POMMEL ATTACK: a.) Any aggressive or offensive action delivered or executed with the pommel of a weapon, whether it lands or not. b.) An attack made, usually in close distance, with the pommel of the weapon. c.) Any aggressive or offensive action, usually in close distance, delivered with the pommel of a weapon.

PONIARD: (also *Poynard, Parrying Dagger,* and *Main Gauche Dagger*) A form of quillon dagger developed during the sixteenth century designed to be held in the left hand with the point above, like a sword. The guards of these daggers were provided with a hilt formed by curved quillons and a Side-Ring, small shell or plate of metal in order to protect the knuckles.

POOP: a.) The rearmost part of a ship; the stern; also, the rearmost and highest deck, often forming the roof of the cabin built in the stern. b.) To strike in a fatal manner.

PORTA DI FERRO: ("Iron Door" guard) Fiore Dei Liberi's low middle-right position, a form of Low guard (point forward, blade down at roughly 45 degrees) leading with the left leg and the blade turned slightly, point back and turned slightly to the right, the hilt turned slightly left. Also called *Porta di Ferro Piana Terrena* or *Tuta Porta di Ferro.*

PORTO DI FERRO MEZZANA: ("Middle Iron Door" guard) Fiore Dei Liberi's term for the Low guard, leading with the right leg. Used to counter-strike and to defend against *Gioco Stretto.*

POSTA: Italian for "position" (fighting posture or stance).

POSTA BREVA: ("Short" guard) Fiore Dei Liberi's thrusting middle guard with the pommel held close to the body. Also called *Spada Distesa* ("lying sword"). A limited "entering" or close-range posture with the blade held more vertical, the hilt pulled in low and the knees bent more, it is used for both parrying and preparing to slice, thrust, or bind.

POSTA DI BICORNIO: ("Two-Horned" position) Fiore's thrusting guard holding the sword horizontally in a high middle position with the left hand in a reverse grip. Suited for thrusting in close.

POSTA BREVE SERPENTINA: ("Short Snake" guard) One of Fiore's *Mezza Spada* postures, essentially a "Middle" guard with the left hand holding the blade at the ricasso, left leg leading.

POSTA DI CODA LUNGA DISTESA: ("Long Lying Tail" position) Fiore Dei Liberi's term for a right "Tail" guard, leading with the left leg and the blade held back and down at 45-degrees.

POSTA CROCE: ("Cross" guard or "True Cross Guard") One of Fiore's *Mezza Spada* postures, with the left hand holding the middle of the blade in a reverse grip. Essentially a low left "hanging" guard.

POSTA DENTE DI CINGHIALE: ("Boar's Tooth" guard or "Wild Boar's Tooth") Fiore Dei Liberi's Low guard leading with the right leg and the sword held forward and down at roughly 45-degrees, the hilt to the outside of the left side of the left knee. Suited to counter-thrusting and to ward off by lifting upward followed by an immediate cut downward.

POSTA DI DONNA SOPRANO E ALTERA: ("Upward Proud Woman's guard" or "Noblewoman's" guard) Fiore Dei Liberi's term for a position with the blade held over or on the right shoulder. In one version it is held horizontal almost resting on the shoulder. In another it is held at a 45-degree angle as if in a shoulder-level "high" guard, but with the opposite shoulder turned more forward. While he only depicts a right-side version, Fiore does list both a left & right Woman's guard (*Posta Dominarum dextra* and *sinixtra*). The Women's guard seems related to horizontal cut, as the posture can be assumed both preliminary to such a blow and as a result of such a blow.

POSTA DI FALCONE: Vadi's name for a guard with the blade held centered close at chest level with the blade out forward at a 45-degree angle. Perhaps similar to Fiore's *Posta Fronte*.

POSTA DI FRONTE: ("Front guard") Fiore Dei Liberi's term for Corona ("crown guard") or a middle position and the hilt held close to the chest or abdomen pointing forward. In Vadi the "Front" guard is shown as held much closer to the body and more vertical with the point directed upward.

POSTA DI FRONTE: ("Front" guard) Fiore and Vadi's term for a form of unstable high middle position poised to greet or intercept a downward blow with the ricasso or cross. Also called *Corona*.

POSTA DI VERA FINESTRA: ("True Window" or "True Royal Window" guard) Fiore Dei Liberi's term for a stance leading with the left leg and the sword held horizontally out to the right, point aimed at the opponent's face. The blade is held with the edge and cross upward and the hilt slightly behind the head, not in front of it or to its side. Essentially equivalent to the German right Ochs stance. While Fiore only depicts a right-side version, he does list both a left & right Window guard (*Posta Fenestrarum dextra* and *sinixtra*).

POSTA DI VERA FINESTRA MANCINA: ("True Left Hand Window" guard) Fiore Dei Liberi's posture of holding the sword over and behind the left shoulder. While called a "window" stance, it is not equivalent to the right-side "window". This position can be interpreted as either form of "High" guard or one with the blade behind the head, horizontal or diagonal. Essentially a left-side Woman's guard.

POSTA LONGA: Fiore Dei Liberi's name for an extended Middle guard, leading with the left leg bent, the rear leg stretched and the arms extended, the blade held more horizontal. Often resulting from a thrust and used for warding, threatening and thrusting to the throat or face as well as slicing to the arms.

POSTA SAGITTARRIA: ("Archer" guard) One of Fiore's Mezza Spada postures, a right "Window" guard with the sword pulled farther back and the left hand holding the blade knuckles up.

POSTA SERPENTINA SUPERIORE: ("Upper Snake" guard) One of Fiore's Mezza Spada postures, a raised Serpentina guard consisting of a right "Window" guard with the left hand holding the blade in a reverse grip.

POSTA VERA CROCE: ("True Cross" guard) One of Fiore's *Mezza Spada* postures, a low right "hanging" position with the left hand holding the blade in a reverse grip.

POSTED STEP: A step made in one count, executed with a posted foot. (I.e. Lunge; Passes Forward and Back; Posted Thwart; Cross; Slip; Half-Passe, Continue, and Return.)

POSTING FOOT: The foot that stays stationary when performing certain types of footwork.

POSTURA: (It.) The position of the body and the weapon; preceding the modern definition of guard.

POSTURE: a.) The particular position of a weapon in drill or combat. Most likely derived from the Italian "postura." b.) The placement and carriage of the limbs and the body as a whole; attitude, alignment, pose.

POTCH: a.) To thrust at. b.) To slap or smack someone or something. Believed to have derived from the Yiddish patshn, meaning to slap.

POWDER: Gun powder.

PRACTICE: The conscious application of technique through discipline of perfect concentration.

PRAT: a.) A prank or trick; a fraud or piece of trickery. b.) To beat about the buttocks.

PRATFALL: (also *Prat-Fall*) a.) A comic or trick fall or tumble; a staged fall most often executed backward onto the buttocks. The combatant squats, taking their knees out of alignment and quickly lowering the torso. Weight and center remain over the feet. Once down in the squat the torso is slightly rocked forward as the feet are kicked out, causing the combatant to drop onto their gluteus and the muscles on the back of the leg. The rock of the torso forward keeps the weight and pres-

sure off the tailbone. b.) A comedy fall; a fall onto the buttocks. See *Prat Fall*.

PRELHAW: (also *Prelhau*, meaning Plunge Strike) From a binding position, a plunging thrust down between the opponent's arms.

PREPARATION OF ATTACK: A blade, body, or foot movement that opens the way for the attack.

PRESENTATION OF CUTTING EDGE: The turning of the true edge towards the target to be attacked.

PRESS: A pressure attack on the opposing blade that pushes it aside and open a line of attack. This lateral displacement of the blade is sometimes referred to as the fourth pris d'fer along with the croisé, bind and envelopment.

PRESSURE: a.) The application of force to something by something else in direct contact with it. (pressure = force/area) b.) Attacks on the blade that utilize lateral pressure to displace the blade. There are two common forms of Pressure Attacks; the *Press*; and the *Froissement*. See *Press* and *Pressure Attack*. c.) An attack on the blade executed by contacting the blade and pressing upon it (varying degrees of pressure may be used).

PRESSURE ATTACKS: Attacks on the blade that utilize consistent lateral pressure to displace the opposing blade. The contact with the blades may utilize more than one point on the opposing blade.

PRESSURE GLIDE: a.) (also *Ruffling, Scrape, Effort* and *Froissement*) The most violent of the Attacks on the Blade consisting of a strong beating or pressing of the blade in conjunction with a fast graze or glissade from forte to foible. b.) (also *Froissement*) An attack on the opposing blade that combines a strong beating or pressing of the blade in conjunction with a fast graze or glissade from forte to foible. Generally used as a preparatory action to an attack. c.) An improper term for a croisé with an expulsion.

PRICK-SONGS: Literally "printed music." The phrase "He fights as you sing prick-songs" used by Shakespeare in Romeo & Juliet refers to Tybalt fighting with studied accuracy, like trained singers who can read from printed music; in contrast to those who sing by ear. It is more than likely then that this reference is a comparison between Tybalt's fencing style and the acquired and practiced skill of reading printed music. This is supported by such a reference offered by Saviolo, a Fencing Master who's work Shakespeare is believed to have been familiar with. "for as a man hath voice and can sing by nature, but shall never do it with time and measure of musicke unless he have learned the arte."

PRIMA: (It.) (also *Prima Guardia*) (from the Latin Primo - "firstly") a.) Agrippa's term for the first guard position that can safely be assumed upon drawing the sword. b.) The single weapon guard that closes the high outside line (standard) and high inside line (across) with the hilt above the head and in front of the body, the blade below the hand, tip directed toward the opponent's right or left shoulder. c.) (Double Fence) The first guard that can safely be assumed upon drawing the rapier and dagger. The rapier assumes the placement of single weapon *Prima* (standard or across); the dagger in single weapon *Terza*.

PRIMA INTENZIONE: (It.) See *First Intention*.

PRIME PARADE: (Small Sword) One of the lower parades, seldom practised, except on emergencies, when an adversary presses vigorously upon you.

PRIME: (also *One*) a.) The transitional rapier and small sword (also modern fencing) parry that closes (protects) the low inside line, the hand is across the body, with the blade below the hand. b.) The cross body guard used in transitional rapier and small sword to close the high, outside line. See *Prima*. c.) The first parry or guard position defending the inside high line. The hand holds the weapon as if it had just been drawn from a scabbard.

PRINCIPALS: The actual combatants in a duel. The offended and offending parties (or their representatives) who will actually fight the duel. See also *Seconds*.

PRINCIPLE OF DEFENSE: (Swordplay) The opposition of forte to foible.

PRINCIPLES, SIX: See *Six Principles*.

PRIS D'FER: (also *Pris de Fer* and *Controlling the Point*) Attacks on the Blade that catch the opposing blade, master it, and hold it or remove it in preparation for an attack. These actions are the *Croisé*, *Bind*, and the *Envelopment* and in some schools the *Press* or *Pressure Attack*. These actions command the opposing blade and may retain it or remove it with the action of an Expulsion. These types of actions were referred to as *Controlling the Point* in sixteenth century swordplay.

PRISE DE FER: a.) A translation into English is, taking of the blade (or iron). Refers to any controlling attack on the blade that takes an opponent's blade from an existing line to a new one or returning to same line. Examples are a *Bind*, a *Croisé*, or *Envelopment*. b.) A "taking" or contacting of the opponent's blade in an offensive or counteroffensive action. See *Pris d'Fer*.

PRIZE: Referring both to the master's prize of the sixteenth century, and the prize fights of the seventeenth century. The masters' prize was a public exhibition and examination for a provost to try for his masters status in the English corporation of Masters of Defence. The test consisted of a proficiency in many different weapons and styles, and were quite popular forms of entertainment. Two members of Shakespeare's company at the Globe were fencing masters; Tarlton the comic and Christopher Sly, the man who first played the part of Romeo. Ben Jonson, the best known contemporary of Shakespeare, was also quite a swordsman, killing fellow actor Gabriel Spence in 1598, in a duel (serving time in prison and having his thumb branded for the crime). Public contests being quite popular, they became exhibits between professional swordsmen, pugilist and wrestlers purely for entertainment and profit. Even with the disbanding of the corporation of Masters of

Defence in 1624, the prize fights continued. Generally speaking, the weapon employed in these later contests was the backsword, inflicting grim enough looking wounds without being anything as deadly as the thrust of the rapier. Other weapons, however, were employed, including the two-handed sword, quarterstaff, the falchion, halberd, and, unbelievably, the flail. In the eighteenth century the sword fight fell way to professional pugilistic matches.

PRIZE FIGHTER: a.) One who professionally performs in public fighting matches or contests. One who fought a prize. b.) A boxer or pugilist who fights in public competition for a prize or stake.

PRIZE-FIGHT: (also *Prize Fight*) A public exhibition and examination for a provost to try for their master's status within the English guild of Master's of Defence. The test consisted of showing proficiency in many different weapons and styles, and were quite popular forms of entertainment. In contrast to the tournaments, where the lists were closed to all combatants except those of noble birth, the tests for degrees in the guild of Masters of Defence were open to all students of the sword.

PRIZER: (also *Priser*) One who fights a prize or fencing match. See *Prize*.

PROGRESSIVE ATTACK: a.) An attack consisting of a number of actions, each continually moving towards the target maintaining the threat. b.) A method of delivering certain compound attacks as one fluid action.

PRONATION: a.) The position of the sword-hand with the palm down. b.) The position of the hand where the palm is turned down, nails of the sword-hand facing the floor.

PROPER ALIGNMENT: Essentially good posture where the various parts of the body - head, shoulders, arms, ribs, hips, legs, feet - are all in correct relative position to one another. See also *Line of Gravity*.

PROPORTION: (also *Keeping Proportion*) A sixteenth century term for assuming prop-

er counter guards to avoid being struck by the opponent. To keep "proportion," was to move with the opponent, keeping due relation of one part to another; such relation of size, etc., between weapons and body placement as renders the two guards harmonious; balanced, symmetrical. Keeping proportion meant assuming the corresponding wards and positions of assault, and thus never giving the opponent an opening or opportunity to attack.

PROPUGNATION: Means of combat, defense.

PROPULSION: Any momentary contact technique, such as a punch, push, shove, concussive explosion or bullet hit which forcefully causesa person to fall.

PROTECT: To guard, defend, shield.

PROVOST: The third level of the four rankings in English schools of Defence.

PUGILISM: The art or practice of hand to hand combat; fist fighting; Boxing.

PUGILIST: A fighter well versed in hand to hand; someone who fights with their fists; a boxer.

PULL: An act of drawing towards oneself with force; including a momentary pluck, wrench, or tug, and a continued exercise of force.

PULL OVER BACK FLIP: A partnered acrobatic that the stand back-to-back, with their hands held above their heads, hands joined or clasped on a staff, pole or similar object. Working together, the base man creates a "table" for the airman to execute a backward roll upon, rolling up and over the base man's back, completing the roll the airman lands facing the base man. The technique gets its name from the joined hand position that gives the appearance that the base man "pulls" the airman up and over.

PUMMEL ATTACK: An offensive action executed in close quarters where the pommel or hilt of the weapon is used to attempt an attack at the opponent's body.

PUMMEL: a.) To attack, strike or bludgeon with the Pommel of a sword. b.) To pound, beat, or strike repeatedly with the fists as with the Pommel of a sword. c.) (also *Pommel*) (Small Sword) The round knob or ball fixed as a counterpoise at the farthest extremity of the hilt or handle of a sword or foil.

PUN: To pound as in a mortar; to consolidate by pounding or ramming down (as earth or rubble, in setting poles, etc., or making a roadway); to dash to pieces. To Pound.

PUNCH: a.) A driving or thrusting blow, generally one delivered with the fist. A strike with the fist (i.e. Jab, Straight, Cross, Hook, Roundhouse, Uppercut, etc.). b.) Offensive striking techniques with the hand(s) that are executed with the hand closed into a fist. c.) An instrument or tool for pricking, piercing, perforating, or making a hole in anything; esp. for making holes or cutting out pieces of a particular shape; also for enlarging a hole already made, hence a term for a dagger. See *Puncheon*

PUNCH BLOCK: a.) A defensive action made with the hand closed, using the fist to strike into the aggressor's attack. The hand is punched into the attack, generally striking the aggressor on the wrist or tendons on the inside of the forearm. b.) Said of any action that blocks a punch.

PUNCH BLOCK: Any action, armed or unarmed, that stops or deflects a punch or blow. Punch Thrust: A thrust driven home with the unarmed hand pushing forward the pommel/butt of the knife.

PUNCHEON: (also Punch) A short piercing dagger.

PUNTA: (It.) Literally "point; tip." The point of a weapon, hence, a thrust or attack with the point.

PUNTA DRITTA: (It.) (*punta*, point, *dritta*, right; hence, a thrust from the right.) a.) An attack with the point, hand in pronation, delivered from one's right. b.) a pronated thrust from the right, from either Terza or Seconda, to either of the opponent's hips or thighs; parries one, two, seven and eight; low three or four; high seven or eight.

PUNTA ROVESCIO: (It.) (also *Punta Reversa*)

(*punta* = point; *rovescio* = turned over; upside down.) a.) A thrust made from the reverse side of the cutting circle, from the left with the hand often in supination. Opposite of *Punta Dritta* or *Mandritti*.

PUNTA SOPRAMANO: (also *Demi-Lunge*) (It. = "thrust over the hand") a.) An attack introduced by Viggiani (1575) in which the lead foot is extended forward, about eighteen inches, accompanied by a supinated thrust with the sword arm and a slight turning in the torso. The first clear development toward the lunge of today. b.) A demi-lunge, whether or not it is accompanied by an attack.

PUNTO: (It. & Span.) a.) Literally "point," hence, the point of the weapon or an attack with the point; a thrust. b.) A term used by the English during the sixteenth century for a stroke or thrust with the point of a sword; Punto Dritto, a direct thrust; Punto Riverso, a back-handed thrust.

PUNTO MANDRITTI: A point attack delivered from the attacker's outside line to the partner's inside line, usually with the hand in pronation.

PUNTO REVERSO: (also *Punto Riverso*) a.) An English bastardization of the Italian Punta Rovescio, a thrust made from the reverse side of the cutting circle; a thrust from the left with the hand in supination. b.) A supinated thrusting attack delivered from the attacker's inside line. c.) A point attack delivered from the attacker's inside line to

PUSH AWAY: A physical action taken from a corps-a-corps or other such close combat technique where one combatant uses their hand, arm, foot, leg or other such body part to force their partner away, outside measure.

PUSH: a.) A continued application of force or pressure made with one or both hands intended to move or drive the victim back or away from the aggressor or in a particular direction. A Shove. b.) To take hold of or touch another person and appear to control their movement away from you. c.) A blow, stroke or knock. More often a thrust of a weapon, or of the horn of a beast. d.) To shove, to drive by force.

e.) An attack or onset.

PUSHOVER: Any opponent or adversary who, can be easily beaten, someone who only takes one push to knock them down. It is believed that this term is actually a double metaphor: "a prizefighter who can be easily beaten is a pushover," says Robert Claiborne, as is "a woman who can be easily had. Whence the figurative sense of anything easily accomplished."

PUT: a.) To place, push or "thrust" a weapon home. b.) A thrust, push, shove. c.) To lay on, as in a blow...

Q

Q-STICK: Slang for Quarterstaff. See *Quarterstaff*.

QUALITY: a.) The characteristics of movement determined by the way energy is used, such as swinging, percussive, suspended, sustained and vibratory movement. b.) A term used for the essential character or distinguishing attribute of sound. The color or timbre of the actor's voice; the features of the sound; rough, voiced, screamed, whispered, etc.

QUARRAL: (also *Quarrel*) A short, heavy, square-headed arrow or bolt, formerly used in shooting with the cross-bow or arbalest.

QUARREL: a.) Any dispute or contest that can not be settled by words; private difference as well as dissension and combat for a public cause and on a larger scale. An armed encounter, fight or brawl. b.) Cause, occasion and motive of dispute. c.) To wrangle, to seek occasion of a fray, to pick a fight. d.) See *Quarral*.

QUARRELLER: (also *Quarreler*) One who picks quarrels.

QUARRELLOUS: Disposed to quarrel.

QUARRELSOME: Disposed to quarrel.

QUART: a.) To assume the fencing posture of *Quarte*. b.) To draw the head and shoulders back, keeping them as far from the adversaries blade as possible, while executing a thrust.

QUARTA: (also *Quarta Guardia)* a.) The single weapon guard assumed with the arm across the body to the inside (about three inches away from the belly), the hand supinated, the tip at roughly armpit level (Standard or Across) closing the high inside line. b.) The double fence guard assumed with the rapier in single rapier Terza (Standard or Across), and the dagger in a placement similar to its parry of High Three, closing the rapier's high inside line.

QUARTE: (also *Four)* a.) The small sword,

transitional rapier and modern fencing guard which closes (protects) the high inside line. b.) (also *Carte*) The fourth parry or guard position, defending the inside high line. c.) The transitional rapier and small sword parry executed with the point higher than the hand, which is supinated, closing the high inside line. d.) An eighteenth century term sometimes given to *Sixte*.

QUARTE OUTSIDE: A seventeenth and eighteenth century term sometimes given to the parry or guard of sixte because the supinated hand position of sixte did not become common until the late eighteenth century.

QUARTE OVER THE ARM: A seventeenth century term for a disengage from the guard of quarte with a supinated thrust delivered in the high line over the opponent's arm. See *Carte Thrust Over the Arm.*

QUARTER: a). To cut to pieces, to slaughter. b). quarter, "to give no", a phrase meaning to offer no clemency or mercy. Phrase thought to stem from Shakespeare, meaning "enter into no relations with" or else "house no prisoner attempting to surrender".

QUARTER-BLOW: (also *Quarter-Stroke*)

QUARTERSTAFF: (also *Quarter-Staff*) A weapon used by English peasantry consisting of a stout pole, from six to eight feet in length, with each end often tipped with iron. The exact sense of quarter is not clear: 1.) The OED suggests that the staff may have been made from a tree of a certain size cleft into four quarters or seqtions which are then shaped to staves. 2.) Possibly a weapon that is one quarter length of a Pike staff. The short end of a pike-staff broken in battle could be used for offensive and defensive action at close quarters.

QUELL: A euphemism for murder.

QUILLON(S): (Fr.) a.) One or both of the arms or branches forming the cross guard of a sword. The guard of the typical medieval sword consisted merely of a pair of straight or only slightly curved branches sticking out perpendicular to the blade. The right angle

of the blade and quillons created a "t" or cross at the guard, leading to the term cross-hilt or cross-guard. The quillons provided the sword-hand with a protective barrier, preventing the opposing blade from sliding down the sword and striking the hand. In the sixteenth century the quillons were extended with the intent to displace or entangle the opponent's blade. The quillons were either straight as in the medieval swords, recurved in S-form, or bent towards the blade. Now in common use. See also *Rudder of the Blade.* b.) The crossbars of the hilt.

QUILLON BASH: (also *Beat-Away*) A standard parry followed by beating or knocking the attacking blade up, out or down with the cross guard of the defending weapon. See *Beat Away.*

QUILLON BLOCK: The sturdy block of metal from which the branches, quillons, knuckle bow, as well as the variety of other loops and rings of the rapier hilt extend.

QUILLON BLOW: (also *Quillon Strike* and *Hilt Strike*) An attack made with the sword, held by the blade swinging the hilt or guard as a club or mace.

QUILLON DAGGER: (also *Poniard*) A form of dagger, developed during the mid-thirteenth century and used in various forms through the eighteenth century, which resembled the hilt and quillon configuration of contemporary swords. See also *Poniard.*

QUINTA: (It.) (also *Quinta Guardia*) The fifth guard position in Double Fence technique assumed with the rapier in Low Terza (Standard) with the hand held roughly ten to twelve inches in front of the body and the dagger held across the body above the rapier, the hand pronated and in front of the body at mid torso, the blade placed over and above the forte of the rapier. The weapons are crossed but not touching.

QUINTAIN: An object or target mounted on a stout post or plank used as a mark for tilting practice. A target set up for exercises of skill for horsemen and footmen, designed to be tilted at with lances, poles, or thrown at with darts or the likes.

QUINTE: (Fr.) (also *Five* or *Fifth*) a.) The modern sabre parry that closes the high line and protects the head. b.) The fifth thrust or parry of the eight taught in the French school. c.) The fifth parry (in Foil and Epee defending the inside low line, in Saber defending the head.)

QUIVER: A case for arrows.

QUOIT: To throw.

R

R & D: Abbreviation for *Rapier and Dagger*.

RABBIT EARS GRASP: (also *Scissors Grasp*) A cliché *corps-à-corps* where both combatants grasp hilts and create an "X" with the blades like a pair of scissors or an old rabbit ear antenna set.

RABBIT PUNCH: A sharp, chopping blow delivered to the back of the neck. Designed to kill a rabbit by breaking its neck with a sharp blow., it is executed with a closed hand which hits with the little finger down and thumb up, in the same manner as a Hammer Punch, to strike like club or hammer. Derived from the way in which a gamekeeper puts a rabbit out of pain. A true punch of the Elizabethan era.

RACCOGLIMENTO: (It.) See *Envelopment*.

RADOPPIO: (It. & Ger.) (also *Raddoppio*) a.) A reprise of the attack executed by lunging and immediately recovering forward and again lunging. b.) See *Reprise*.

RAFFINE: A swordsman bully who will provoke a duel on the slightest pretext or cause.

RANGE: The relative scope or extent of movement. Technical range of motion is determined by body size and joint flexibility.

RAP: a.) A severe blow or stroke with a sword, dagger or other such weapon. b.) A painful stroke or blow with a branch, stick or other such rod, not causing serious hurt.

RAPIER: a.) The long, thrusting sword developed in Italy in the 1480's, introduced to the court of Mary Tudor by fashionable Spanish noblemen, and widely used throughout Western Europe until the mid seventeenth century (the late eighteenth century in Spain, Italy, and Germany to a lesser degree). Originally used for both cut and thrust attacks (actually being poorly designed for either), the rapier became a weapon chiefly used for thrusting. In an attempt to protect the sword hand from a thrust, over a hundred distinct hilt configurations were developed (including the Two-Ring Hilt, Swept-Hilt and Cup-Hilt). Though quite popular in Spain, the long thrusting Espada Ropera (literally meaning "dress sword") did not sit well with England's preferred style of swordplay. The French, as early as 1474, referred to the weapon as the epee rapiere, a contemptuous term for the ridiculously long Spanish sword. This initial contempt for the sword and its style was intensified when the Italian "masters" came to England to instruct the "true art of defense" to the uneducated Englishmen. While many of the English nobles and gentlemen were quite taken by the new, fashionable and "scientific" art and masters of the Italian Spada (sword), the English masters of defense were not as impressed. They found the sword impractical in war and capricious in civil disputes (as often both duelists would be seriously wounded or killed). The common Englishmen, being a true "sword and buckler man" saw the foreign sword as a threat to their heritage and as an insult to their ideals. It is no wonder that when the rapier finally gained acceptance, they Anglicized the name rapier, from the French rapiere. The rapier was one of the first swords to be considered primarily a "civilian" weapon. Within a few decades of its first appearance in the 1480's the rapier had become an essential part of every Spanish and Italian gentleman's proper attire, (regardless of their actual skill at swordplay). In comparison to the military sword of the day, the rapier was a lighter weapon with a narrower double-edged blade with a sharp point. Through the later half of the sixteenth century, and into the seventeenth, the blade became narrower and lighter and eventually practical for nothing but point work. In an attempt to protect the sword hand from a thrust of the adversary's blade different bars, rings, branches and arms were added to the hilt at varying angles. In the mid-seventeenth century the Spanish developed the cup hilt which completely protected the hand. At the time of its introduction, the rapier, as a long and slightly awkward weapon, needed a second weapon that could move quickly enough to respond defensively to an oncoming attack. This weapon could be a buckler, dagger, cloak, or when all else failed even an unarmed hand. At the turn of the century, however, the rapier had become light and fast enough for the swordsman to discard the second weapon and use the rapier for both defense and offense. The superiority of the point finally led to the evolution of the lunge. This transformed the entire science of defense from circular patterns of footwork into a linear method of gaining and breaking ground. This new style of rapier play, as introduced by such masters as Nicoloetto Giganti and Ridolfo Capo Ferro, gave birth to a new and exciting form of swordplay now recognized as the springboard for the modern art of fencing. Well over 200 years of continuous use throughout Europe serve as admirable testimony to the utility, versatility, and style of this remarkable weapon. b.) This weapon has been referred to by a sorted collection of names, most derived from previous weapons or those similar in use (thrusting with the point). It also received many other names from phonetic renderings and mispronunciations of foreign terms for the sword and like weapons. The term "rapier," however, has come to be the most common name for this particular weapon. Originally referred to as the Spanish Sword by sixteenth century Englishmen. The actual term "rapier" is not traceable to one definite source, but it is most commonly linked to the French rapiere which itself can be traced to the Spanish espada ropera. Some, however, believe that the term derived from the Spanish raspar which means "to scrape or scratch" others from the German rappen meaning "to tear out"; the later being less plausible as the rapier was generally a thrusting weapon and introduced to Germany through Spain.

The term "rapier" was actually never used in Italy, and the general term espada referred to just about every type of sword in Spain. In Germany rapier, and in Russia the word rapira, has evolved to mean the modern fencing foil. Only in France and England has the term been preserved to represent the original weapon. c.) The long, narrow weapon that combines the advantages of the cut and the thrust. It originated in Italy in the early sixteenth-century and was destined to replace the broadsword. d.) The sword of choice and the main topic of discussion in Di Grassi's "True Art." As a weapon, he divided it into four parts, basically the Guard or Hilt, the Forte of the Blade, the Middle and the Foible (including the tip). He determines that the first two parts are to be used for defense and the latter two for offense.

RAPIER AND CLOAK: (also *Spada e Capa*) A method of fighting using a common cloak or robe for defense.

RAPIER AND DAGGER: (also *Rapier & Poniard*) a.) The fashionable style of swordplay during the later half of the sixteenth century and into the early portion of the seventeenth century where the rapier was held in the right hand, used chiefly for offensive purposes and the dagger was held in the left for warding or deflecting blows. The evolution of swordplay eventually lead to the discarding of the dagger as the rapier became capable of being manipulated both offensively and defensively. See also *Rapier*.

RAPIER BLADE: During the Age of the Rapier, its blade was originally long (up to six feet in length), flat, and generally heavy. As the point became more dominant during the Age of Transition, however, the blade became much lighter and more manageable. In most cases the blade is broken down into several parts: Tip, Foible, Middle, Forte, Shoulders, Ricasso, and Tang. The flat of the blade tapers to two edges (the True Edge and False edge) and was often grooved or channeled (Fullers or Fluting) to lessen the weight without jeopardizing its structural integrity. See *Rapier, Age of, Transition, Age of, Rapier* and *Transitional Rapier*.

RAPIER GRIP: a.) The handle of the rapier; that which the hand is clasped around. See *Grip*. b.) The manner of holding the rapier. Although there are a great variety of ways to handle the rapier, there are generally two standard methods. In both the hand clasps around the handle, the thumb on one side of the grip, the fingers on the other. The index finger (forefinger) is placed above the lower quillon, inside the pas d'âne, comfortably wrapped around the ricasso with its pad near the quillon block. The last three fingers lightly grip the handle, bringing it to bear against the palm of the hand. Here the hand can be placed in (1) an Opposition Grip and (2) a Relaxed Grip. 1.) The thumb is placed onto the false, or back edge of the ricasso, in opposition to the grip of the index finger. 2.) The thumb rests on the tip of the index finger. c.) The manner of holding the rapier as taught by seventeenth century English Fencing Master Joseph Swetnam can be done in three ways 1.) The Natural Fashion in which the thumb is placed against the ricasso of the blade inside the hilt (in the manner of holding a dagger), the surest grip for both cut and thrust; 2.) The Whole Hand in which the hand is wrapped around the grip between the pommel and the cross guard, the thumb locking in the fore finger; 3.) The Stokata Fashion (also Stokata Grip) where the thumb and fore finger wrap about the neck of the pommel and the last three fingers about the pommel, extending the reach of the rapier.

RAPIER HILT: The protective guard (consisting of a variety of bars, rings, branches and arms) placed between the sword's grip and exposed blade in an attempt to shield the sword hand from the opposing blade. There are basically three types of guards; the Two-Ring Hilt, Swept Hilt and Cup-Hilt. Within these, there are a vast variety of configurations.

RAPIER, AGE OF THE: (Circa 1550-1625) The beginning of the Golden Age of Sword-play where armor began to be abandoned, the sword became a part of the attire of every gentleman, and schools and masters of the science of fence were becoming established in most western countries developing practical ways of managing the sword. This period marks the beginning of the dueling craze and the clash of station and style in swordplay. The fact that the sword was always carried meant it could be used in a flash for self-defense or to settle a matter of honor. Duels and brawls were fought over no greater pretense than the type of weapon a someone carried. This period also marks the intrusion of foreign masters and their foreign blades into the traditional practices and weapon of English swordplay. "True" Englishmen took great insult to the imported "scientific" practices of the Italians and Spaniards.

RAPIERE: (Fr.) A disrespectful term for the ridiculously long sword common to the bully and braggart.

RAYKES: A term from the 15th century English great-sword text by J. Ledall, likely referring to "draw cuts" from a high guard.

RAZE: To strike or cut as with a razor.

READY STANCE: A relaxed stance from which offensive and defensive actions can instantly and equally be made.

REAR FOOT: See *Lag Foot*.

REAR LUNGE: The action of forming a lunge without forward motion by extending the rear leg and arm into lunge position. Not a *Backward Lunge*.

REARING LUNGE: A lunge where the combatant rears back like a horse before they spring forward. When the torso rocks back on an awkward weight shift and the lunging foot raises considerably from the floor before lunging forward.

REBATE: A blunted weapon where the tip has been turned back upon the blade.

RECOIL: a): The force transmitted to the attacker when their technique is blocked by, or lands on, an opponent. b). The backward shock of a firearm as the gunpowder ignites, the kick of a gun.

RECOVER: a.) To get or take back again into one's hands or possession; to regain possession of something displaced, lost or taken away. b.) The act of regaining or returning to the ascribed on guard position or ready stance after leaving the said position by choice or force. c.) Return to the On Guard position.

RECOVER BACKWARD: a.) To move back into an on guard stance or ready position. b.) To arrive at an En Guarde position from a lunge by bringing the forward foot backward.

RECOVER FORWARD: a.) To move forward into an on guard stance or ready position. b.) To arrive at the En Guarde position from a lunge by bringing a rear foot forward.

RECOVERED FOOT: The foot that returns to proper En Garde placement after performing a step.

RECOVERED STEP: A step, made in two counts, where the foot returns to proper En Garde placement after performing a step. (i.e. Advance/Retreat; Recoveries Forward and Back from a Lunge; Recovered Thwart; Half-Passe, Change and Return)

RECOVERING: (also *Recover* and *Recovery*) (Small Sword) "The act of resuming your guard posture after having made a longe at your adversary. A quick and easy recovery to guard, forming the most natural parade is an essential branch to your safety."

RECOVERY: a.) The action of returning to an on guard position or ready stance. b.) To arrive at an En Garde position from a lunge by bringing the forward foot backward.

RECOVERY FORWARD: a.) To arrive at an En Garde position from a lunge by bringing the rear foot forward. b.) See *Recover Forward*.

RECREANT: One who yields or gives up in combat; a cowardly or feint hearted person.

REDDING: (also *Redding-Up* and *Redding Up*) The action of separating combatants.

REDDING-BLOW: (also *Redding-Stroke*) A blow received by a person trying to separate combatants. See *Redding*.

RED-HANDED: A term derived prior to the use of firearms, where, an assassin or murderer would generally use a sword or dagger to slay their victim. In this process, the killer would most likely get blood on their hands, and, if they were caught prior to washing off the blood, they were caught "red-handed." The term is now applied to being caught in the very act of crime (murder or otherwise), having the evidences of guilt still upon the person.

REDIRECTION BLOCK: A defensive action where the hand or arm intercepts the attack and then immediately displaces or removes the opponent by mastering the energy of the initial attack.

REDOPPIO: (in German *Underhau*) Diagonal rising cut.

REDOUBLE: a.) To re-engage in combat with twice as much effort, energy, attacks; to strike twice as hard and fast as before. b.) To repeat an attack or blow.

REDOUBLEMENT: a.) A new attack made against an opponent who has failed to riposte. Generally made while still in the lunge from the previous attack. b.) A renewed attack after a missed or successful parry, in a different line from the original attack. c.) A new action, either simple or composed, made on an opponent who has parried without riposting or who has merely avoided the first action by retreating or displacing the target.

REFUSING THE BLADE: To avoid crossing or engaging swords with the opponent by means of a Change Under, Change Over, Vertical Change or other *Changement*.

REINFORCED PARRY: a.) (also *Split Parry*) A defensive action of the sword and unarmed hand where the unarmed hand takes hold of the sword's blade (approximately one third of the way from the tip) to strengthen and brace the parry against the opposing blade. See also *Dagger Reinforcement Parry*. b.) Any parry that is given extra support from another source, be it the unarmed hand, another weapon,

shield, etc. A bolstered or braced parry.

REITSCHWERT: (literally "cavalry sword") A German name for a military cut & thrust sword of c 1500-1700. Also called a *Degen* or "knight's sword".

RELAXING THE CUT: An exercise that works the mechanics of the flick or wrist cut of the rapier by executing several cuts in quick succession. This helps the combatant feel and understand how the tension and relaxation of the fingers, thumb and wrist work in the final stage of the cut.

RELEVÉ: (Fr.) Literally meaning "relifted." A term from ballet meaning the rise to the ball (or demi-pointe) of the foot. The rise is sometimes called elevé when it is made without the benefit of a preceding plié.

REMISE: (Fr.) a.) A parried attack that is renewed without withdrawal of the weapon arm. If a riposte is not immediately offered by the defensive combatant, a disengage, coupé or half-disengage may be immediately executed, allowing for a continuation of the attack. b.) The act of making a simple and immediate offensive action following the original attack, without withdrawing the arm, after the opponent has parried or retreated, when the latter has quitted contact with the blade without riposting or has made a riposte which is delayed, indirect, or composed. c.) A direct action of the blade, without withdrawing the arm, which continues the attack in the same line without a change of line with such an action as a disengage or coupé. If the action is indirect, it is a Redoublement. d.) A renewed attack after a missed or successful parry, in the same line as the original attack.

RENVERS: (Fr.) Literally to "reverse," "to turn upside-down," "to turn the wrong way," "to turn back." a.) A cutting attack delivered from the left side of the body. b.) A cutting attack made with the back or false edge of the blade.

REPERCUSSION: The recoil of the aggressor's fist, foot, etc. after impact; the fact of being forced or driven back by a resisting body.

REPLACEMENT: a.) See *Remise.* b.) See *Transfer Parry.*

REPLACEMENT BEAT: a.) (also *Replacement Beat Parry*) A double fence replacement parry where the primary parry stops the attacking blade and the secondary parry engages the attacking blade and beats it away. b.) A Return Beat or Counter Beat attack. See *Beat Attack.*

REPLACEMENT PARRY: A double fence parry where the attacking blade is stopped with a single weapon parry and then a second weapon engages the attacking blade and takes the place of the first parry.

REPLY(S): See *Riposte.*

REPRISE: a.) The process of renewing a parried attack when the opponent fails to offer a riposte. Generally the arm is drawn back to the cue position, and then the renewed attack is made in the same line as the original. This may be the renewal of an initial attack, or a riposte if the opponent fails to offer a counter-riposte. b.) A renewed attack after coming back to the en-guard position, usually forward but can be back.

REPRISE D'ATTACK: (Fr.) a.) A new attack executed immediately after a return to the "on guard" position. The recovery to the guard may be either forward or back. b.) See *Reprise.*

REPRISE TO THE FORE: Linear footwork that combines a Recovery Forward and a Lunge. There are two counts in this action, one-recover, two-lunge. The sword arm stays extended.

REPULSE: A beating back of the enemy.

RESISTANCE: (Small Sword) The act of opposing your adversary's blade either inwards or outwards according to the thrust you may make, by which you are covered on the longe. See *Opposition*, and *Covering.*

RESPONSE HIT: A counterattack in hand to hand combat where one blocks and attacks the opponent before their attacking limb has recovered to a guard or ready position.

RESPOST: See *Riposte.*

REST: a.) Generally a noticeable pause in action or movement. b.) A support for a horseman's lance. c.) A support for a firearm, forked at the upper end and provided with a spike at the other so as to secure it to the ground. Most common with the older and heavier muskets; employed to steady the barrel, insuring a more accurate aim.

RESTING GUARD: A variation on the single weapon guard position of Terza where the pommel is placed on the right thigh allowing the sword arm a moment's rest.

RESTORATION: The re-establishment of the English monarchy with the return of Charles II (1660).

RETIRE: a.) To retreat or surrender ground; yielding ground. To retreat from battle or danger. b.) A term for the Retreat.

RETREAT: a.) An action in the footwork of fencing used to step back, moving the rear foot first and then the lead foot (without crossing them). Opposite of *Advance.* b.) From the en garde position. The rear foot steps backward, followed by the front foot. c.) An action in the footwork that carries the body backward by moving the rear foot first and then the lead foot (without crossing them). Opposite of *Advance.* d.) To withdraw in the face of opposition; retiring or moving backward from danger. See *Retire.* e.) An off-line action of footwork where the rear foot steps backward, followed by the front foot.

RETREATING: (Small Sword) "The act of stepping backward, keeping a steady position on guard; the left foot should move first, and the right foot is instantly to follow." See also *Retreat.*

RETURN BEAT: A beat executed in immediate reply to the opponent's beat.

RETURN STEP: The second step of a Halfe Passe where the stepping foot returns to its original En Garde placement.

RETURN: [In French *riposté*] (Small Sword) When you deliver a thrust intantly after parrying one made by your adversary- If your parade has been well formed, your return must be well delivered. There are various sorts of returns, either by the complete longe, the complete extension, the extension of the arm only, or a return of the wrist. Straight returns, or those that touch your adversary at the moment of parrying before he can recover to guard are by far the best. The straight return of octave thrust, after parrying your adversary's, is one of the best returns in fencing.

RÉVÉRENCE: (Fr.) See *Salute*.

REVERSAL: (MA) To break or release from a specific hold or lock and turn that lock back onto the aggressor so that they find themselves in a similar position.

REVERSE: (At times *Reverso*) a.) A cutting attack delivered from the left side of the body; a backhanded stroke or cutting attack. b.) To turn a sword, knife or dagger in the hand from an overhand to a underhand grip, or vice versa. c.) To suddenly change the direction of an action of the blade, body, footwork or any other action within a fight or fight sequence. d.) The butt–end of a lance. e.) See *Reversal*.

REVERSE BLOWE: a.) (also *Reverse*) Di Grassi's term for a cut delivered from the non–weapon bearing side of the body. A backhanded cut. See also *Reverso Tondo*. b.) Sometimes used to describe a cut made with the reverse or false edge of the blade.

REVERSE GUARD: A guard position in Broadsword play assumed with the unarmed side leg forward.

REVERSE KNIFE HAND: (also Ridge Hand) An open-handed strike, associated with martial arts, made with the inside edge (thumb side) of the hand. See *Knife Hand*.

REVERSE PASSATA SOTTO: A flamboyant technique that combines a grand volte and the passata sotto. A sort of low line bum–in–the–face.

REVERSE PUNCH: a.) A linear or driving punch, associated with martial arts, that begins with the hand supinated, and as the punch is delivered the hand rotates to prona-tion, adding extra torque to the impact. b.) A term sometimes applied to a strong punch, utilizing the hips and characterized by having the opposite leg forward to the fist used; i.e. left punch/right leg forward and vice versa.

REVERSE ROUNDHOUSE KICK: (also *Heel Hook*) A kick in which the heel, or sole of the foot, that travels towards the target via a circular path. See *Roundhouse Kick*.

REVERSED GRIP: a.) To hold a weapon in a manner directly opposite to that which is intended. b.) A manner of holding a knife or sword where the blade is carried below rather than above the hand. See *Underhand Grip*.

REVES: (Span.) A cutting attack with the false edge of the blade.

RHYTHM: a.) The visible and audible variables of rate within beats and phrases of a fight. b.) The temporal pattern produced by the grouping and balance, or imbalance and unpredictability, of sounds and dialogue during a fight. The strong and weak elements in the flow of sound and silence.

RICASSO: (It.) a.) The thick portion of a blade's tang situated between the pas d'âne and the quillon block used to place the index finger, and sometimes the second finger, around when holding the rapier. The ricasso is necessary for the correct handling of the sword. b.) The flattened part of the tang of the blade, immediately above and within a guard. c.) The thick unsharpened part of a blade that is next to the hilt. d.) 1. "n the Italian foil, which preserves the plate, the section of the blade between that and the grip is called the *Ricasso*. 2. That part of the blade between the cup guard and the quillons of the Italian foils and duelling swords.

RICAVATIONE: (It.) a.) Fabris' term for the *Double Changement*. Like the counter change-ment, the double changement may be either a coupé or a disengage. b.) (also *Ricavzione*) See *Doublé*.

RIDGE HAND: An open-handed strike, associated with martial arts, made with the inside edge (thumb side) of the hand. See *Reverse

Knife Hand.

RIDING THE BLADE: a.) The act of going with or following a *pris d'fer* or other blade taking action for offensive or defensive purposes, usually tactical. b.) To purposely keep blades joined during movement or manipulation.

RIGHT BLOWE: a.) Di Grassi's term for a cutting attack delivered from the weapon bearing or "right" side of the body. See also *Man Dritto Tondo.* b.) Sometimes used to describe a cut made with the right or true edge of the blade.

RIGHT CROSS: a.) A right-hand punch that travels from the right to the left, across the opponent's face. It is delivered with a twist of the waist and upper body to the left. b.) (also *Right Hook*) A punch delivered with the right hand up high at shoulder level. Turn at the waist as you deliver this punch, stepping forward with your left foot and shifting your weight form the ball of your right foot to the left leg. The right cross is frequently a knockout punch for a right-handed boxer. Probably the most important thing to remember is to turn your body to the left at the waist as you throw this punch. The difference between a potent right cross and a weak one lies in twisting properly and shifting your weight and power into the punch. When you throw the right cross, remember also to keep your left low to protect the torso. The right cross is usually the second half of the classic "one- two" combination, however, the right cross can also be effectively used as a lead punch. See *Cross.*

RIGHT DOMINANT: a.) Having the right hand and/or foot forward in an on guard or ready stance. Generally referring to the lead foot in the on guard stance. b.) To have more control in, or to be more dexterous with the right hand.

RIGHT FOOT STANCE: An En Garde that places the right foot on the Forward 45 right, and left foot on Back 45 left of the Imaginary Star, the upper body facing the Line of Engagement.

RIGHT OF WAY: a.) A conventional rule of play for foil and sabre. b.) The convention in Foil and Saber fencing which interdicts the causing of a double hit.

RIGHT-DRAWN: To unsheathe one's sword in a just cause.

RIMESSA: (It.& Ger.) See *Remise.*

RINVERSO TONDO: (It.) (also *Reverso Tondo*) A cutting attack with the false edge of the blade across the eyes in a plane horizontal to the floor.

RIP: (also *Gash*) a.) A violent attack made with the edge of the blade after the knife has penetrated the body with a successful thrust or stab. Once the blade is in the body the edge is forcefully pulled through the flesh, tearing open the body creating a deep laceration. b.) To cut or tear open. A wound to the body made with the edge of a bladed weapon that is more violent and damaging than a drawn cut. c.) To shred or tear fabric or paper.

RIPOSTE: a.) A counter attack launched by the combatant after successfully completing a parry. b.) The offensive action following the parry of an attack. It may be immediate, delayed, or delivered in any line. Any type of blade action may be used, simple or compound; the riposte may be executed from the en garde position, or with a step, Balestra, Lunge or Fleche. c.) A return attack made by a defender immediately following a successful parry.

RISER: A raised fuller ridge providing rigidity and strength on a blade.

RISING BLOCK: a.) A block delivered upward to defend against a descending diagonal or vertical attack. b.) A deflection block, made with either arm, which protects the head.

RISING PARRY: (also *Beat-Aside, Intercept Parry* or *Beat-Down Parry*) A defensive action with a sword that beats the offensive blade aside during the execution of an attack. The rising parry is generally used in defense to a vertical or diagonal attack to the head. The defending blade is brought up to intercept the attacking blade and knock it aside before it lands on its intended target. The rising parry is generally executed with an evasive step. See *Beat-Aside*.

RIVERSO: (also *Manverso*) (It) A left to right cut.

RIVERSO SQUALEMBRATO: (It) A descending diagonal cutting attack delivered from the non-weapon bearing side.

RIVERSO TONDO: (It) A pronated horizontal cutting attack delivered from the non-sword bearing side. *Riverso Tondo Alto* is directed to the opponent's shoulder, *Mezzo* to the hip, and *Basso* to the thigh.

RIVET: a.) A pin of iron driven through a hole, to keep different pieces of armor together. b.) To fasten armor with such a pin. c.) See *Capstan Rivet*.

ROCKING: a.) The back and forth movement of the body during the execution of stationary footwork. b.) In active footwork; a partial advance or retreat (traveling about ½ the distance of a standard footwork) on the part of the combatants.

ROCOCO: a.) Old fashioned, antiquated. b.) Said of blade-play having the characteristics of the furniture or architectural workmanship of Louis Quatorze or Louis Quinze, typified as meaningless decoration; excessively or tastelessly florid or ornate.

ROD: The instrument of chastisement for children (or men compared with children).

ROISTING: Bullying, blustering.

ROLL: a.) A technique often associated with gymnastic exercises in which the body is either placed into a tuck position and turned in a forward or backward circle about an axis parallel to its direction of motion or it is laid out prone and the body is turned about the physical centerline.

ROLL OUT: A flip, throw or fall that is completed with a clean roll, to either side, backward or forward, where the combatant immediately recovers to a kneeling or standing position.

ROLL WITH THE PUNCH: (also Rolling with the Punches) To allow the head and neck to respond properly to the dynamic energy of a punch, slap or blow. The immediate snap or turn of the head at impact.

ROLLING FALL: (also *Tumbling Fall*) A drop (usually forward) in which a person turns heels over head, rolling the length of the spine along the floor.

ROMPRE: (Fr.) See *Breaking Ground*.

ROMPERE DI MISURA: (Fr.) See *Breaking the Measure*.

ROOM TO SWING A CAT, NOT ENOUGH: For punishment and discipline onboard a ship, the cat-o'-nine-tails was used to whip the sailors. The lashes were always dealt out on deck, since below deck there was not enough room to swing a cat.

RONDACHE: (also *Targa*) Larger, less common renaissance battle shields worn on the arm, metal, or wood.

ROTA: A countering technique described by Filippo Vadi (c. 1480). A cut wherein the back edge (fil falso) is quickly raised to smack or deflect an opposing blade prior to an immediate descending cut with the forward edge. The word "rota" comes from the verb "*rotare*", which means "to turn".

ROTATION: a.) The act of turning or rotating a limb (wrist, hand, head, arm, leg, etc.), the body, a weapon or other object, in one direction or another. To turn circle-wise. b.) The act of rotation, or turning, usually 360° in a gymnastic flip, roll or throw.

RONDELLA: (It.) A round buckler, usually metal or leather.

ROTELLA: (It.) A small hand shield similar to the English buckler.

ROUND HOUSE: See *Roundhouse Punch, Roundhouse Kick, Roundhouse Knee*, etc. .

ROUND KICK: A common term for the *Roundhouse Kick*.

ROUND PARADES: (Small Sword) Compound movements, performed with circles of like magnitudes. As the diameters of the circles are demonstrated to be equal to the distance of the wrist from one opposite parade to another that is six inces, so is the periphery of these circles equal to about nineteen inches. See also *Circular Parry*.

ROUND PARRY: See *Circular Parry*.

ROUNDEL: A small round shield.

ROUNDHOUSE: See either *Roundhouse Kick* or *Roundhouse Punch*.

ROUNDHOUSE KICK: A kick delivered from a chambered position of the knee that uses the top of the foot and is generally executed in a horizontal plane.

ROUNDHOUSE PUNCH: (also *Round House Punch, Round-House Punch, John Wayne Punch, Wide Hook Punch* and *Hay Maker Punch*) a.) A large, dynamic, hooking punch that travels in a wide arc across the victim's face, from either right to left, or vice versa, delivered with a rotation of the hips, waist and upper body in the direction the punch is delivered. The roundhouse is often thrown in a wild manner and was made popular in old "Westerns" like those of John Wayne. b.) A large, dynamic, hooking punch that travels in a wide arc across the victim's face, from either right to left, or vice versa.

ROUT: a.) To defeat an opponent and put them to flight in disorder. b.) Uproar, brawl. c.) Disordered flight from a battle or fight.

ROVERSI: (It.) a.) A sixteenth century term for a cutting attack delivered from one's left to the opponent's right side. b.) a cutting attack delivered from the left side, the hand in pronation, delivered to the opponent's right.

ROVESCIO: (It.) (also *Punta Rovescio*) A thrusting attack delivered in supination from one's left to the opponent's right side.

ROW: A noisy disturbance or quarrel; a violent dispute or commotion. Noise, din, clamor.

RUDDER OF THE BLADE: A quaint nickname given to the quillons, which can be used by the combatant to determine where the blade is directed, and help "steer" the blade to its correct placement. See *Quillons*.

RUFFIAN: a.) A brutal, boisterous, mischievous fellow. b.) To play the ruffian, to be boisterous, to rage.

RULES OF DEFENSE: a.) According to English fencing master Joseph Swetnam, there are seven principal rules whereon true defense is grounded. 1.) A good guard. 2.) True observing of distance. 3.) To know the place. 4.) To take the time. 5.) To keep the space. 6.) Patience. 7.) Often practice. b.) In Elizabethan swordplay it was thought that the best defense was a good offense. The manuals of the period speak of the rules of Time, Distance and Proportion. See *Time, Distance* and *Proportion*.

RUMBLE: a.) A street fight between rival gangs. b.) Any large fight whether in scope or numbers. c.) Commotion, bustle, tumult, uproar.

RUN: a.) A continuous series or succession of parries and ripostes. b.) To pierce or stab a person; to "run" them through. c.) To take flight; to retire rapidly; to abscond or desert. See *Cobb's Traverse*.

RUNNING-BUTTOCK: A peculiar throw over the hip made use of in wrestling and formerly in pugilism. See also *Buttock*.

RUSSIAN LUNGE: See *Flying Lunge*.

S

SABER: See *Sabre*.

SABRE: (also *Saber*) a.) A weapon said to be originated by the Turks, adopted by the Hungarians, and became known to western Europe during the eighteenth century, eventually becoming the weapon of the Household Cavalry. From the sixteenth to the eighteenth centuries Turks raided their border countries on fast ponies using their heavy curved weapons, which were very effective for cutting attacks. The Hussars (Hungarian light horsemen), Poles and Austrians resorted to the use of sabres of their own design to combat the marauders. The first mention of the sabre in print is in Marcelli's manual (1686). In the eighteenth century the small sword was deemed the gentleman's weapon; the sabre, practiced by the cavalry of all nations in the eighteenth and early nineteenth century, was considered to be rather a crude affair and was reserved mainly for the military. b.) The only cut and thrust weapon in modern sport fencing; with which the point and the edges (the entire true edge and first two-thirds of the false) may be used on the offensive.

SABREUR: (also *Sabrer*) One who fights with a sabre. Often applied to a soldier in the cavalry who is distinguished for bravery in war rather than skill.

SACK: To loot or plunder.

SAFETY: (also *Safety-Bolt* and *Safety-Catch*) A contrivance for locking the trigger of a gun, so as to prevent accidental discharge.

SALLE: (Fr.) Literally a "hall" or "room". Used in reference to the salle d'armes ("room of arms"), the school or studio where fencing lessons are given, skills practiced and bouts held.

SALTO IN DIETRO: (It.) A jump backward from the position of the grand lunge.

SALUTE: (also *Révérence*) a.) The formal exchange between combatants prior to a duel or fencing bout. This ceremony was first introduced around 1653 by the French Master, Charles Besnard; consisting of a conventional series of guards, appels, thrusts, parries, etc. b.) A formality in modern sport fencing which displays good sportsmanship between the competitors. The modern salute is executed with the weapon, to the opponent, the officials, and spectators. c.) A courteous gesture to the opponent, jury, and audience, at the start and finish of a bout. The salute may be simple or elaborately choreographed as in the civilian and military versions of the "Grand Salute." d.) A courtesy exchanged by the combatants at the start and/or conclusion of an encounter.

SAVATE: (Fr.) French form of kick-boxing based loosely on French small sword play and sport fencing. Sometimes called "Fencing with the Feet." The sport version is called Boxe Francaise.

SBASSO: (It.) See *Low Line Evasion* and *Passata Sotto*.

SCABBARD: The case or sheath that serves to protect the blade of a weapon when not in use. Generally consisting of a stiff body of wood covered with leather, with metal mounts that the sword itself rests in. Scabbards may also be made of metal.

SCALED: Said of armor manufactured with small plates of metal layered like the scales of a fish.

SCALY: Said of scale armor; abounding in, covered with, or consisting of scale armor.

SCANDAGLIO: (It.) The testing and probing of one's opponent. Actions (feints, beats, etc) to test and discover the opponent's nature.

SCANNATURA: (It.) A parry with the hand accompanied by a simultaneous counter attack. First described by Capo Ferro in 1610. See *Hand Parry*.

SCATHE: To injure, to do harm.

SCHERMA: (It.) See *Fencing*.

SCHIAVONA: An Italian cage hilt cut & thrust

sword, usually with a ricasso for fingering.

SCHIVAR DI VITA: The action of voiding the opponent's sword by moving the body out of line.

SCHLAGER: (Germ.) The weapon that replaced rapier play of German students in the early 1830s. See *Schlager Blade.*

SCHLAGER BLADE: (Ger.) a.) A light, long, flat and strong fencing blade with a rounded point, thick shoulders and a substantial tang, designed specifically for edge-to-edge play. b.) The balde of the weapon that replaced the rapier of German students in the early nineteenth century. The blade of the weapon, still used in student "duels," is long and flat with a rounded point, and is of excellent design for edge to edge play.

SCHLAGER DUEL: A formal fight executed with schlagers and by the strict rules set for such a fight.

SCHLAGPARADE: (Ger.) See *Beat Parry.*

SCHOLAR'S PRIVILEGE: In English schools of Defence, the excluding of attacks to the face during practice with novices.

SCIMITAR: A short, curved, single-edged sword, used among Turks and Persians.

SCISSORS KICK: (also *Flying Snap Kick*) A fast kick, executed from a leap, where one leg is carried past the other (while in the air) like a pair of scissors, whipping the leg up from the hip and knee in a form of Snap Kick.

SCISSORS PARRY: a.) A term generally used to describe double fence cross parries where the crossed weapons resemble a pair of scissors. See *Cross Parry.* b.) Any cross weapon parry. c.) (also *Scissoring*) Sometimes used to describe a double fence cross parry where the cross of the blades has closed like a pair of scissors.

SCOOPING THE PARRY: (also *Scooping*) An increased arc in the blade's path (especially in semicircular parries) that carries the hand through the plane of the intended attack. A dangerous practice because the attack may arrive at the target before the hand has finished moving into place, accidentally striking the hand.

SCORCH: a.) A mark or impression produced by a superficial burn. b.) To strip off (skin or bark), to flay.

SCORE: A crack, cut, notch, or scratch; a line drawn with a sharp instrument.

SCOTCH: a.) A gash, cut or slash. A slight cut or incision. b.) To cut or gash.

SCOURGE: a.) A whip or lash; used with reference to the torturing of human beings, or as the symbol of punishment and vindictive affliction. b.) To whip, to lash for punishment or torture.

SCRATCH: a.) A slight tearing or incision of the skin produced by a sharp instrument such as the finger nails or the tip of a blade. b.) A scraping or slashing attack made with one or more fingernails of the open hand, usually delivered to exposed skin or other such sensitive body areas. c.) An attack made by 'raking' one or more fingernails over a piece of flesh. d.) A light, flicking cut generally made with the tip of the knife rather than the edge. e.) Sometimes applied slightingly to a trifling flesh-wound. f.) A line or mark drawn as an indication of a boundary or starting-point; in Pugilism, the line drawn across the ring, to which boxers are brought for an encounter. g.) A skirmish, a trivial fight.

SCRIMER: A term believed to be coined by Shakespeare, meaning a person who partakes in swordplay; a fencer. (Possibly from the French escrim)

SCROOGE: British slang for the *Froissement.*

SCUTCHEON: (also *Escutcheon*) The shield or shield-shaped surface on which a coat of arms is depicted; also in wider sense, the shield with the armorial bearings; a sculptured or painted representation of this.

SECOND: a.) The guard or parry defending the outside low line with the hand holding the weapon in pronation. See *Seconde.* b.) Literally in reference to the "next," the person coming after the first, or principal duelist. Generally one or more friends of the parties involved in a duel whose duty was to convey the challenge and see to arranging the details of the actual encounter. During the hay-day of dueling, several conventions concerning the second developed, notably seconds were often expected to engage one another in combat, sometimes in an orderly fashion, sometimes like a brawl where any victorious member could then come to the aid of anyone he chooses. In more "civilized" duels a second could be expected to face the opposing principal, as well as his second(s) if his friend should not be able to continue.

SECOND CAUSE: See *First and Second Cause.*

SECOND COUNTER-RIPOSTE: The defender's second riposte.

SECOND INTENTION: a.) A tactical attack designed to score on the counter riposte. b.) An action made with a preconceived trap in mind, such as a false attack intended to draw a riposte.

SECOND STRING: During the Middle Ages archers would often carry a spare bowstring in case the first became damaged or broke. The term for such a replacement has carried into modern sports with its second string players and team. In the case of the medieval bowman, the second string was a replacement generally equal to the first while the athletic second string is a replacement, but generally inferior to the first. "Second string" now carries its latter meaning: a replacement implicitly inferior to the first.

SECONDA INTENZIONE: (It.) See *Second Intention.*

SECONDA: (It.) (also *Seconda Guardia*) (from the Latin Secundo - "secondly") a.) (also *Seconda Proper*) The singe weapon guard assumed with the arm and blade held completely horizontal to the floor, the hand in pronation with the arm fully extended, the body square to the opponent, tip at shoulder level (Standard or Across). b.) (also *Double Fence Seconda*) The extended guard of the sword-bearing hand where the rapier hand assumes Seconda proper and the dagger is held in Dagger Terza with the dagger hand

placed roughly ten to twelve inches in front of the body just above waist level.

SECONDE: (also *Second*) a.) The guard and parry in small sword, transitional rapier and modern fencing that closes (protects) the low outside line, taken with the point lower than the hand, which is pronated. b.) Often applied to the Transitional Rapier Parry of Two.

SECONDE PARADE: (Small Sword) "A lower outward parade, the nails being reversed, as in tierce; and it forms the same angle with guard point as semicircle, and has for its opposite the inward parade of prime."

SECONDE THRUST: (Small Sword) "The natural and corresponding thrust to the parade of seconde; but it is often delivered after parrying your adversary's thrust with tierce- The nails are turned downwards when you thrust seconde, in the same manner as when you form that parade, and your adversary's blade is opposed outwards."

SEGNO: A training aid consisting of a circular wall or floor diagram of 8 intersecting lines representing all possible cutting angles and thrust, or when placed on the floor, stepping positions for the feet.

SEGNO CUTS: Fiore Dei Liberi described seven cuts or blows, two *Fendenti* (right or left downward cuts from a high position) two *Sottani* (right or left upward cuts from a low position), two *Mezani* or *Mezzane* (horizontal cuts), and *Ponte* (the straight thrust). Filippo Vadi taught the same six cuts and one thrust, but called his horizontal cuts Volanti. Vadi's right-to-left cuts are Derito and his left-to-right cuts were *Manreverso*. While Filippo Vadi speaks of "seven cuts", he lists only three (*Fendente, Volanti*, and the *Rota*), but as each of these can be employed either left or right, along with *Punte* (his thrust) they make for seven attacks. Neither Fiore Dei Liberi nor Fillipo Vadi distinguished between different angles vertical or diagonal) of cut, all descending cuts were *Fendenti*. Pietro Monte advised *Manudextri* (blows from right to left) and *Manusinistri* (from left to right). Monte taught only 2 primary cuts: both diagonal rising cuts from either right or left (and a thrust, *Stocchata Vel Puncta*). These cuts and thrusts were invariably used in swift combinations of 2 to 3 strokes.

SEIZURE: To grasp or take hold of the opponent's sword hand, hilt or weapon with intent to disarm them. See also *Grasp*.

SEMICIRCLE PARADE: (Small Sword) "A lower inward parade. In performing it from either of the guards, the point froms a curve resembling a half circle. The angle that this parade makes with guard point is forty-five degrees nearly. Octave Parade is the opposite and outward." See also *Semicircular Parry*.

SEMICIRCLE THRUST: (Small Sword) "Generally termed the thrust of low carte, Is the natural thrust corresponding to the parade of semi-circle- It is a lower inward thrust, and you oppose your adversary's blade inwards."

SEMICIRCULAR PARRY: A defensive action of the blade where the hand maintains its same relative placement and the blade moves from one position to another in a semicircular path. The starting and ending point of the blade are in the same vertical plane, changing line but remaining on the same side of the body. The point of the blade describes an arc, not a straight line, as the parrying movement follows a semicircular path from one position to another.

SENSING THE STEEL: (also Sentiment de Fer) A kind of intuition, or "sixth-sense," that stretches the fencer's tactile sensibility up to the very point of the blade granting the fencer's hand a special guessing instinct that warns them of the intentions and the will of their opponent, allowing the fencer to anticipate them. This process of feeling the blade and reading the opponent's attack may well have been the reason blades were originally engaged in combat. As early as the works of di Grassi, the idea of joining the blades to "feel" the opponent's movements was suggested.

SEPARAZIONE: (It.) To separate engaged blades.

SEPTIME: (also *Seventh*) a.) The guard and parry of small sword and modern fencing that closes (protects) the low inside line, with the point lower than the hand, which is in supination. b.) The guard or parry defending the inside low line with the hand holding the weapon in supination. c.) Often applied to the *Transitional Rapier Parry of Seven*.

SEPTIMO: A lifted parry of seven that prepares the defender for an immediate riposte into the low line.

SEQUENCIAL PARRIES: a.) A term in Double Fence for two separate parries (1- primary, 2- secondary) executed against the same attack. The primary parry leaves the opposing blade before the secondary parry is engaged. b.) A term sometimes applied to the Transfer Parry. c.) Parries executed in numerical order, one after the other.

SERE: (also *Sear*) A term used to describe someone as a coiled spring; derived from the catch of a gun-lock which keeps the hammer at full or half cock, thus a person ready to go off at any time.

SERPENTINE ARM BAR: A joint lock made with the whole arm where the aggressor's arm is wrapped around one or both of the victim's arms like a serpent, trapping it in the armpit and applying pressure to the elbow with the trapping arm's hand.

SESSA: (also *sa-sa*) A cry of incitement in fencing; an exclamation of uncertain meaning, possibly derived from the French cessez or sessez (or the German sasa), meaning "cease," or the Spanish cessa meaning "be quiet."

SESTA: (It.) (also *Sesta Guardia* and *Double Fence Sesta*) The Double Fence guard where the rapier hand assumes the placement of single rapier Low Terza (Standard), the hand drawn back to the side of the body at waist-level and the dagger in a variation of single weapon Terza (Standard) with the arm extended forward, the hand at roughly chest level.

SET UP: a.) A feint attack with the edge aimed at a target on the opponent other than that which is the real object of the attack. b.) Returning to, recovering to, or assuming the correct position and placement for a specific sequence or a particular move. c.) Moving or manipulating an opponent into a particular position or place for the execution of a pre-planned move or sequence.

SEVEN, PARRY OF: a.) Defense for an attack to the non-weapon bearing thigh. The hilt and hand below waist level, palm towards the opponent, blade below the hand, its forte at the level of the non-weapon bearing leg's quadriceps, just above the knee. b.) (also *Parry Septime*) Protecting the low inside line with the point down, the hand in supination. c.) Broadsword defense against a Low Inside Cut, made with the palm of the lead hand facing up and the blade angled down. This parry has a beautiful diagonal sweep from guard.

SFORZO: (It.) See *Froissement*.

SGUALEMBRATO: (It.) A descending diagonal cutting attack; Man Dritto from the right, Reverso from the left. See *Man Dritto Squalembrato* and *Reverso Squalembrato*.

SHAFT: The long slender rod forming the body of a quarterstaff, spear, lance, arrow, etc., hence, a term for a quarterstaff, spear, lance or arrow.

SHAKE: a.) The preliminary formality of shaking hands, with a bidding farewell to the opponent, between two duelists. b.) An aggressive act made by one or more people to a single victim where they are grabbed and violently shook towards some effect; generally to disturb or unsettle the victim.

SHAKE OFF: The ability or apparent ability to take a powerful hit or blow and simply "shake off" its effects and keep on going.

SHARP: To have a keen edge or point; being well suited for cutting or piercing; a blade tapered to a fine edge or point; opposite to blunt.

SHARP-POINTED: Having a sharp point.

SHEARING CUT: A descending diagonal attack with the sword intended to meet a hanging parry and slide down the defending blade in a manner similar to the closing of a pair of scissors.

SHEARING PARRY: A defensive blade actions designed to deflect an attack, allowing the offending blade to slide or graze down the defending blade rather than stopping or opposing the attack. See *Hanging Parry* and *Shearing Cut*.

SHEATH: The case, covering, home or lodging for the blade of a weapon when not in use; usually close fitting and conforming to the shape of the blade, the blade is generally thrust into the sheath by way of an opening at its top. See *Scabbard*.

SHEATHE: a.) To put, place or thrust a sword (dagger, etc.) into its sheath or scabbard. The action of putting into a sheath. b.) To hide; to cover; to put up in general. c.) To put, place, thrust or bury a sword (dagger, etc.) into an enemy's body, to the hilt, as in a sheath. d.) To fit or furnish a bladed weapon with a sheath.

SHEATHED: Said of any bladed weapon put into or encased in a sheath.

SHEATHING: a.) The process of placing a sword (dagger, etc.) into its sheath or scabbard. b.) The process of having a sheath made.

SHELL: a.) The coquille or guard. b.) (Small Sword) That part of the hilt or handle of a sword or foil next the blade, serving both for an ornament and guard. Shells that are made with pierced or open work are esteemed the most serviceable, as they are apt to entangle your adversay's point that with an abrupt turn of your wrist there is a probability of either disarming him or breaking the foible of his blade. See also *Shell-Guard*.

SHELL-GUARD: A portion of a sixteenth century sword hilt named for its resemblance to an open seashell. The shell was seated below the shoulder of the blade, atop the pas d'ane, and could be affixed to one or both sides of the hilt.

SHIELD BOSS: (also Shield-Boss) a.) A metal

fixture usually mounted in the center of a shield intended to deflect or break the blow of an opponent. Many of these bosses had hooks, spikes and other such devices that could be used to trap and break the opposing weapon as well as being used as an offensive weapon themselves. In referring to the buckler, many fifteenth and sixteenth century fencing manuals refer to the spike or point emitting from the center of the buckler. Such a spike proved profitable in close-quarter combat. "It shall be also verie profitable, that in the midst of the Buckler, there be a sharpe poynt or stert of Iron, to the end the enimie may be stroken therwith when occasion serveth." [Di Grassi ff - 84-85] b.) A person armed with or carrying a shield.

SHIELD: a.) In ancient and medieval warfare, and still in that of primitive peoples, an article of defensive armor (made of various materials, as metal, wood, wickerwork covered with skins or leather, etc.) carried in the hand or attached by a strap to the non-weapon bearing arm of a soldier, as a protection from the weapons of the enemy. The form has varied greatly in different periods and countries; the principal types are (1) the circular shield, usually convex in front, with a boss in the center; (2) the oblong shield, either flat, or, more commonly, having the form of a portion of a cylinder; and (3) the shield with curved sides tapering to a point at the lower end, which was the prevailing form in Europe during the Middle Ages. In the Middle Ages the "armorial bearings" of a knight were depicted on their shield, and decorated shields, made for display and not for warlike use, were often hung on walls in churches or other buildings as a memorial of a knight or noble. b.) An article of this kind larger than the buckler, which was usually carried in the hand, and smaller than the pavis, which was held by an attendant in front of a knight or archer. c.) To guard, to protect as if with a shield.

SHIN BLOCK: A defensive action made with the shin and/or the muscle groupings of the

lower leg, generally made by bending at the knee and lifting the leg up to oppose a kick or similar attack.

SHIN KICK: A kick or kicking action generally associated with the martial arts, made with the shin of the leg rather than with the foot.

SHOCK: To meet with force, to encounter, to face.

SHORT FORM: A hand position for quarterstaff that divides the staff into three equal sections.

SHORT SWORD: (also *Short-Sword* and *English Short Sword*) a.) A common term for the traditional English single-handed broadsword; in most popular use from around the beginning of the sixteenth century until the turn of the seventeenth century. A sword with a stout, short blade, roughly the length of a man's arm, furnished with a simple cross hilt, pas d'âne, side-ring and often a knuckle bow. Intended to be used with a buckler for defense and the strong and swift cut on the offense. This was the traditional weapon of England, used in conjunction with the buckler; in most popular use from around the beginning of the sixteenth century until the turn of the seventeenth century. The sword and buckler was replace by the rapier and dagger, which become popular during the mid sixteenth century. Stout, true blooded Englishmen, however, disapproved of the Italian and Spanish rapier play and held fast to their heritage and beliefs in the sword and buckler; some, well into the first quarter of the seventeenth century. The sword and buckler was generally considered out of fashion in the court and among nobles in England by the end of the first half of the sixteenth century. See *True English Fight* and *Sword and Buckler*. b.) A term often mistakenly applied to the short bladed Roman *Gladius*. c.) A sword that is not long.

SHOULDER CUT: (also *Full Cut* and *Standard Cut*) a.) Large, sweeping, cutting attacks delivered with the whole arm from the shoulder. See also *Piston Cut.* b.) Any cutting attack delivered to the shoulder. c.) A term used in sabre fencing for a cutting attack made to the weapon bearing side of the body at roughly chest level. In a proper on guard stance the foot of the weapon bearing side is carried forward, slightly turning the body to the inside and exposing the bottom of the outside deltoid muscle to the cut more than the non-weapon bearing shoulder. Opposite of a *Chest Cut.*

SHOULDER RAM: (also *Shoulder Smash*) A hard, driving strike in which the shoulder is used like a battering ram, hitting the victim with the point of the shoulder.

SHOULDERS: a.) A step or notch in the blade of the sword where it narrows from forte to tang designed to meet flush and flat to the hilt of the sword (on the quillon block and often the pas d'âne) to minimize torque and strain on the tang of the weapon. See *Tang* and *Slop.* b.) The target in cutting and thrusting attacks situated on the arm at the notch where the deltoid and biceps meet (at roughly chest level).

SHOVE: A strong or violent thrust or push with the feet, hands or body, quickly moving a body away from the agent. See *Push.*

SHUNT: A sudden striking or knocking away of a parried blade with the hilt of the sword. See *Beat Away.*

SHUNT DISARM: The use of a Shunt or Beat Away against the opposing blades forte to facilitate a disarm. Often executed from a Bind Over or Heavy Parry.

SHUTO: (MA) See *Knife Hand.*

SIDE KICK: a.) A kick using the heel or edge of the foot, delivered out from the side of the body. b.) A form of push kick using the heel or edge of the foot, delivered out from the side of the body.

SIDEARM: a.) A weapon worn at the side, such as a pistol, knife, dagger, sword, etceteras. b.) An additional weapon used in conjunction with a sword or rapier. Such as a cloak, dagger, buckler, target, etceteras.

SIDE-RING: (also Side Ring) A ring or rings placed on the side of the hilt intended to protect the knuckles and the backside of the sword hand. See *Parrying Dagger, Upper Side-Ring,* and *Lower Side-Ring.*

SIDESTEP EVASION: Evasive actions that remove the body from the cutting plane of a diagonal or vertical swipe by lunging either to the left or to the right and leaning the torso into the lunge, creating, with the body, a parallel plane to the attack outside the cutting plane. See *Traverse Evasion.*

SIEGE: a.) The act of besetting a fortified place. b.) The term is also used metaphorically for any strong endeavor to gain entrance, assault or attack to the senses; generally in cases of love and death.

SIMPLE ATTACK: a.) An action comprised of two separate attacks; an Indirect Attack (such as a changement, attack on the blade or pris d'fer) that removes the opposing blade and opens the line for an immediate Direct Attack. Although this action is comprised of two separate attacks, Indirect and Direct, it is assumed to be the simplest attack possible in swordplay because a Direct Attack launched on an effective guard will either meet the defending blade or impale the aggressor. Thus, the simplest attack is to displace the opposing blade and then strike in one swift motion. b.) An attack made with one movement either direct or indirect. c.) An attack executed in one fencing "time", such as a thrust, disengage, coupe, counter-disengage, and counter-coupe.

SIMPLE BEAT: See *Direct Beat.*

SIMPLE CHANGEMENT: Any blade movement made from one guard position to another that does not require manipulation around, over or under the opposing blade.

SIMPLE FOOTWORK: Base elements of footwork that involve the execution of one component, such as the *Advance.*

SIMPLE PARRY: Any parry made by a simple lateral movement carrying the blade horizontally across the body.

Simultaneous Attacks: Two attacks launched at the same time.

Single Feint Attack: (also *Simple Feint Attack*) The feint of a direct attack, followed by a deception of parry and ending with an actual direct attack in a different line.

Single Fight: a.) A fight or combat consisting of two participants; personal combat; a duel. b.) Something unmarried couples do with reckless abandon.

Single Hand Choke: A strangling action usually made from the front, executed with a single hand, the fingers on one side of the neck and the thumb at the throat.

Single Passe Backward: (also *Single Pass Backward*) A walking step backward that places the front foot behind the rear foot. See also *Pass Backward*.

Single Passe Forward: (also *Single Pass Forward*) A walking step forward that places the rear foot in front of the leading foot. See also *Pass Forward*.

Single Rapier: The rapier alone. In many sixteenth and seventeenth century schools of fence, the single rapier was considered the foundation of the science of arms and the best possible style to introduce to a novice.

Single Stick: a.) Fighting, fencing, or exercise with a stick provided with a guard or basket and requiring only one hand. See also *Back Sword*. b.) (MA) A fighting stick, baton or jo light enough to be used in one hand, often wielded with a second weapon such as a dagger or knife, but is used alone to function both offensively and defensively.

Single Sword: Any sword light enough to be used in one hand, generally wielded with a second weapon such as a dagger or buckler, but is used alone to function both offensively and defensively. See *Transitional Rapier* and *Single Rapier*.

Single Time: (also *Stesso Tempo*) a.) Where the parry and riposte are one action rather than two separate actions. Opposite of *Double Time*. b.) The idea and practice of the Elizabethan swordsman that the best defense was a good offense. Inasmuch that to parry and defend in one action was much wiser, swifter, and truer than to defend in one action and then counter attack in another; in the manner of the Transitional Rapier and Small Sword. c.) The time it would take to complete one simple attack.

Single Weapon: a.) Working with only one weapon, be it rapier, sword, dagger, etc. Mechanics or techniques concerned with the management of a solo weapon. b.) The handling of a weapon in a solo manner whether or not there is a second weapon in the other hand.

Sit Throw: A wrestling or grappling technique that takes hold of the victim by the hands or arms and uses the aggressor's foot as a fulcrum for leverage against the victim's center by placing it on their stomach and then sitting down on the other leg, pulling the victim off balance and throwing them over the aggressor's head by extending the leg placed on their stomach.

Sitting Down: See *Demi-Plie*.

Six, Parry of: a.) The single weapon defensive action for a thrusting attack to the mid torso, the hand supinated (picking up the attacking blade with the false or back edge) with the blade above the hand. Due to the delicate nature of this parry, it is generally only used in transitional rapier play and small sword fence. b.) (also *Parry Sixte*) a.) Protecting the high outside line (the same as a parry Tierce or 3), except the hand is held in supination. Usually used against a thrust. b.) Defense for a descending vertical or diagonal cut to the head with the blade held above the head, the hand and hilt held on the non-weapon bearing side of the body. Sometimes called "5A.". d.) roadsword defense against a Shoulder Cut or thrust, made with the point up, the hands a little higher than the waist and pushed out slightly away from the body; the blade points almost straight up, defending the outside high line with the false edge of the blade. Being a false edge parry, this parry is not commonly used for broadsword.

SIXTE: (also *Sixth*) a.) The guard in small sword, transitional rapier and modern fencing that closes (protects) the high outside line; taken with the point higher than the hand, which is supinated. b.) The parry in transitional rapier and small sword executed with the point higher than the hand, which is supinated, closing the high outside line. c.) The guard or parry defending the outside high line with the hand holding the weapon in supination.

SKATING PARRY: (also *Slide Parry*) A Beat Parry executed down the opposing blade toward its foible rather than out in opposition.

SKIFTING: (also *Skiffing*) a.) To move lightly and quickly; to skip, run, glide, etc. b.) To shift, change or move the body. A term for movements of the head, body and/or feet, either to the right, left or backward in order to dodge an attack. See *Avoidance* and *Slipping a Punch*.

SKIRMISH: a.) An irregular engagement between two small bodies of troops, esp. detached or outlying portions of opposing armies. b.) A petty fight or encounter. c.) To engage in a skirmish or irregular encounter; to fight in small parties. d.) A mode of fighting.

SLAP: a.) A smart blow, especially one given with the open hand, usually to the face; or with something having a flat surface; a smack; an impact of this nature. A slap can be delivered either Forehand or Backhand. 1. Forehand Slap: An open hand blow delivered with the palm and fingers of the hand, generally swung across the plane of the face. 2. Backhand Slap: A slap delivered with the back rather than the palm of the hand. b.) Attack made with either side of the open hand usually "delivered" to the face. c.)

SLASH: a.) A strong cutting stroke delivered by a sweep or stroke with the edge of the knife, producing a long and deep or severe cut, gash or wound. b.) See *Swipe*. c.) To strike and cut with a sharp weapon.

SLAUGHTER: a.) The act of slaying or killing. b.) To slay, to kill, to murder. c.) Great destruction of life, massacre.

SLAUGHTERER: A murderer; a slayer.

SLAUGHTERMAN: A slayer, destroyer, murderer.

SLAY: a.) To violently kill; to strike, smite or deliver a mortal blow; to put to death by means of a weapon. b.) A metaphor for any annihilation, destruction or ruin.

SLAYER: One that slays; a killer.

SLEEPER HOLD: (also *Sleeper Lock* and *Sleeper Choke*) A popular hold in "pro-wrestling" matches where the victim is taken from behind, one arm wrapped about the neck and its hand placed in the crook of the free arm's elbow. The free arm then locks the hand in place by bending the arm and places its hand on the back of the recipient's head; forcing it down and forward into the strangling arm; thus cutting off the air supply and putting them to "sleep."

Slice: (also Draw Cut) A clean and easy cutting stroke delivered by drawing the edge of the knife along the surface of an object, producing a thin, shallow cut or wound.

SLIDE PARRY: (also *Slide Back Parry*) A Beat Parry executed down the opposing blade toward its foible rather than out in opposition. See *Skating Parry*.

SLING: A missile weapon with which stones are thrown.

SLINGING STEEL: Slang for crossing swords in offensive and defensive play whether as an exercise or for rehearsal. Swordplay.

SLIP: a.) An evasive action executed either to the right or left used to avoid both ascending and descending diagonal swipes. The feet remain stationary and the torso leans away from the attack, straightening the leg and creating a diagonal at roughly forty-five degrees to the floor. b.) A movement of the head or body, either to the right, left, forward or backward, used to avoid a punch or minimize its impact. See *Slipping a Punch*. c.) A circular step that takes the body off-line to either the right or left and ending with the legs crossed. See also *Demi-Volte*. d.) See *Slip Backward* and *Slip Forward*. e.) A Posted Circular Step, Traversing to the Back 45 degree line, taking the body Off-Line to either the right or left and ending with the legs crossed. f.) A accidental or apparently accidental stumble or shifting of the feet that takes the individual off balance, sometimes to the floor.

SLIP BACKWARD: a.) An evasive action that removes the body with a sloped pace backward on a diagonal, roughly forty-five degrees off the parallel tracks of linear footwork. The evasive step can be executed to either the right or left with either foot leading. The foot is lunged backward and to the side, executing a demi- or grand lunge to the rear onto the diagonal path of the sloped pace. The trunk of the body remains facing forward but leans into the lunge following the line of the straightened lead leg. If the torso is turned away from the opponent, be sure to maintain visual contact. b.) An accidental or apparently accidental stumble that carries the individual backward, sometimes to the floor.

SLIP FORWARD: a.) An evasive action that removes the body with a sloped pace forward on a diagonal, roughly forty-five degrees off the parallel tracks of linear footwork. The evasive step can be executed to either the right or left with either foot leading. The foot is lunged forward and to the side, executing a demi- or grand lunge onto the diagonal path of the sloped pace. The trunk of the body remains facing forward but leans into the lunge following the line of the straightened lag leg. If the torso is turned away from the opponent, be sure to maintain visual contact. b.) A accidental or apparently accidental stumble that carries the individual forward, sometimes to the floor.

SLIP STEP: An off-line action of footwork where the moving foot slips behind the stationary foot.

SLIP TO THE 90: A Slip stepping farther through to the 90 degree line to either the right or left. A specific type of Slip to the 90 Right is also called a Demi-Volte.

SLIP TO THE FORWARD 45: A Slip stepping deeper around the Imaginary Star to the Forward 45-degree line to either the right or left. A specific type of Slip to the Forward 45 Right is also called a *Volte*.

SLIPPING: Gaining reach by sliding the hand down the grip to the pommel when striking with a cutting blade (also throwing out a one handed thrust with a pole arm).

SLIPPING A PUNCH: A movement of the head or body, either to the right, left, forward or backward, used to avoid a punch.

SLISH AND SLASH: Much swinging and cutting of weapons.

SLIT: To cut lengthwise

SLOGAN: A term derived originally from the Scottish Gaelic sluag-ghairm, meaning the ferocious, terrifying war-cry or battle cry emitted by fierce Scottish Highlanders or Borderers, or by the native Irish, usually consisting of a personal surname or the name of a gathering-place.

SLOP: a.) Said of careless swordplay with uncertain attacks and parries. b.) A term for poorly fitted or manufactured parts of a sword or poorly assembled weapons with gaps, shims or wedges to make it all fit.

SLOPED PACE: a.) (also *Croked Pace*) Any footwork executed on the four diagonal planes that run at a forty-five degree angle to linear tracks of straight pace footwork. Sloped Paces may be taken forward to the right (NE), backward to the right (SE), backward to the left (SW), and forward to the left (NW). See also *Ten Directions of Footwork*. b.) Side steps on the imaginary circle, to either the right or the left, where the feet do not cross one another.

SMALL STEP: (also *stretto passo* or *piccol passo*) An advance or retreat that is more a shuffle than a proper step.

SMALL SWORD: a.) The last form of the rapier, first adopted by the French between 1650 and 1660, coming into fashion in England around the Restoration period, in Spain and Italy (and Germany to a lesser degree) in the late eighteenth century, and continuing in use in the European community for as long as swords were worn as part of civilian dress. A sword with a light, triangular, fluted blade (used only for thrusting) with a very simple hilt consisting of two half shells, or an elliptical plate, and a smaller guard for the hand and fingers. b.) The light, thrusting weapon that superseded the transition rapier at the turn of the eighteenth-century. c.) The Restoration period sword form taught as one of the eight testing disciplines of the SAFD. d.) A term mistakenly applied to the *Short Sword*.

SMART: a.) Painful, pungent. b.) To feel a pungent pain. c.) To cause pain.

SNAKE HAND DISARM: See *Wrap-n-Trap*.

SNAP KICK: A fast kick, generally from the hip and knee, which relies upon a spring-like delivery. Depending on the technique or discipline, the actual attack can be made with the heel, toe, ball or instep of the foot.

SNUFF: Quarrels.

SOFT PARRY: (also *Short Parry,* rarely *Flick Cut*) Defensive actions against standard thrusting attacks that meet the arm of the aggressor instead of the "Hard" steel of their blade. The "parry" places the flat of the blade's foible or middle onto the middle of the aggressor's forearm, usually on the inside. The movement of the defensive hand is an exaggerated execution of a standard parry, much like an extended parry.

SOMERSAULT: a.) A roll or tumble (usually forward) in which a person travels lengthwise across the floor, turning heels over head and returning to the primary starting position. The roll is executed down the back, rolling the length of the spine along the floor. b.) A leap or spring in which a person turns heels over head in the air and alights on his feet; esp. such a feat as performed by acrobats or tumblers. A forward flip. c.) Forward or backward rotation through the air.

SORTIE: A dash or sally by a besieged army or military force upon an investing force.

SOUTHPAW LEAD: Slang for a left dominant guard or stance.

SPADA: (It.) Literally "Sword." Generally referring to the rapier.

SPADE DA FILO: (Sp.) Sharp or edged blade.

SPADA DA GIOCO: (also *Spade da Marra*) (Sp.) Practice sword, as opposed to sharp or edged blades (*Spade da Filo*).

SPADA DI MARRA: (also *Spada Nera*) (Sp.) Historical Spanish practice rapiers which were untipped (also Italian *smarra*, and *fioretto* or foil)

SPADA IN ARME': ("Sword and Armor") Italian for combat in plate armor or "heavy armor" (called *Harnischfechten* in German).

SPADA LIBERA: - (It.) Literally "Sword Free." Keeping your sword in such a way (by space or leverage) that the opponent does not have leverage on it or the "advantage of the sword."

SPADA E PUGNALE: Italian for "sword and dagger", usually a rapier & dagger. See *Rapier and Dagger*.

SPADA SOLA: (It.) Literally "Sword alone." See *Single Rapier*.

SPANISH BLADE: a.) A superior blade; one of the best blades available. Toledo, Spain was considered to be one of the best manufacturers of sword blades during the Elizabethan era. b.) A rapier furnished with a blade manufactured in Spain. See *Spanish Sword*.

SPANISH DAGGER: A form of parrying dagger that appeared in the second quarter of the seventeenth century, consisting of a bigger weapon, with a longer, heavier blade, long straight quillons (often reaching 11 inches or more tip to tip), a long and stout blade (with total lengths of 19 inches or more) and a wide triangular guard that curved from the quillons to the pommel, protecting the combatant's hand and knuckles.

SPANISH GUARD: a.) (Single Rapier) The on-guard position for the sixteenth and seventeenth century Spanish style of fence is Seconda Proper with the legs practically straight, the upper torso upright and the left hand outside the body at about waist level. It is in this position that the Spaniards traversed their Mysterious Circle. b.) The cup-hilt of the Spanish rapier.

SPANISH SCHOOL: The fantastical style of swordplay created by Commander Jeronimo de Carranza and first put into print in 1569. The system based its principals on seemingly irrelevant mathematical principles and used angles, arcs and related tangents to explain its superiority. It was claimed that a comprehensive knowledge of geometry and natural philosophy within the established principles would lead to victory. Don Luis Pacheco de Narvaez, a student of Carranza, became the master of the Spanish school in the later part of the sixteenth and early seventeenth century. He offered his own reproduction of Carranza's work, where he verbosely expounded the dignified, but unrealis¬tic principles of the Spanish school, basing his system on the imaginary circle.

SPANISH SWORD: A term for the rapier used by Englishmen exposed to the Spanish weapon in the court of Mary Tudor, preceding the introduction to the Italian weapon and school.

SPARRING: Fight training that simulates conditions in an actual bout or combat.

SPARRING PARTNER: A person with whom you spar during training.

SPEAR HAND: [MA] a.) A jabbing or thrusting technique in unarmed combat that utilizes the finger tips. b.) An open-handed strike, associated with martial arts, that utilizes the finger tips for jabbing or thrusting techniques similar to a thrust with a spear.

SPEAR: A pole-arm of considerable length with a stout wooden shaft and a sharp pointed head of either iron or steel; designed solely for piercing with the point; a lance. A shorter and lighter weapon of the same design was used for throwing.

SPECTACLE: A specially arranged or prepared exhibition, especially on a large scale, de-signed to impress those viewing it; a grand display; an entertainment of marvelous scale and proportion.

SPEED: The velocity or rate at which a fight is moving. The degree of quickness of movement, both of sword and body, usually as a result of exertion, clarity, swiftness; also the power or rate of progress.

SPENT ACTION: A term used by George Silver for the condition of activity, at work, in practical or effective operation of the body and weapon that has been completed, or is deprived of force or strength. See also *Action*.

SPIGOLI: (It.) See *Edge*.

SPIN: a.) An act or spell of revolving or whirling round; a circular or rotatory movement. b.) (also Full Turn) An extended grand volte that turns the combatant 360 degrees on the foot as a single axis, like a drafting compass.

SPIT: a.) To put as on a spit. b.) A deliberate expectoration of saliva, or the illusion thereof, from the mouth. Often made at or onto someone as a sign of hate or disgust.

SPONTOON: A form of half-pike or halberd carried by officers in the infantry during the eighteenth century.

SPOOF: A parody of something; a hoax; humbugging.

SPOTTER: In target practice, one who notes the point where a shot strikes; a marker.

SQUABBLE: To quarrel, to brawl.

SQUALEMBRATO: A diagonal cut down or up (*Mandritta Squalembrato* = right-to-left, collar-to-waist cut; *Riverso Squalembrato* = left to right).

SQUARE: To quarrel.

SQUARER: A quarreler.

SQUAT DUCK: (also *Duck*) A deep bend in the knees that lowers the torso, displacing the head from target of a horizontal attack.

SQUIRE: a.) In the military organization of the later Middle Ages, a young man of good birth attendant upon a knight. b.) A gentleman ranking just below a knight under the feudal system of military service and tenure c.) allusion to a popular romance entitled

`The Squire of low degree'. d.) A NCO – Non Commissioned Officer.

STAB: a.) To drive, to plunge, to thrust or kill with the point of a weapon. b.) To make or offer a thrust with the point of a weapon. c.) An attack made with the point of the knife delivered from a reverse or underhand position

STABILITY: Firm balance during the execution of technique or in a particular stance.

STACCATA: (also Staccado & Steccata) Lists to fight or joust in. See *Field of Play*.

STACCATO: Clear-cut detached or disconnected engagements of the blades.

STAFF: (also *Stave*) a.) A stick, pole or club used for support or as a weapon; a quarterstaff. b.) The shaft of a lance, and the lance itself. (to break a staff = to break a lance in tilting, combat with a lance...)

STAMP: Attack made with the foot 'sandwiching' a part of the victim's body between something immobile and the attacker's foot.

STAMPING KICK: (also *Stomp Kick*) A kick with the heel, ball or flat of the foot that is generally directed downwards; such as at the knee, shin or instep.

STANCE: a.) The specific positioning of the feet and body as part of correct physical placement for a particular technique or form of combat. b.) See *Postura*.

STANCE & BALANCE: Always stand with your weight centered and knees slightly bent. This stance allows for freedom of movement in all directions. If your weight is leaning on one leg or the other, it will be hard to change directions when needed.

STAND: To hold one's position against an opponent or enemy; to make a stand; to fight.

STANDARD: The normal or common application of a technique. Applied to guard, parry, footwork and offensive/defensive positions that are regular or prevalent placements.

STANDARD CUT: See *Shoulder Cut*.

STANDARD PARRY: See *Opposition Parry*.

STANDING LUNGE: A thrust with the sword arm punched forward by a weight shift onto the lead leg and a slight turning in the torso.

STANDING VOLTE: An evasive action of the body where the upper body pivots ninety degrees as the lower body "rocks" away from the attack (generally a thrust) without moving the feet. If a thrust comes to the left, the body rocks to the right and the torso is turned to the right and vice versa for an attack to the right.

STANDING-TUCK: (also *Standingtuck*) A rapier placed upright.

STAND-UP BOXER: A boxer who fights from the classic stand-up stance.

STAND-UP STANCE: A fighting posture and placement in boxing that has the fighter.

STAR: An imaginary series of 8 lines on the floor that radiate out from a central apex, beneath the combatant, consisting of 45-degree relationships like the points of a compass or lines of an astrex. The points of the star indicate the variable planes of movement that a combatant can take. See *Imaginary Star*.

STAVES: More than one staff, the plural of staff.

STEAL: (also *Stealing the Time* and *Stealing Time*) See *Counter Attack* and *Time Hit*.

STECCADA: (also *Stoccata*) (It.) A thrusting attack under the opponent's sword arm, much like McBanes Boar's thrust.

STECCADO: A thrust or thrusting attack with the rapier.

STECCATA: (It.) See *Field of Play*.

STEEL: a.) An alloy of iron and carbon, in various proportions (generally from 0.5% – 1.5% carbon; if more carbon, it becomes Cast Iron and loses its elastic properties), distinguished from Iron by certain physical properties, especially greater hardness and elasticity, rendering it suitable as material for armor and cutting instruments such as swords, daggers, etc., hence, a generic term for the blade, or the entire weapon, nondescript to any period or weapon. (Various other elements may be added for specific properties, including tungsten, manganese, nickel molybdenum, etc.) b.) Said of a person, or a person's character, in relation to the strong and dependable characteristics of steel. Hard, firm; thoroughly trustworthy; dependable.

STEELED COAT: A coat made of steel. Armor.

STEELY POINT: A point or tip made of steel.

STEP OUT: (also *Traverse*) An evasion to the side. See *Side Step Evasion.*

STEP-IN-PARRY: (also sometimes *Jam Parry*) A defensive action against a cutting attack that combines the mechanics of a standard parry while moving in to the close.

STESSO TEMPO: (It.) Literally "single" or "same time." "Simultaneous time." The common practice of the sixteenth century Italian school of executing the parry and riposte in one action. Opposite of *Dui Tempi*. See also *Single Time.*

STICCIO: (It.) See *Glide.*

STICK: a.) To stab, to pierce. b.) A staff; a rod. c.) See *Baton* and *Single Stick.*

STILETTO: A short dagger with a blade thick in proportion to its breadth.

STITCHBLATT: (literally "thrust leaf") (Gr.) The small pierced plates on some hilts.

STOCATTA: Attack Low.

STOCCADO: The point of a sword or dagger, hence, a thrust with such a point.

STOCCATA LUNGA: (Literally "Elongated Thrust") Gigantti's term for the lunge. See *Grand Lunge.*

STOCCATA: (also *Stucatho*) A thrust in fencing.

STOCCHATA VEL PUNCTA: Pietro Monte's "thrust" or straight thrust delivered from either side from a high or low position and which he considered the most effective of all attacks.

STOCCO: (It.) Italian name for the *Estoc* or *Tuck*, a late Medieval edgeless, two handed, broad-bladed thrusting sword for piercing plate armor.

STOCK: a.) A term coined by the English during the sixteenth century for the rapier, or merely a thrust by such a weapon. Possibly deriving its name from the Italian Stoccada or the French estoc (or stoccata). b.) The wooden portion of a musket, cross bow, fowling piece; the handle of a pistol. The wooden shaft of a pole arm; the haft.

STOMP KICK: See *Stamping Kick.*

STOMP: A heavy stamping of the foot.

STONE-BOW: A type of cross bow designed for the shooting of rocks or bullets.

STOP CUT: a.) A counter offensive cut designed to strike the opponent before the final movement of the opponent's attack is executed. b.) Sometimes applied to the *Stop Short*. c.) Any attack with the edge that has a pause or moment of stillness at the parry. A cutting attack that does not instantly move on to the next attack or parry. d.) (also *Ricochet Cut*) A term sometimes used for the Piston Cut, a cut executed to read as a real cut to the audience but which stops prior to connecting with one's partner. See *Piston Cut.*

STOP HIT: A counter offensive action, cut or thrust, designed to strike the opponent before the final movement of the opponent's attack is executed.

STOP PARRY: See *Jam Parry.*

STOP SHORT: a.) A feint with the edge of the blade that resembles a proper full arm cut, but the actual attack is abruptly brought to a halt, prior to executing the final two-thirds of the cut. b.) To suddenly halt during or immediately after gaining ground for offensive or defensive reasons.

STOP THRUST: A counter offensive thrust designed to strike the opponent before the final movement of the opponent's attack is executed.

STORM: To rush, charge or attack with redoubled forces and intent.

STOSS: (Ger.) See *Thrust.*

STRAIGHT ARM PARRY: A parry executed with a straight or locked arm. See *Extended Parry.*

STRAIGHT ATTACK: An attack executed from an open guard position where the opposing blade is neither an immediate threat nor closes the immediate line of attack. A *Direct Attack.*

Straight Pace Backward: Any footwork straight backward on the linear tracks of footwork. Footwork that carries the combatant straight back.

Straight Pace Forward: Any footwork straight forward on the linear tracks of footwork. Foot work that carries the combatant straight forward.

Straight Punch: A direct, linear punch, generally made to the face, delivered from the rear or back shoulder and foot. The combatant delivers a straight punch by extending the arm straight forward from the rear shoulder (thumb up at roughly 10 o'clock), and twisting the hand (thumb slightly to the inside) on impact. Generally the combatant steps into the attack by taking a short step with the leading foot as they deliver the punch. The arm is then returned to the position that the punch began. When throwing a straight punch, the lead hand is generally kept high to protect the face. Opposite of a *Jab*.

Straight Thrust: A direct and simplest form of attack with the point of a weapon.

Straight: (also *Straight Punch*) A jabbing punch to the face from the rear hand; so called because it travels straight to the target.

Stramazone: (It.) (also *Stramazon*) a.) A ripping cutting attack with the rapier, that is delivered vertically downward with the edge of the blade nearest the point. A "knock-down" blow. b.) A fast, light cutting attack to the face.

Strangle: To choke; to kill or attempt to kill by stopping respiration.

Strangle Hold: (also *Choke Hold*) Offensive or defensive actions which decrease or stop a person's intake of air by obstructing or crushing the windpipe with force or pressure applied by the hand(s), arm(s), leg(s), or other such implements.

Stratagem: An artifice in war, a trick to deceive the enemy (a deed as well as a practice).

Stresso Tempo: Simultaneous attacks.

Strike: a.) To make or give a blow. b.) To beat with the hand, a stick or other object or weapon. c.) Used of any hurt inflicted or offered with any weapon.

Stringering: Maintaining contact or opposition with the opponent's blade so as to control it.

Stripe: The wound (or its scar) made with a lash, whip or stroke of a sword.

Stroke: a.) An attack or blow with a weapon or the hand, inflicted on or aimed at another person. Sometimes applied to the thrust of a weapon. See *Cutting Attack.* b.) The killing blow. c.) Fighting, giving battle.

Stromacione: (also Stromazone) A tearing tip-cut to the face, used to harass or distract.

Struck: Subjected to an attack, blow or stroke; wounded, stricken.

Struggle: A resolute contest, whether physical or otherwise; a continued effort to resist force or free oneself from constraint; a strong effort under difficulties.

Stuck: A variation on the spelling of stock, a sixteenth century English term for the rapier, or a thrusting attack with such a weapon. See also *Stoccado.*

Style: a.) A personal or characteristic manner of executing a fight. b.) An esthetic creative choice based on the actual mechanics of the weapon or form of combat.

Substitution of Target: Replacing or covering valid target area with invalid target area (in Foil and in Saber only). Hits made on such a substituted surface may be scored valid.

Successive Parries: a.) A series of parries, successful or unsuccessful, executed one right after the other. b.) Several unsuccessful parries following one another until the attacking blade is found.

Sucker Punch: (also *Blind Side Punch* and *Cold Cock*) a.) A strong punch delivered to an unsuspecting victim.

Suffocate: To kill by stopping respiration; to choke.

Suffocation: Death caused by choking.

Supination: The position of the sword-hand with the palm up.

SURRENDER: To resign; to yield.

SUSPENSION: A quality of movement that occurs in a moment of resistance or frozen time, such as the instant a combatant thrusts home and lands, but before the blade is again withdrawn. That moment of acknowledgment or registration of an act or action.

Sustained Movement: A quality of movement that is smooth and unaccented. There is no apparent start or stop, only continuity of energy and flow.

SWAG: a.) A big blustering fellow. b.) A swaying or lurching movement; the swinging or bouncing of a sword, in its hanger, on one's hip.

SWAGGER: To talk blusteringly; to quarrel or squabble with; to boast or brag. To rant; to be noisy and boisterous.

SWAGGERER: One who behaves as if they were superior to others; a person with a defiant or insolent disregard of others; a person who carries himself as if among inferiors, with a superior or insolent air; a blusterer, bully, boaster.

SWAGGERING: Bullying, boasting; the action of a swaggerer.

SWASH: a.) To fence with, or to make the sound of clashing swords or of a sword striking a shield; to bluster with, or as with weapons. b.) A heavy forceful blow, usually sounded with a crash. c.) The whistling sound created as a heavy or forceful blow as it "cuts the air." d.) A swaggering bravo or ruffian; a swashbuckler.

SWASHBUCKLER: [swash b.) + buckler = the striking of a buckler with a "crash."] a.) Literally one who makes a noise by striking his own or his opponent's shield with his sword. b.) An Elizabethan term for a reckless swaggering bully much given to dueling with his sword and buckler; a swaggering bravo or ruffian. (From the popularity of the swashbuckling films of Errol Flynn et al, the term has been subject to upward revaluation making the swashbuckler a gallant swordsman and gentleman)

SWASHBUCKLING: Acting like, or characteristic of the conduct of a swashbuckler.

SWASHER: A swaggering bravo or ruffian; a blustering braggart; a swashbuckler.

SWASHING: a.) Ostentatious, showy or blustering behavior; swaggering, swashbuckling. b.) A stroke or blow delivered with great force. Perhaps the stramazone. See *Swashing Blow.*

SWASHING BLOW: (also *Washing Blow*) A large, sweeping stroke or blow delivered with great force, intended more to batter than cut the opponent.

SWEEP KICK: A low-line kick delivered to the feet, ankles or calves of the opponent, designed to kick their legs out from under them. The kick itself seems to "sweep" along the floor, and if executed correctly "sweeps" the victim off their feet.

SWEEPS: a.) A term for a slash or slashing attack with the blade. See *Swipe.* b.) See *Sweep Kick.*

SWEPT-HILT: A guard consisting of several curved branches and side-rings interconnecting with one another, giving the guard a grace of design matched by few other swords. There are generally at least two side-rings on the guard sweeping down from the pas d'âne with branches stemming to the knuckle bow. The larger ring is referred to as the Upper Side-Ring, and the smaller as the Lower Side-Ring.

SWING STEP: (also *Swinging Steps, Compass Steps,* and *Pivot Steps*) Footwork used to change the angle or direction the body faces by swinging one foot and pivoting on the other, thus turning the body. The stepping foot describes a portion of a circle and, like a drafting compass, pivots around the axis of the stationary foot.

SWING: A stroke, blow or cutting attack with or without a weapon.

SWINGBUCKLER: (also Swinge-Buckler & Swing-Buckler) A variation of swashbuckler; a reckless swaggering bully, much given to dueling with his sword and buckler.

SWINGE: A stroke or blow with a weapon; to thrash, beat or flog.

SWINGING MOVEMENT: A quality of movement established a fall with gravity, a gain in momentum, a loss of momentum, and the repeated cycle of fall and recovery (like that of a pendulum).

SWISHY-POKEY: A modern slang term for the small sword; making fun of its delicate blade movements and style of point work.

SWITCH STEP: (also Switch) A piece of footwork that changes the leading or dominant foot without gaining or loosing ground.

SWITCHBLADE: (also *Switch-Blade* and *Switch-Blade Knife*) A pocket knife with a blade released by pressing a "switch" or similar device on the handle.

SWORD & BUCKLER: a.) Armed with, using, or pertaining to a sword and buckler. b.) The traditional weapons of England: in most popular use from around the beginning of the sixteenth century until the turn of the seventeenth century. The sword and buckler was replace by the rapier and dagger, which become popular during the mid sixteenth century. Stout, true blooded Englishmen, however, disapproved of the Italian and Spanish rapier play and held fast to their heritage and beliefs in the sword and buckler; some, well into the first quarter of the seventeenth century. The sword and buckler was generally considered out of fashion in the court and among nobles in England by the end of the first half of the sixteenth century. c.) The weapon of servants, fools and oafs on stage. d.) An insult. To say someone was a sword and buckler man was indeed a great disparagement. The traditional weapon was, by the turn of the century, identified only with the lowest class of men, ruffians and soldiers.

SWORD & DAGGER: a.) A style of swordplay where a sword is carried in the right hand for offense, and a dagger carried in the left for warding, parrying or deflecting the adversary's attacks. See also *Rapier and Dagger.*

b.) Armed with, using or pertaining to the sword and dagger.

SWORD & LANTERN: a.) A style of swordplay where a combatant would use their lantern as a defensive weapon for warding, parrying or deflecting the adversary's attacks. At night the lanterns hood could be opened and closed by the combatant, aiding them in the attack while blinding the opponent. See *Hoodwink.* b.) See also *Lantern Hand.*

SWORD & SHIELD: The Medieval and Renaissance double fence style that has the combatant armed with cross-hilt, backsword or similar weapon and a shield upon the other arm. This form of swordplay is prominent in Shakespeare's history plays.

SWORD CANE: A hollow cane or walking stick housing a steel blade which may be drawn or shot out an end and used as a sword.

SWORD CARRIAGE: The complicated waist belt and suspension rigging for the Elizabethan rapier.

SWORD CASE: a.) A wooden or metal and wood case designed to carry a single sword. In some instances the case was designed to carry two identical swords; a case for dueling swords. b.) A term for the scabbard or sheath of a sword.

SWORD GRIP: a.) The handle of a sword; that which the hand is clasped around. See *Grip.* b.) The manner of holding a sword. There are generally two standard methods of holding a sword furnished with a simple Cross-Guard and no Pas d'ane. In both the dominant hand clasps around the handle near the cross-guard, the thumb on one side of the grip, the fingers on the other. The thumb curls around the grip and rests on the tip of the index finger. The last three fingers lightly grip the handle, bringing it to bear against the palm of the hand. This is the manner of holding a Single-Handed Sword (or Short Sword) or a Hand-and-a-Half Sword with one hand. If two hands are to be used, the non-dominant or unarmed hand is clasped onto the grip, beneath the first, in opposition to the dominant hand. The thumb to the opposite side of the grip to the other, the fingers also opposing the others. The thumb of the second hand curls around the grip and rests on the tip of the index finger in the same manner as the first. For a Hand-and-a-Half Sword, the last three fingers lightly grip the pommel, cradling it in the palm of the hand. For a Two-Handed Sword, the lower part of the handle is lightly held with the last three fingers, the little finger near the pommel. c.) The manner of holding the sword as taught by the sixteenth century gentleman George Silver, where the handle is held along the hand, resting the pommel in the hollow part of the palm heel toward the wrist, the forward part of the handle held between the forefinger and thumb, outside the middle joint of the forefinger, it being held something straight out, griping round the handle with the lower three fingers, the thumb held straight out upon the handle, so that the point may be held out straight from the hand. In Silver's opinion this is the best way to hold the sword in Variable Fight. In Gardant and Open Fight, the handle should be griped in the hand with the thumb wrapped around the hand, gripping the forefinger.

SWORD HANGER: The lighter and less complicated belt, hook and chains used to carry the civilian small sword.

SWORD KNOT: A thong or lace that attaches the hilt of the sword to the combatants wrist; designed to help prevent loss or disarmament in battle. Now a decorative ribbon or tassel hung from the hilt of military sabres chiefly as a mere ornament or badge.

SWORD OF FASHION: The civilian sword, most often the small sword, but sometimes the rapier. See *Small Sword*.

SWORD, AGE OF THE: (Circa 1450-1550) The period where the sword became the paramount weapon above the heavy cutting and crushing weapons of the Middle Ages. From the mid-fifteenth century to the mid sixteenth century the practice of the sword,

with less armor and more agility by the combatant, where new designs in the weapon and stronger disciplines in its practice were developed.

SWORD: a.) A weapon, generally carried at one's side, used by hand, adapted for cutting and/or thrusting. Comprised of a handle or hilt and a straight or curved blade with either one or two sharp edges and/or a sharp point. b.) A symbol used on ceremonial occasions to represent honor, rank or position of authority; a symbol of regal power. c.) See also *Broadsword, Gladius, Rapier, Short Sword, Small Sword* and *Transitional Rapier*.

SWORD-ARM PROTECT: (also *Sword-Arm Protect Parry*) A hanging parry executed to protect the sword bearing side of the body. The hand and hilt are on the right side of the body at roughly ear level, palm back, away from the opponent, the blade is below the hand, sloped down with the tip at roughly four o'clock.

SWORD-ARM: The arm with which the sword is wielded; generally the right arm.

SWORDBELT: (also *Sword-Belt*) The wide, tight waist-belt with vertical straps ending in snaphooks, used in the nineteenth century to carry sabers and officers swords.

SWORD-BLADE: See *Blade*.

SWORD-BREAKER: a.) A term for any type of dagger provided with special contrivances designed to entangle and entrap the opponent's blade. These include daggers where the actual quillons, or an internal set of struts, are angled sharply forward towards the blade so that the opposing blade might be caught between the dagger's blade and quillon; those with the true edge of the blade deeply serrated much like a comb or rake, with some twenty horizontal teeth which could entrap an opponent's sword blade; and another such device where the blade divided longitudinally into three parts which folded together to resemble a conventional blade. When a spring catch is pressed, however, the blade sprang open, a long piece on either side shooting outward to form a type of trident. The prongs of the blade function like the struts of other blade-breaking hilts, catching the enemy's sword. b.) A device designed to catch a sword blade and break it; a notch, hook, etc. on a dagger, buckler, etc. manufactured for breaking the blade of an adversary's sword.

SWORD-BROTHER: A fellow swordsman; a comrade in arms.

SWORD-CATCHER: A term used for special dueling daggers with extended prongs and quillons capable of grabbing and trapping a rapier blade, some had spring-locked triggers, they were uncommon (and possibly more menacing than practical).

SWORD-CRAFT: See *Swordsmanship*.

SWORD-CUT: a.) A blow, stroke or attack dealt with the edge of a sword. b.) A wound or scar produced by a blow, stroke or attack with the edge of a sword.

SWORD-CUTTLER: (also *Sword-Cutler*) A cutler who makes sword-blades or swords.

SWORDER: a.) One who habitually fights with a sword; a fighter, combatant, swashbuckler, prize fighter or gladiator. b.) A sword for hire; a mercenary, assassin, cut-throat; One who kills others with a sword.

SWORD-GIRDLE: See *Swordbelt*.

SWORD-HILTS: The portion of the sword comprised of the guard, grip and pommel. The handle of the sword. See also *Hilt*.

SWORDING: Exercising or practicing with a sword; fencing.

SWORDMAN: (also *Swordsman* and *Swordmen*) A man skilled in, or addicted to, the use of a sword; a man of the sword; a sword fighter.

SWORDPLAY: The exchange of offensive and defensive actions (cuts, thrusts, blows, strikes, parries, etc.) with swords, whether in practice or in combat; fencing.

SWORDSMAN: (also *Swordman* & *Swordmen*) A person skilled in, or addicted to, the use of a sword; a man of the sword; a sword fighter.

SWORDSMANSHIP: The art of using, or skill in the use of the sword.

SWORDSTER: A person addicted to the use of, or practice with, the sword.

T

Tac au Tac (Riposte): (Fr.) A riposte made immediately after a percussive parry by bouncing forward off the opponent's blade.

Taglio: (It.) A term used by the Italian fencing master Salvator Fabris (late sixteenth early seventeenth century) for a cutting attack.

Tagliata: (It.) See *Coupé*.

Tah-Tahs: A term derived from the French term that describes a detached parry done in time with *Tac au Tac*. See *Baronial Hall*.

Taiaha: a.) A Maori (A member of the Polynesian people inhabiting New Zealand) martial art employing a spear/staff weapon. b.) A long-handled Maori club with a sharp tip.

Taille: The edge of the blade. See *Edge*.

Tajo: (Span.) A cutting attack. See *Cut*.

Taking the Blade: (also *Taking the Opponent's Blade*) See *Pris d'Fer*.

Tang: (Originally referred to as the "tongue" of the blade) The portion of the blade that extends from the forte and shoulders, passes through the guard and grip of the sword and fastens in some way to the pommel. It is the strength and stability of the blade and must be of suitable width to support the percussive use of the weapon.

Tap: a.) A slight blow. b.) A touch in fencing.

Tap Parry: a.) See *Beat Parry*. b.) Sometimes applied to a *Detached Parry*.

Targe: (It.) (also *Target*) A round or squarish shield, fitted with two enarmes, one strapping across the forearm and the other held in the left hand. Introduced during the Middle Ages as an infantry weapon, the target was used through the sixteenth century by footmen and archers.

Target: a.) That part of the body towards which an attack (armed or unarmed) is directed. b.) The area of the fencer's body which is specified by the rules as a legitimate scoring surface. c.) (It.) A light round shield or buckler; a small *Targe*.

Technique: A term for a specific move or action; especially in martial arts.

Temper: a.) To bring steel to a suitable degree of hardness and elasticity or resiliency by reheating it to the required temperature after quenching (impressing it while hot, in some liquid, usually water) and allowing it to cool under appropriate conditions in order to achieve a crystalline structure which posses the desired properties of hardness and elasticity. Too hard a temper can cause a blade to fracture; too mild a temper, and the edges of the blade chew up and become like a saw. b.) The degree of hardness and elasticity imparted to steel, namely to a sword. The quality of a sword. c.) A term used to describe the qualities of tempered steel in a person. One's disposition, constitution, temperament.

Temperament: (also *The Humors*) In Medieval England a person's character was determined according to a philosophy that judged the relative proportions of "humors" in their body. These include the choleric (hot-tempered / irritable) , melancholic (sad / unhappy), phlegmatic (dull / indifferent), and sanguine (cheerful / light-hearted) humors. The mettle of their character was how these humors were forged within them, thus creating their temperament or constitution. This philosophy was still in common use in Elizabethan England where the plays and literature of the period made common use of the terms. Shakespeare and many of his contemporaries make many references to characters concerning their temperament by use of the humors. In theatrical character exploration there is a fifth humor added to the list, the "harlequin" (fool / buffoon) humor.

Tempo: a.) (also Fencing Tempo) The amount of time required to execute one simple fencing action. b.) A general term describing time relationships of fencing actions, related to cadence

Tempo Indivisable: (It.) Literally "indivisible time." When the parry and riposte follow one another with no pause whatsoever. or rhythm. c.) The pace or speed at which movement progresses; relatively slower or faster.

TEMPS PERDU: Fencing actions (usually composed) executed with a pause or syncopation.

TEN DIRECTIONS OF FOOTWORK: The ten directions that any piece of footwork can take a combatant during a fight. Each direction generates out from a central position, like the points on a compass. No matter which direction the fight takes, the center of the compass is always below the combatant, their chest and torso always facing "North." Any footwork forward on the linear tracks moves North, these are known as Straight Paces Forward. Movements straight backward, or "South," are known as Straight Paces Backward. Movements taken to the right, or East, are called Traverse Right, and action to the left, or West, are called Traverse Left. The diagonals of the footwork compass North East (NE), South East (SE), South West (SW) and North West (NW) run at a forty-five degree angle to the North-South, East-West tracks and are known as Sloped Paces. Circle steps are the ninth and tenth direction of movement on the compass. They are referred to as Circular Pace Right and Circular Pace Left. All tracks of the feet are the same width apart, and may be moved upon in the same manner as traditional footwork. See also *Star* and *Imaginary Star*.

TENSION RELAXATION: Avoid becoming too tense when performing the fight. excessive tension gets in the way of body control and quickly tires you out.

TERZA: (also *Terza Guardia*) (from the Latin *Tertio* - "thirdly") a.) The standard single weapon On Guard position in historical rapier fence assumed with the hand just above the waist (held in pronation, supination, or vertical/middle position), the arm bent at roughly 90 degrees, the blade angled up with the tip at roughly the opponent's arm-

pit level (Standard or Across). b.) The double fence guard assumed with the rapier in single weapon Terza (Standard or Across) with the dagger also held in single weapon Terza (Standard). The hands may be held in pronation, supination, or vertical/middle position.

TERZA-BASSA: (It.) See *Low Terza*.

TERZO: Italian term for the middle portion of a blade.

THRASH: (also *Thresh*) A term for a sound beating or drubbing, derived from the beating of corn from the husk with a flail; from thrashing corn.

THREE FEET: (also *Three Leg* and *Three Leg Stance*) Fencers slang for the *Low Line Evasion* or *Passata Sotto*.

THREE FEET TO THE SIDE: A diagonal avoid executed with an extended torso and the left hand placed on the floor for balance.

THREE, PARRY OF: a.) Defense for a horizontal attack to the weapon bearing shoulder with the hand and hilt at roughly waist level on the weapon bearing side, knuckles toward the outside, the blade above the hand, its forte at the level of the notch in sword bearing arm where the deltoid and biceps meet. b.) (also *Parry Tierce*) Protecting the high outside line with the point up, the hand in pronation. c.) Broadsword defense against a Shoulder Cut, made with the point up, the hands a little higher than the waist and pushed out slightly away from the body; the blade points almost straight up, defending the outside high line.

THREE-POINT STANCE: A stance in swordplay with an increased depth and reduced width than that of the standard four-point stance, narrowing the parallel tracks of linear and circular footwork from shoulder width to approximately one foot. Because the parallel tracks are closer, the push and pull of the legs in footwork is focused on a tighter area, allowing for a greater concentration of effort. Such a stance allows for strong, quick movements of the feet such as the advance and retreat.

THROTTLE: To choke.

THROW: a.) Any fast or sharp action that uses leverage on the victim's joints or body to take them off center and bring them down from an erect position. In some forms of wrestling the throwing down of an opponent finishes a bout or round. b.) (also *Flip*) An offensive movement which controls or appears to control the victim's center, giving the illusion of lifting them off their feet and returning them to the ground – usually into a break fall or roll. c.) Forcible propulsion or delivery from or as from the hand or arm; a cast. To project or propel through the air, and connected uses; to cast, fling, hurl, drive, shoot (away from the propelling agent).

THROW IN THE TOWEL: (also *"Throw in the Sponge"*) As fight fans know, a sponge and towel are essential tools of a prizefighter's handlers, to cool him off between rounds. And as they also know, throwing the towel (earlier, the sponge) into the ring is the traditional sign that the fighter is too badly hurt to continue. In any context, it means to surrender.

THROW OFF: a.) A term for the *Bind Away.* b.) A strong blade taking action that upon its completion propels the attacking sword, and its barer, off in the direction the defending sword sends it. c.) A *Flip* or *Throw* in unarmed combat.

THRUST: a.) An act, or the action of thrusting. An attack, lunge, strike or stab with a pushing or piercing action with the point of a blade, or pointed instrument, generally involving a full extension of the weapon arm. An attack with the point of the weapon, opposed to a blow with the edge. b.) An attack made with the point of the weapon. c.) An attack made with the point of the knife delivered from an overhand position. d.) (Small Sword) Offensive attacks upon an adversary, chiefly executed with a lunge. Thrusts are divided in the same manner as the parades, simple and compound, upper and lower.

THRUST OF THE WRIST: (Small Sword) Delivered to an adversary while recovering to

guard, after he has parried a first thrust, and is slow in making a return.

THRUST UNDER THE ARM: A cowardly or villainous attack made under the arm of an individual who attempts to part the combatants, thus taking the victim by surprise. Such an action is not merely a stage device such as that used in Shakespeare's Romeo & Juliet, for in Joseph Swetnam's treatise on the "Science of Defence," Chapter III deals with such "fearfull examples of murther."

THRUSTING HOME: a.) An attack with the point that closes measure and lands, or intends to land on the opponent. b.) A term for the "kill" or killing thrust.

THRUSTING ON THE CIRCLE: A drill in blade-play that takes the combatants through a series of thrusts, parries and ripostes while executing circular paces on the tracks of the imaginary circle.

THUMBS DOWN: A mistranslation of the Latin phrase pollice verso, thumbs turned. When gladiators fought in the Roman arena, a wounded man unable to continue fighting would appeal to the spectators for mercy. If they thought he'd put up a good fight, the audience might make the gesture pollice primo (thumbs pressed); if not – or if they were just feeling nasty – it would be pollice verso, and the wounded man was finished off. Historians have argued for generations over precisely what gestures these expressions signified; the popular "translation" comes from a painting by the nineteenth century French artist, Jean Leon Gerome: it showed the end of a gladiatorial contest, with scowling spectators holding out their fists with the thumbs turned down. Ever since, to turn thumbs down on something figuratively condemns it to death.

THUMP: a.) To beat with something blunt, to cuff. b.) The sound of something being struck with a blunt instrument.

THWACK: a.) To beat to bang. b.) The sound of a hard knock or blow.

THWART: a.) To step across or transversely;

walking or passing from side to side; cross-wise. b.) (also Diagonal Evasion) An evasive step that takes the body 45° off-line to either the right or left, ending with the legs open. c.) An off-line action of footwork where the same body action as the lunge is used in conjunction with a defensive action. d.) A step that takes the body diagonally off-line to either the right or left, ending with the legs open. e.) A Posted or Recovered Traverse on the Forward 45 degree line, taking the body Off-Line to either the right or left and ending with the legs open.

THWART THE 90: A Thwart stepping farther around the Imaginary Star to the 90 degree line to either the right or left.

THWART TO THE BACK 45: A Thwart stepping deeper around the Imaginary Star to the Back 45 degree line to either the right or left.

TIERCE: (also *Third*) a.) The small sword, transitional rapier and modern fencing guard that closes (protects) the high outside line; taken with the hand in pronation and with the point higher than the hand. b.) The transitional rapier and small sword parry taken with the hand in pronation and with the point higher than the hand, closing the high outside line. c.) The guard or parry defending the outside high line with the hand in pronation.

TIERCE GUARD: (Small Sword) The outside guard, the blades being crossed on that side. See *Guards*.

Tierce Parade: (Small Sword) The upper outward parade, and the opposite to carte; and it was anciently the third parade in fencing. This is a favorite parade for disarming your adversary by crossing the sword (see *Disarms*). Tierce is performed by the gradual descent of the wrist outwards, the nails reversed downwards, the point always receding to its identical direction.

TIERCE THRUST: (Small Sword) An awkward thrust and seldom practised. In performing it the nails are turned downwards as in seconde, and in this manner delivered towards the breast, opposing your adversary's blade on the outside.

TIE-UP: A boxing term for a bear hug executed in a clinch, where one combatant locks their opponent's arms against their body in an attempt to prevent striking while inside.

TIGE: (It.) Another term for the ricasso of a blade. See *Ricasso*.

TIGHT: Said of two or more combatants fighting inside measure.

TILT: a.) A combat or encounter, generally for exercise or sport, between two knights or horsemen armed with lances, or the like, with the objective of knocking one's opponent from his saddle; a joust. b.) The striking of a lance in a tilt, hence, the thrusting of a weapon, as in a tilt. To strike or thrust at with a weapon. c.) A place for holding tilts or jousts; a tilting ground or yard; the lists.

TILTER: a.) A participant in the tilt or joust. b.) A combatant; a fencer. c.) A slang term, used in the sixteenth century for the rapier.

TILT-YARD: (also *Tiltyard*) A place for holding tilts or jousts; a tilting ground or yard; the lists.

TIME: a.) The practice of Elizabethan and modern fencers that minimizes the offensive and defensive motions of the body to those strictly necessary, both in number and in extent; and also balances those motions carefully with those of the opponent, in order to seize instantly any opportunity while minimizing the possibility of being struck. b.) Di Grassi's notion of moving the hand, weapon and feet all in one action, at the same time, to better gain advantage and avoid injury. c.) The period of time taken to execute any one action of the blade, arm, or foot.

TIME ACTION: A stop hit executed by closing the line in which the attack is to completed.

TIME CUT: See *Stop Cut* and *Time Action*.

TIME DISENGAGEMENT: The action offered by Fabris to deny the opponent an engagement of the blades. "Time" refers to timing the action so that it is executed at the last possible moment prior to engagement and therefore gaining the advantage. See also *Absence of Blade* and *Refusing the Blade*.

TIME HIT: a.) A counter attack which lands while at the same time preventing the opponent's attack from reaching its objective. See *Time Action*. b.) The practice of Elizabethan gentleman George Silver of striking on the advance of an adversary in a manner that they do not have ample time to defend against the opposing attack. In response to an advance of the opponent, he breaks time down into three options: 1.) To cut or thrust at the opponent, as they close measure but before they attack: a Stop Hit. 2.) To Parry and immediately Riposte, remembering the rules of offensive and defensive play (the Four Governors). 3.) To evade backward, avoiding their attack and then immediately delivering a cut or thrust. In all of these, Silver feels that it is important for the combatant to remember that on their adversary's first motion toward them, they must move backward a little to be prepared in due time to perform any of his aforesaid actions.

TIME THRUST ON THE EXTENSION: (Small Sword) The act of delivering a thrust to an adversary, when he has made a full lunge, by yeilding forward on the extension before he can possibly recover to guard, or form any parade to oppose it. This is parying and thrusting at the same moment. See also *Time Thrust*.

TIME THRUST: (in French *coup de tem*) (Small Sword) The act of delivering a thrust to an adversary in the momentary duration of time employed by him in executing any feint or design performed by him. See also *Stop Thrust*.

TIMING: a.) The synchronization of each action and its corresponding reaction throughout a fight; the coordination of which incorporates both the speed at which actions are performed as well as the action-reaction speed of intrinsic partnered movements. b.) To acknowledge an opportunity or opening and execute the correct action at the best possible moment.

TIP: a.) The pointed or rounded end of a sword blade or dagger. See *Point*. b.) To give a slight blow, knock or touch to; to tap lightly.

TIP CONTROL: See *Point Control*.

TO THE HILTS: a.) An active form of coming to the close where the offensive and defensive weapons join and meet guard to guard as the combatants close measure. This type of corps-a-corps may be executed either from an offensive or defensive position. b.) Meaning to "go all the way" or "go all out." Derived from swordplay and refers directly to the hilt of the sword. "To the Hilt" is a term for a thrusting attack that is delivered and lands in one's opponent and, is further, driven into the victim's body "all the way" up to its hilt.

TOASTING-IRON: A contemptuous term for a sword; mocking its resemblance to an iron fork used to toast bread or cheese.

TOCASA: (Span.) See *Hit*.

TOCCATA: (also tocco) (It.) Literally "a touching," from toccare "to touch." Originally applied to a composition for a keyboard instrument, intended to exhibit the touch and technique of a performer; later applied to the touch and technique of a fencer, and finally to that of a touch or hit in fencing. See *Hit*.

TOE KICK: a.) Any strike with the foot that is driven by the action of the leg and makes contact with the point or toes of the foot, whether point or flexed. b.) Sometimes applied to a kick made with the instep of the foot, toes pointed out and forward.

TOE, BALL, HEEL: a.) The correct mechanics for avoiding tripping when moving the foot forward. The toe and the ball of the foot are lifted off the floor, and the hell is advanced forward, skimming the floor, completing the action by securing the heel, ball and then toe of the foot back on the floor. b.) The correct, and safe, method of landing on the feet from a jump, throw or flip. The combatant should never land *Flat Footed*.

TOLEDO: a.) Spanish town renowned for its rapier blades during the Elizabethan era. b.) A present day manufacturer of non-practical, decorative weapons and armor designed only for display and not for theatrical combat. See *Wall-Hanger.*

TONDO: (It.) Literally "around" or "compass." A circular cutting attack delivered in a horizontal plane. See *Man Dritta Tondo* and *Reverso Tondo.*

TOOL: a.) An archaic term for a weapon of war; one's weapon. b.) The cutting part of a blade or knife.

TOP MAN: (also *Air Man*) The gymnast or combatant who is lifted or flipped. The "Flippee". The one who actually flies, flips or is lifted over the base man.

TOUCH: a.) A very light hit, knock, stroke or blow. b.) A valid hit in fencing, scored within the prescribed target area.

TOUCHÉ: (Fr.) A rather outdated vocal acknowledgment to a touch or hit received in fencing practice.

TOUR D'EPEE: (Fr.) a.) An attack consisting of a coupé and disengage, or a disengage and coupé, avoiding the defender's weapon. b.) See *Circular Feint.*

TOURNAMENT: a.) Originally a martial sport or exercise of the Middle Ages in which a number of armored and mounted combatants divided into parties or teams, fought with blunted weapons under certain restrictions for the prize of valor; a place of practice, sport and exercise for knights. b.) A encounter or trial of strength in combat; a prize fight.

TOURNAMENTS OF CHAMPIONS: Public exhibitions where knights would come together to display their skills at arms. Developed in the twelfth century, many of the early tournaments were mock battles between two bodies of armed horsemen called a mêlée. Later came the joust, a trial of skill in which two horsemen charged each other with leveled lances, each attempting to unhorse the other. The melee continued side by side with the joust into the sixteenth century. See *Champion.*

TOURNEY: a.) To take part in, or to tilt in a tournament. b.) A *Tournament* or *Tournament of Champions.*

TRAINED STEEL: (also *Trained Blade*) The slight bow or bend in the foible of a fencing blade which allows the blade to give on a hit rather than pierce; the blade arches as denoted in the classically executed hit and then returns to true after completing the attack.

TRAMAZONE: (It.) See *Stramazone.*

TRANSFER BEAT PARRY: A form of transfer parry where a successful primary parry is completed with one weapon, followed with a secondary beat parry. Any double fence parry may be executed as a transfer beat.

TRANSFER BLOCK: (also *Replacement Block*) A block that uses both hands/arms, one after the other, to deflect and control the offending hand, arm or leg. One hand begins the block, the other is then used to complete the block, "checking" the offending limb and freeing the first hand for a counter attack.

TRANSFER HEAVY PARRY: A transfer parry where the primary parry is executed with the dagger and as the parry is transferred to the rapier it instantly takes the offending weapon to the floor in the manner of a heavy parry.

TRANSFER PARRY: (also *Replacement Parry*) A double fence parry that uses both weapons, one after the other, to deflect and control the offending blade. One blade begins the parry, usually the rapier, either breaking a thrust to one side or the other, or slowing the attack of a cut but not completing the parry itself. The other weapon, usually the dagger, is then used to complete the parry, "staying" the offending blade and freeing the rapier for a counter attack. There is a split second of mutual contact as one blade transfers the parry over to the other. The primary defending blade does not leave contact with the offending blade until the secondary weapon is in contact with that blade. It is an exchange or transfer of the parry, not two separate parries executed on the same blade.

TRANSFER PRIS D'FER: (also *Replacement Pris d'Fer*) a.) A variation on the transfer parry where a pris d'fer is instantly executed by the secondary weapon after the primary weapon has successfully completed the parry. b.) A double fence technique that uses both weapons, one after the other, in the execution of a pris d'fer on the opposing blade.

TRANSITION: Moving of the blade from one line or placement to another. See also *Changement*.

TRANSITION, AGE OF: (Circa 1625-1675) The second phase of the swords "Golden Age" where the rapier decidedly tended towards simplification, but had not yet assumed the definite shape of the small sword. In the early parts of this period, the protective shell guard started to increase in size until this buffer reached the form of the cup guard or Cup-Hilt. Many rapiers, however, still used the complex guard of swept rings and counter guards to protect the sword hand. Blades were diminished in size, and although the point was paramount, they still often maintained an edge. This was not as much for use in cutting attacks as to prevent the opponent from executing a disarm by taking hold of the blade. The average blade length of the weapon was generally between thirty to thirty-five inches long. During the early part of this period, the dagger had, for the most part, been abandoned, leaving the left hand free for the play of the weapons. Some schools taught the fencer to trust solely in the rapier for defense, others let the left-hand function as a defensive weapon, and still others taught a method of fencing with both hands upon the sword known as shortening the sword. Because of the variance in methods, gentlemen had their choice of masters and techniques, and fenced in the style of their particular fancy. See also *Transitional Rapier*.

TRANSITIONAL FOOTWORK: a.) Footwork executed from the narrower base of the three-point stance, allowing for the style of gaining and breaking ground generally associated with the quick exchange of point work of the Transitional Rapier. b.) Any footwork used as a shift between two specific pieces of choreography.

TRANSITIONAL PARRIES: (also *Transitional Rapier Parries*) Stylized parries that represent the form of defense that complements the thrusting style of the transitional rapier. The hand placement and general mechanics remain the same as standard rapier parries, differing mainly in the angle of the defending blade. In high line parries the point is angled forward at roughly forty-five degrees and slightly away from the body. In the low lines the blade is also angled forward and away from the body. The blade still travels out to the parry and the forte still defends the intended target. The blade is kept forward as a threat to one's opponent and to facilitate a quicker thrust after successfully parrying an attack.

TRANSITIONAL RAPIER: The form of rapier in fashion during the second and third quarter of the seventeenth century. A rapier with a smaller, lighter blade designed mostly for point work, a razor sharp point (the edges were kept sharp only to prevent the opponent from seizing the blade), and a less complex hilt configuration then that of the earlier rapiers. See *Transition, Age of*.

TRANSITIONAL SCIENCE OF FENCE: From 1625 to 1675 many treatises were penned dealing with the matters of dueling and the art of swordsmanship but little new material was offered in rapier play. The Spanish cared very little about the advancements in rapier play and were quite satisfied with the techniques of Carranza and Narvaez. The Italians, confident in their form, did little to improve upon the works of Fabris and Capo Ferro. The French, however, excelled in the practice of puncture play, and it is to them that the torch was unwittingly passed as the rapier gave way to the small sword. See also *Transition, Age of*.

TRANSPORT: a.) (also sometimes *Transport Parry*) A croisé into the high line with an expulsion, executed from a successful parry. b.) A checking action made on the opponent's hand, arm or leg, executed by blocking the attack and then moving it vertically from a high line to a low line, or vice versa, but on the same side as the block took place (similar to a *Croisé* in fencing). c.) See *Pris d'Fer*.

TRANSPORT PARRY: a.) A defensive maneuver with a bladed weapon that lifts or lowers the opposing blade to a different line than that being attacked. Using the mechanics of a standard parry coupled with a vertical or diagonal movement of the hand and blade, to transport the opposing blade to a point other than that which was attacked. These are done to manipulate the opposing blade to a position that better facilitates an effective riposte. Most transport parries move in a vertical plane. b.) A parry executed with a pris d'fer, usually a croisé. See *Transport*.

TRAP: a.) Any act or action which attracts by its apparent easiness and proves to be a trick or deception. b.) Any act or action, armed or unarmed, by which a combatant, their limbs and or weapons are unsuspectingly caught, stopped, secured or pinned. c.) An act or action that immobilizes an opponent's limb(s) and or weapon to effect an attack or disarm. d.) (also *Trap Door*) A movable covering of a pit, or of an opening in a floor, designed to fall when stepped upon; hence applied to any similar door flush with the surface in a floor, ceiling, or roof.

TRATTEGIO: (It.) See *Finger-Play*.

TRAVERSE: a.) Any footwork executed directly to the right/East (Traverse Right) or left/West (Traverse Left) instead of movement forward or backward on the linear tracks. See *Ten Directions of Footwork*. b.) An off-line "advance" or "retreat" in any direction. When moving to the right the right foot leads; when moving to the left the left foot leads. c.) Any foot movement that takes the combatant off line. d.) An evasive step that takes the body 90° off-line to either the right or left, displacing the body from the plane of attack. e.) To run a weapon through something; to pierce, stab.

TRAVERSE EVASION: (also *Traverse Right* and *Traverse Left* and *Sidestep Evasion*) An evasive action that removes the body from the cutting plane of a vertical or diagonal swipe by lunging either to the left (west) or to the right (east) and leaning the torso into the lunge, displacing the body from the plane of attack.

TRAVERSING: See *Traverse*.

TRAVERSONE: (It.) A diagonal chest cut; banderole.

TRENCH: a.) A ditch cut and earth thrown up for defense (used only in the plural). b.) A cut or wound that is open like a trench.

TRENCHANT: Having a keen edge; adapted for cutting; sharp, sharp-pointed. Coming from trencher a plate or board that meat was served and cut upon, also trenching, meaning the cutting of meat.

TRENCHED: Deep cuts. Possibly from the word "trenching" meaning the cutting of meat or from the deep "trenches" cut in a battle field.

TRENCHING WAR: War that cuts trenches in the surface of the land to throw up earth works for defense.

TRIAL BY COMBAT: An attempt to control personal feuds and disputes by settling issues through personal combat. Developed near the end of the sixth century the concept being to pit the accuser against the accused in mortal combat. The winner of the contest was in the right since God would not let evil prevail. In theory, accused and accuser had to fight in person, but women, invalids and men over sixty were exempt, and eventually priests also were excused from trial by combat. From the Norman Conquest until the reign of Henry II of France, trial by combat was the only honorable means of deciding a matter of right. The trial by combat was eventually replaced by the trial by jury.

TRIANGLE TARGET: a.) One of three systems of body targets in on-line fencing. The targets, when joined with imaginary lines form a triangle; one center chest (at the sternum) and the other two located on opposite thighs at approximately groin level. The chest target is parried by 3, 4 and 6, the thigh targets work for both the parries of 2 and 8 as well as 1 and 7. b.) A variation on the three point on-line system of body targets. For safety reasons the triangle is inverted, with two chest levels targets (one to the right and the other to the left) and once central target at mid-torso just above groin level. The targets, when joined with imaginary lines form a triangle. The inversion of the triangle is to keep upper body attacks away from the face and throat. The chest targets are parried by 3, 6 and 4, the low-line targets work for the parries of 2, 8, 1 and 7.

TRIP: a.) A stroke or catch in combat or wrestling by which one causes one's antagonist to loose his balance and fall. b.) A sudden catching of the foot that causes one to loose balance and stumble or fall. c.) A light and lively movement of the feet; a tripping gate or tread, this type of step in dance. d.) A move that gets a victim to the floor without getting them airborne. Trips are made either by "blocking" the foot that is about to move or "sweeping" away the foot that is about to land.

TRIPLÉ: (Fr.) A compound attack in any line that deceives a direct parry and two counter parries.

TROMPEMENT: (Fr.) a.) The deception of the opponent's parry or parries in the course of executing a compound attack. From the French tromper meaning "to deceive, delude or cheat." b.) Evasion of partner's attempt to parry the blade whilst in the course of executing a compound attack.

TROPHY: (derived from the Greek *tropaion*) Arms, standards, other property, or human captives and body parts captured in battle, commemorating military victories of a state, army or individual combatant. Upon victory in battle, the ancient Greeks would strip the weapons from the fallen enemies and hang them from a tree or pillar, dedicating this trophy to some particular god.

TROVARE DI SPADA: (also *occupare la spada*) (It.) The art of placing your sword against the opponent's (without touching his blade) so that yours would have the advantage of a lever at the moment they meet. Engaging the blades.

TRUE: a.) Accurately shaped, fitted, or placed, exact in position or form, as a blade, instrument, a part of mechanism, or the like. As in when a tempered blade is bent, it returns to true. b.) See *True Art*.

TRUE ART: The Elizabethan philosophy of superior practice and skill in the techniques of striking the opponent while safely defending one's self.

TRUE EDGE: That part of the blade which, when the weapon is held correctly, is naturally directed towards one's opponent. It is with this edge that most cutting attacks are delivered, and most parries received.

TRUE ENGLISH FIGHT: a.) Sword and Buckler play. b.) In Elizabethan England the educated English gentleman recognized the advantages of the foreign rapier, but the general English populace would not accept an Italian or Spanish concept as being above their own. The sword and buckler did not give way to the needle-sharp rapier until the mid-sixteenth century, and not until the 1580's did the English Masters of Defence begin to include the rapier and dagger as one of the weapons for which they tested proficiency. They did, however, still cling to the practice of the traditional weapons, believing that a great deal of skill was required to deliver a cut, and that the cut was better suited in an open brawl because the thrust required some distance to execute. he general English populace still preferred the rough, "manly" methods of fighting, scorning the tricks and dodging style of the rapier's subtle, "mathematical" craft. At the turn of the century, however, the English gave in, the edge slowly gave way to the superiority and efficiency of the point. It was found and proven that, as one began to deliver a cut, their opponent could "beat their time" by thrusting home upon the preparation of the cut.

Truncheon: a.) A short thick staff; a club, a cudgel. b.) The shaft of a spear. c.) A fragment of a spear or lance; a piece broken off from a spear.

Truncheoner: One armed with a club or cudgel.

Tuck: a.) The gymnastic term for the position of the body when the knees are curled forcefully against the chest, bringing the body into a curved, tight position. b.) (also *Tucke*) A sixteenth century term for the rapier, or a thrusting attack with such a weapon. Possibly an English phonetic blunder for the Italian *Stocaada* or *Stocco*, the French *Estoc* or the German *Stock*.

Tumble: An act of acrobatic tumbling; an acrobatic feat.

Tumult: Commotion, agitation, uproar, brawl.

Tunnel Vision: A condition in which there is a major loss of peripheral vision; also, one in which anything away from the center of one's field of view escapes attention.

Turners of Accent: A contemptuous term for those Englishmen who abandoned traditional practices to learn the techniques and terms of the foreign fencing schools.

Turning Kick: See *Roundhouse Kick*.

Turk's Head: Name given to the "turban-like" metal band or collar fitting between the pommel and handle, or handle and quillons of some swords, they were often merely ornamental.

Tutte botte principali: Principle cuts and thrusts.

Twiddle: (also Twydle) a.) To lightly or delicately rotate, or describe a circle with, the tip of the blade in a manner where one can parry an attack and return to the original position

of the blade; a circular parry. b.) Sometime used to describe an endless series of parries and deception of parries; so that the blades move about one another much like the action of twiddling thumbs.

Twist: See *Croisé*.

Two Behind, Parry of: A parry of 2 executed inside measure, with a pass forward on the left, carrying the parry behind the back to defend the non-weapon bearing hip.

Two on One: A fight, armed or unarmed, where two combatants fight another simultaneously.

Two, Parry of: a.) Defense for an attack to the weapon bearing hip where the hand and hilt are just above waist level on the weapon bearing side of the body, knuckles turned to the outside, the blade is below the hand, its forte at the level of the weapon bearing hip. b.) (also *Parry Seconde*) Defending the low outside line with the point down, the hand in pronation. c.) Broadsword defense against a Flank Cut, made low to the outside, point down and slightly in. The lead wrist should be unbroken and the shoulder relaxed. From guard, parry 2 is executed with a semicircular sweeping action.

Two-Hand Battle: A single combat, a duel.

Two-Hand Choke: (also *Two Hand Choke*) See *Double Hand Choke*.

Two-Hand: a.) (also *Two-Hander*) Said of a weapon wielded with two hands. b.) Any action executed with two hands.

Two-Handed Parry: a.) Said of any parry executed with two hands. b.) See *Reinforced Parry*.

Two-Handed Sword: (also *Two-Handed Broadsword*) A long, broad bladed sword designed to be wielded with both hands.

Two-Ring Hilt: One of the earliest guard configurations of the rapier developed from the medieval cross-hilt, having two side-rings to protect the back of the sword-hand. The rings were circles or semi-circles of steel mounted at the bottom of the pas d'âne and at the quillon block. For further protection against the thrust, counter guards were added to the hilt. The guard configuration, however, is fairly simple and does not afford a great deal of hand protection in actual rapier play.

TWO-TIME: An offensive action executed in two periods of fencing time. Not to be confused with "double time" or "deux temps," which signifies the distinct separation of parry and riposte.

U

UMBO: The bowl-like metal protrusion of a buckler or shield in which the hand fits inside.

UMKREISUNG: (Ger.) See *Circular Parry*. **UMKREISUNG UND FINTE:** (Ger.) See *Circular Feint*.

UNARM: a.) To take off or remove one's armor; to assist in putting off armor or to lay down one's arms. b.) To deprive of arms or armor; to disarm.

UNARMED: a.) Not armed; having no armor or weapon. b.) Unarmed Combat. See *Hand to Hand*.

UNARMED COMBAT: Fighting without weapons. See *Hand to Hand*.

UNBATED: Not bated, buttoned or blunted; sharp.

UNBATTERED: Not bruised or injured by blows.

UNBUCKLE: To unfasten the buckle or buckles of one's helmet; to remove or tear off one's helmet.

UNCOVERED: A position where the line of engagement is not closed. See *Open Line(s)*.

UNDER ROTATION: The act of not rotating far enough during a flip, throw or roll and thus, not landing correctly.

UNDER STOP THRUST: A term for the *Passata Sotto*, or other low line evasion executed with a stop thrust.

UNDERHAND GRIP: (also *Ice Pick Grip* and *Reversed Grip*) A way of holding a dagger or knife with the blade held beneath the hand (gripped with the thumb at the pommel) and managed as a stabbing weapon. Opposite of *Overhand Grip*. See also *Reverse Grip*.

UNDERTAKER: A person who aids or assists; a helper; a second. One who takes up a challenge for another.

UNFENCED: Defenseless.

UNFOUGHT: Not fought.

UNGORED: Not wounded or hurt.

UNHAND: To loose from the hand, to let go.

UNICORNE GUARD: (also *Fore-Hand Guard*) (Backsword) A guard position in Backsword play put forth by English Fight Master Joseph Swetnam. The blade placement is similar to Agrippa's *Prima Guardia*, Saviolo and Di Grassi's *High Ward*, with the sword held on the sword bearing side of the body, the hand and hilt held at roughly ear level, knuckles up, the blade angled in, its point directed at the enemy's face.

UNRIP: To rip; to cut open.

UNSHEATHE: To dislodge or remove a sword from its sheath or scabbard.

UNSHEATHED: A weapon that is not covered or housed in a sheath or scabbard.

UP TO SCRATCH: In old-time bare-knuckle prize-fighting the contestants had to be "brought to scratch" – an actual line scratched on the earth – at the beginning of each round; a fighter who wasn't up to scratch forfeited the match. If you're not feeling up to scratch, you're in no mood for fighting – or, probably, for much else. See also *Scratch*.

UPPER ARM BLOW: A close quarters strike made by driving the muscle group of the shoulder and upper arm into the opponent.

UPPER PARADES: (Small Sword) Parries made in the high line.

UPPER SIDE-RING: (also *Upper Port*) The smaller of the two side-rings found on the two-ring and swept-hilt rapier hilts situated the furthest from the weapon's pommel. See *Side-Ring* and also *Lower Side-Ring*.

UPPERCUT: a.) A left or right blow with the fist delivered with an upward motion in which all the weight is concentrated on the front foot. It is primarily used in infighting because it does not require much room to throw the punch. It is a way to get through the opponent's inside defense without creating an opening for a counter-punch. Dropping the hip and shoulder the punch is thrown from the waist (without a wind up), in an upward motion, in a short arc up to the opponent's jaw. If thrown from the right, the combatant's weight should be concentrate on their right foot, and for the left uppercut, on the left foot. b.) An ascending punch to the point of the jaw. c.) A left or right blow with the fist delivered with a bent arm in an upward motion.

V

Vambrace: (also *Vantbrace*) Armor for the front part of the forearm.

Vanguard: A military term for the foremost division of an army; the forefront or van.

Vault: a.) A spring or jump into the air in order to avoid an attack at the feet. See *Jump*. b.) Any leap or jump in the air.

Variable Ward: Silver's low guard (also a name for all other manner of guards not *Open, Close,* or *Guardant*).

Vaward: See *Vanguard*.

Veney: A practice bout to a number of hits in free play or mock combat.

Venie: (also *Venew, Venue* & *Veney*) A English term from the sixteenth century for a hit or thrust in fencing; a wound or blow.

Venue: (also *Veny* and *Venie*) A thrust or hit in fencing; a stroke or wound with a weapon

Verdadera Destreza, la: A Spanish system of fencing. The word "destreza" literally means "skill." However, the full name is perhaps best translated as "the true art." While Destreza is primarily a system of swordsmanship, it is intended to be a universal method of fighting applicable to all weapons. This includes sword and dagger; sword and cloak; sword and buckler; sword and round shield; the two-handed sword; the flail; and polearms such as the pike and halberd. Its precepts are based on reason, geometry, and incorporate various other aspects of a well-rounded Renaissance humanist education, with a special focus on the writings of classical authors such as Aristotle, Euclid, and Plato. Authors on Destreza also paid great attention to what modern martial artists would call biomechanics. The tradition is documented in scores of fencing manuals, but centers on the works of two primary authors, don Jerónimo Sánchez de Carranza and his follower, don Luis Pacheco de Narváez. The system of combat is tied to an intellectual, philosophical, and moral ideal.

Vertical Attack: Any cutting attack that travels from a high line to a low line, or viseversa, in a plane that is perpendicular to the floor. See also *Vertical Swipe*.

Vertical Changement: A changement executed from a free guard position by passing the point to an open line by moving either up or down. The vertical passage of the point is a slightly curved line that moves out from its point of origin in a shallow arc that rounds back in to its point of completion.

Vertical Jump: (also Jump) a.) The classic cliché for the dashing swordsman to jump over an adversary's attack at the feet. b.) To leap up onto a structure above that which the combatant leapt from (such as a table, chair, platform, etc.).

Vertical Knee Strike: An attack with the bent leg that travels upward in a vertical plane, intending to strike with the point of the knee. Often delivered to the recipient's groin, extended arm, and face. See also *Knee Strike* and *Knee to the Face*.

Violence: The exercise of physical force (whether intentional or unintentional, armed or unarmed) so as to inflict injury on, or cause damage to, persons or property; or forcibly interfering with personal freedom.

Violent: a.) Having some quality or qualities in such a degree as to produce a very marked or powerful effect (esp. in the way of injury or discomfort). b.) Intense, vehement, very strong or severe.

Void: (also *Voyd* or *Voyded*) To evade or avoid an attack rather than directly parry, often by a simple side step or pass, used preferably to parrying. See *Evasion*.

Volte: a.) A method of removing the body from the line of attack by swinging the rear foot back and to the side, turning the body out of the line of attack. This may either be a Demi Volte: A half volte which removes the body from the line of attack by swinging the rear foot back and to the side, directly behind the forward foot, turning the body parallel to the line of attack; or a Grand Volte: A full volte that removes the body from the line of attack by compassing the rear foot back and around the forward foot, turning the body approximately one-hundred and eighty degrees. Often executed with a counter attack such as a *Stop Thrust* or *Stop Hit*. See *Demi-Volte* and *Grand Volte*. b.) (also *Bum in the Face*) A method of removing the body from the line of attack by swinging the lag foot back and to the side, so that the trunk is turned 180★ to the line of attack. c.) A specific type of Slip to the For. 45 right, removing the body from the Line of Engagement. d.) A turning or rotating of the fencer's body.

WALK: Generally used of a tour in dancing (at a masquerade). The term is applied to the footwork in fencing, hence the reference to a fight or bout of swordplay.

WALKING FOOT: a.) An exercise designed to help the combatant develop fluid horizontal movement in footwork by moving the initiating foot with a walking or "rocking" action. b. The foot in motion during a step or piece of footwork.

WALKING SWORD: A civilian sword; a sword to be worn with civilian dress in contrast with the heavier swords of war; a sword to be worn while walking.

WALKING THE LINE: An exercise designed to help the combatant keep their feet on track while traversing linear footwork by following actual lines on the floor.

WALKING THE PLANK: a.) A form of torture associated with pirates where a prisoner (usually bound and tied) was forced to walk a gangplank off the ship and over the open sea. b.) An exercise designed to help the combatant keep their feet on track while traversing linear footwork by having them perform linear footwork on two 2x4 planks.

WALL BOUND: A blade-play exercise that helps maintain measure and places the combatant's focus on the management of the point by working a series of stationary drills with their back up against a wall.

WALL OF STEEL: A term used for the protective barrier created by a parry with the sword. See also *Defensive Box*.

WALL-HANGER: A decorative sword, available at most knife shops and costume houses, that is made only as ornamentation and is in no way designed, engineered, or constructed for combat. A sword meant only to hang on the wall.

WARD: a.) An archaic term for the guard

when it was as much an offensive position as defensive. The ward was a position of observation for the purpose of discovering the approach of danger and effectively launching a counter attack. b.) A defensive posture or movement; to parry, repel, fend off, turn aside a stroke or thrust, blow, attack, weapon. c.) The part of a hilt of a sword that protects the hand; the guard.

WARDER: a.) A ceremonial symbol of office, command or authority, in early use, a staff or wand, and later a baton or truncheon, used to give the signal of commencement or cessation of hostilities in a battle or tournament. b.) One who wards off blows, a person on the defensive; one who parries. c.) A guard, a keeper, a sentinel.

WAR-MAN: A professional soldier or warrior.

WAR-PROOF: a.) Said of soldier or combatant whose skill and valor has been tried and proven in war. b.) Unable to be damaged or destroyed by the actions or effects of war.

WARRIOR: A soldier.

WASHING BLOW: See *Swashing Blow.*

WASTER: A wooden stick used as a practice sword, also called a *bavin*, later a *wiffle*.

WATCH PARRY: Slang for the parry of High One and sometimes the standard parry of one; where the hand and wrist are placed as if the combatant was looking at their watch.

WATER WORKS: An exercise designed to help the combatant develop fluid horizontal movement in footwork by carrying a full glass of water in the sword hand.

WATERFALL PARRY: See *Hanging Parry.*

WAYLAY: To lie in wait for; to ambush.

WEAPON: Any part of the body, extension thereof, or object that can be used for offensive purposes.

WEAPON BEARING SIDE: The side of the body that brandishes or carries the weapon. 1.) A weapon carried in the right hand makes the right side the weapon bearing side and a weapon carried in the left hand makes the left side the weapon bearing side. 2.) In Double Fence the weapon indicates its side (i.e. a rapier in the right hand makes the right side of the body the Rapier Bearing Side, a dagger in the left hand makes the left side of the body the Dagger Bearing Side, and so on). 3.) In two-hand play (i.e. Broadsword) the hand nearest the guard is considered the lead or weapon bearing hand, and thus the weapon bearing side of the body.

WEAPON-BEARING LINES: a.) Lines of attack as determined by the weapon-bearing side of the body. b.) In double fence techniques lines are determined by the sword-bearing and dagger-bearing side. Lines are to the inside and outside of the weapon, not to its right or left. Hence those parts above or below the specific weapon bearing hand and on the inside or the outside of that hand define their lines of attack. An attack coming above either hand is still in the "high line"; and below, in the "low line"; but now the area between the two hands, is the "inside line"; and the exterior of the hands, is the "outside line." See *Lines of Attack.*

WEAPONED: Provided with a weapon (a sword).

WELL-ARMED: (also *Well Armed*) Well furnished with weapons of offense and defense.

WELSH HOOK: A weapon with a curved or hooked blade; a bill-hook.

WHETSTONE: A stone on which a thing is sharpened...

WHIP: a.) An instrument for flogging or beating, consisting either of a rigid rod or stick with a lash of cord, leather, etc. attached, or of a flexible switch with or without a lash. b.) Such an instrument used for driving horses, chastising human beings, and other purposes. c.) To strike suddenly with a lash; to punish with a whip. A blow or stroke with, or as with, a whip; a lash, stripe, a flogging. d.) To drive by lashes of a whip. e.) To move suddenly and quickly like the lash of a whip.

WHIPPER: One who whips another.

WHIPSTOCK: The handle of a whip.

WIDE EPÉE BLADE: See *Giant Epée Blade.*

WIDE PARRY: a) A parry made, by accident or by device, outside the regular perimeters of proper defense. Such actions are generally made with an extended or straight arm. Such extended defensive actions also make it easier for the adversary to deceive the parry and strike home before the arm and blade are recovered and brought back into the body. This is true in modern as well as historical fencing. b.) See *Extended Parry*.

WIDE STANCE: An En Garde that places the feet wide apart and allows the upper body to face the Line of Engagement. Feet may either be in a; 1.) Neutral Stance (feet on 90 left and 90 Right), 2.) Right Stance (right foot on the forward 45 right, and left foot on back 45 left), or 3.) Left Stance (Left foot on forward 45 left and back foot on back 45 left).

WIDE WARD: See *Broad Ward*.

WIDE: a.) (also *Reinforced Parry, Wide Parry,* and *Split Parry*) A two handed parry, generally in broadsword, where the right hand is kept on the grip of the sword and the left grasps the foible of the blade. The middle of the blade is then used for defense, the sword held more like a quarter-staff than a sword. The wide parry is generally used as a defensive maneuver for a vertical cutting attack to the head. It may, however, be used to defend any of the standard targets. b.) Said of a parry that is extended out, beyond the proper defensive range. An extended or straight arm parry. c.) Said of a thrust that is delivered outside and away from its intended target, both on and off-line.

WIELD: To use with the hand, to manage weapons...

WIND UP: The chambering of the hand, arm, foot, leg, limb, etc. in preparation for delivering a blow.

WING BLOCK: (MA) a.) An Arnis and Escrima defensive action in stick and blade play that defends the head and arm in the same manner as the Hanging Parry. b.) A defensive action made with the muscle groupings of the upper arm. The arm is bent, like the wing of a bird, the hand near the near the shoulder, presenting a shield against strong blows; taking the attack on the back of the forearm and outside of the upper arm.

WRANGLE: To quarrel; to brawl.

WRANGLER: a.) Opponent, adversary. b.) A term in motion picture lingo for one responsible for the care and handling of a specific prop or properties.

WRAP-N-TRAP: (also Serpentine, Silver's Disarm, Snake Hand Disarm and Angelo's Disarm) A secured disarm introduced by George Silver that uses the left arm and hand to grasp the sword. The unarmed-hand snakes around the blade and comes up on the inside near the hilt. The arm is wrapped around the blade like a serpent, trapping it under the arm and in the grasp. From this position the sword can be secured and disarmed.

WRAPPING IT UP: Slang for the *Envelopment*.

WRAPPING THE EIGHTS: An exercise in blade manipulation that has the combatant execute a series of full arm molinellos on both sides of the body in the pattern of a large figure-eight. It is called "Wrapping the Eights" because the pattern is carried around on both sides of the body instead of being drawn in front of the body like a standard exercise of figure-eights.

WRESTLE: a.) To strive with strength and skill to throw a person to the ground by grappling with them; to endeavor to overpower and lay down another, especially in a contest governed by fixed rules, by embracing their body and limbs and tripping or overbalancing them. b.) Used as a metaphor for the contending of emotions, one against the other till one or the other falls.

WRESTLER: One who wrestles.

WRESTLER'S BRIDGE: Position of the body on the floor, or landing out of a roll, or throw. The feet are flat on the floor, and the back is arched, to a greater or lesser degree, the weight on the shoulders and feet. This protects the spine and coccyx from injury due to hard contact with the floor.

WRESTLING: To endeavor to overpower or lay down another by seizing and holding their body and/or limbs in order to control, trip, overbalance or throw them.

WRIST BLOW: A cutting attack delivered from the wrist, the quickest and lightest attack to be made with the edge of the blade according to the seventeenth century English Fencing Master Joseph Swetnam. See also *Wrist Cut.*

WRIST CUT: (also 1/3 cut) a.) The fastest and tightest cut delivered in swordplay made only from an action of the hand and wrist. The attack consists of the final third of the cutting arc supplemented by a flicking action of the wrist and fingers. This flicking action allows the blade to travel in a succinct cutting arc while still controlling the power of the attack. b.) A cutting attack delivered to the wrist.

WRIST LOCK: A hold applied to the wrist to immobilize it, or as a lever to be used for a throw. See *Joint Lock.*

X

X BLOCK: a.) A block where both hands/arms are used together and are crossed, the one over the other, catching the attacking limb in the open "V" between the hands. b.) Another term for the *Cross Parry.*

X PARRY: See *Cross Parry*

Y

Z

YERK: To thrust or strike with a sudden and quick motion. A smart blow or stroke; to strike smartly, as with a whip or rod. The sound of such a blow; the crack of a whip, a thud.

YIELD PARRY: (also *Ceding Parry* and *Yielding Parry*) a.) A parry executed against a flowing attack without separating the blades. The ceding or yielding parry is a particular method of execution used against thrusts and cuts off a *Froissement*. The yield consists of not resisting the pressure, but waiting to parry until the final stage of the attack when the focus shifts from the pressure to the attack. At that time, without losing contact, the pressured blade is quickly drawn back, pressing its forte against the offending blade's foible. b.) (also *Ceding Parry*) A parry executed against the cut or thrust made at the end of a successful glissade. To distinguish a yield parry from a normal parry, both the offensive and defensive blades remain engaged from the initial attack on the blade through the successful parry. c.) A technique of parrying using the force of the opponent's pressure on the defending blade, to divert the defending and attacking blades into another line, while closing that line.

YIELD: a.) To give up or surrender; the action of giving in; submission. b.) To deliver, to render, to give up, to surrender. c.) To give way, to succumb.

YIELDER: a.) One who surrenders. b.) One who gives up.

ZONE: (also *Close to the Oblique*) Footwork that takes the body diagonally off-line (45° to either the right or left) and inside measure, ending with the legs open. The technique is usually in response to an offensive action, to gain tactical advantage for both defensive and offensive purposes.

ZWAGGERER: See *Swaggerer*.

ZWEITE INTENTION: (Ger.) See *Second Intention*.

"Beauty is power; a smile is its sword."

John Ray

THE MASTER OF VERONA

ROMEO & JULIET IS THE GREATEST LOVE STORY EVER TOLD. EVERY STORY HAS A BEGINNING. A SWEEPING NOVEL OF RENAISSANCE ITALY, THE MASTER OF VERONA FOLLOWS PIETRO ALAGHIERI, ELDEST SON OF THE POET DANTE, AS HE'S CAUGHT UP BY THE CHARISMA AND GENIUS OF VERONA'S RULER, CANGRANDE DELLA SCALA. PIETRO RISKS BATTLES, DUELS, AND MURDER TO IMPRESS HIS NEW LORD. AT THE HEART OF THE STORY IS AN INFERNAL PLOT AGAINST CANGRANDE'S BASTARD HEIR, AND THE RIVALRY OF TWO FRIENDS OVER THE AFFECTIONS OF A GIRL - A RIVALRY WILL SEVER A FRIENDSHIP, DIVIDE A CITY, AND SPARK A FEUD THAT WILL SOMEDAY PRODUCE THE STAR-CROSS'D LOVERS. BASED ON THE PLAYS OF WILLIAM SHAKESPEARE, THE POETRY OF DANTE, AND THE HISTORY OF ITALY, THE MASTER OF VERONA IS A NOVEL OF BRUTAL WARFARE, LOST FRIENDSHIP, AND DIRE CONSPIRACY, COMBINING TO CREATE AN EPIC JOURNEY INTO THE BIRTH OF THE RENAISSANCE THAT RECALLS THE BEST OF BERNARD CORNWELL AND DOROTHY DUNNETT.

"Intricate plotting, well-staged scenes, and colorful descriptions enhance head-spinning but lively entertainment." - Kirkus Reviews

"A novel of intricate plot, taut narrative, sharp period detail and beautifully realized characters." - Publisher's Weekly

"Be prepared to burn the midnight oil. It's well worth it." - Historical Novel Society

"A delightful romp through the backstory of 'Romeo & Juliet.'" - Chicago Sun-Times

"Shakespearean actor David Blixt traces the genesis of the famous feud between the Montagues and Capulets in this sharp, arresting novel that is completely impossible to put down." - MICHELLE MORAN, Nefertiti and Madame Tussaud

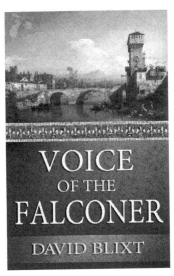

VOICE OF THE FALCONER

ITALY, 1325. EIGHT YEARS AFTER THE TUMULTUOUS EVENTS OF THE MASTER OF VERONA, PIETRO ALAGHIERI IS LIVING IN EXILE IN RAVENNA, ENDURING THE LOSS OF HIS FAMOUS FATHER WHILE SECRETLY RAISING CESCO, BASTARD HEIR TO VERONA'S PRINCE, CANGRANDE DELLA SCALA. BUT WHEN WORD OF CANGRANDE'S DEATH REACHES HIM, PIETRO MUST RACE BACK TO VERONA TO PREVENT CESCO'S RIVALS FROM USURPING HIS RIGHTFUL PLACE. BUT YOUNG CESCO IS DETERMINED NOT TO BE ANYONE'S PAWN. WILLFUL AND BRILLIANT, HE DEFIES EVEN THE STARS. AND FAR BEHIND THE SCENES IS A MASTERMIND PULLING THE STRINGS, ONE WHO STANDS TO LOSE - OR GAIN - THE MOST. BORN FROM SHAKESPEARE'S ITALIAN PLAYS, THIS NOVEL EXPLORES THE DANGER, DECEIT, AND DEVILTRY OF EARLY RENAISSANCE ITALY, AND THE TERRIBLE CHOICES ONE MUST MAKE JUST TO STAY ALIVE.

"David Blixt is one of the masters of historical fiction. Dramatic, vivid, superbly researched, VOICE OF THE FALCONER captures Renaissance Italy in all its heady glamour and lethal intrigue. This is a novel to savor - and then read again!" - C.W. GORTNER, The Queen's Vow and The Tudor Conspiracy

"David Blixt is a man of many talents--an actor, director, author. In his hands, history comes to bright, blazing life." - SHARON KAY PENMAN, The Sunne In Splendour and Lionheart

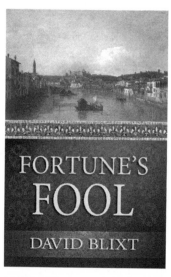

Fortune's Fool

ITALY, 1326. WHILE THE BRILLIANT AND WILY CESCO IS SCHOOLED IN HIS NEW DUTIES AT THE HAND OF A HARD MASTER, PIETRO ALAGHIERI TRAVELS TO AVIGNON, CURRENT SEAT OF THE PAPACY, TO FIGHT HIS EXCOMMUNICATION. HE DOESN'T KNOW AN OLD FOE HAS BEEN WAITING TO RUIN PIETRO'S LIFE AND SEIZE CONTROL OF VERONA ITSELF. BACK IN VERONA, SEPARATED FROM EVERYONE HE TRUSTS, CESCO MUST CONFRONT HIS AMBITIOUS COUSIN, A MYSTERIOUS YOUNG KILLER, AND THE HOLY ROMAN EMPEROR HIMSELF. A HARROWING SERIES OF ADVENTURES REVEAL A SECRET LONG HIDDEN, ONE THAT THREATENS CESCO'S ONLY CHANCE FOR TRUE HAPPINESS. INSPIRED BY SHAKE-SPEARE, DANTE, AND PETRARCH, FULL OF RENAISSANCE INTRIGUE AND PASSION, THIS THIRD NOVEL IN BLIXT'S ACCLAIMED STAR-CROSS'D SERIES REFLECTS THE HEIGHTS OF DRAMA, EXPLORING THE CAPRICIOUS WHIMS OF LADY FORTUNE, WHO HAS HER FAVORITES - AND HER FOOLS.

"This is one of the most exciting, and satisfying, reads that I have immersed myself in for a long time. David Blixt is a gem of a writer." - Helen Hollick, The Pendragon Chronicles

"For anyone who has yet to read David's novels, you are about to hit the literary lottery. Yes, he's that good." - Sharon Kay Penman, The Sunne In Splendour

"David Blixt is a master of historical fiction. Dramatic, vivid, superbly researched, this series captures Renaissance Italy in all its heady glamour and lethal intrigue." - C.W. Gortner, The Tudor Conspiracy

HNS Editor's Choice

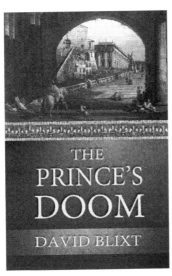

THE PRINCE'S DOOM

ITALY, 1328. THE LONG-AWAITED EXPLOSIVE FOURTH NOVEL IN THE STAR-CROSS'D SERIES! VERONA HAS WON ITS WAR WITH PADUA, BUT LOST ITS WAR WITH THE STARS. THE YOUNG PRODIGY CESCO NOW TURNS HIS TROUBLED BRILLIANCE TO DARKER PURPOSES, EMBRACING A RIOTOUS LIFE AND CHALLENGING NOT ONLY THE LORD OF VERONA AND THE CHURCH, BUT THE STARS THEMSELVES. TRYING DESPERATELY TO SALVAGE WHAT'S LEFT OF HIS SPIRIT, FOR ONCE PIETRO ALAGHIERI WELCOMES THE PLOTS AND INTRIGUES OF THE VERONESE COURT, HOPING THEY WILL SHAKE THE YOUNG MAN OUT OF HIS TORPOR. BUT WHEN THE FIRST BODY FALLS, IT BECOMES CLEAR THAT THIS NEW GAME IS DEADLY, ONE THAT WILL DOOM THEM ALL.

Brag Medallion Recipient 2015

Finalist for the 2015 M.M. Bennetts Award for Historical Fiction

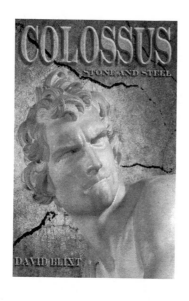

COLOSSUS: STONE & STEEL

JUDEA, 66 AD. A ROMAN LEGION SUFFERS A SMASHING AND CATA-STROPHIC DEFEAT AT THE HANDS OF AN ANGRY BAND OF HEBREWS ARMED WITH ONLY SLINGS AND SPEARS. KNOWING EMPEROR NERO'S REVENGE WILL BE SWIFT AND MERCILESS, THEY MUST DECIDE HOW TO DEFEND THEIR LAND AGAINST THE ROMAN INVASION. CAUGHT UP IN THE TUMULT IS THE MASON JUDAH, INADVERTENT HERO OF BETH HORON, WHO NOW FINDS HIMSELF RUBBING SHOULDERS WITH PRIESTS, REVOLUTIONARIES, GENERALS, AND NOBLES, DRAFTED TO HELP DEFEND THE LAND OF GALILEE. DENIED THE CHANCE TO MAR-RY WHERE HE WILL, HE TURNS ALL HIS ENERGY INTO DEFENDING THE BESEIGED CITY OF JOTAPATA. BUT WITH A GENERAL SUFFERING DELUSIONS OF GRANDEUR, FRIENDS FALLING EACH DAY, AND THE ROMAN MENACE AT THE WALLS, JUDAH MUST BRAVE A NIGHTMARE TO SAVE THOSE HE LOVES AND PRESERVE HIS HONOR. FIRST BOOK OF THE COLOSSUS SERIES.

Colossus: The Four Emperors

Rome under Nero is a dangerous place. His cruel artistic whims border on madness, and any man who dares rise too high has his wings clipped, with fatal results. For one family, Nero's whims mean either promotion or destruction. While his uncle Vespasian goes off to put down a rebellion in Judea, Titus Flavius Sabinus struggles to walk the perilous line between success and notoriety as he climbs Rome's ladder. When Nero is impaled on his own artistry, the whole world is thrown into chaos and Sabinus must navigate shifting allegiances and murderous alliances as his family tries to survive the year of the Four Emperors. The second novel in the Colossus series.

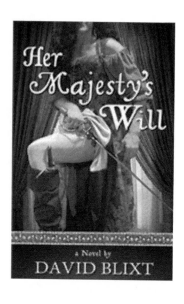

HER MAJESTY'S WILL

BEFORE HE WAS FAMOUS, HE WAS A FUGITIVE. BEFORE HE WROTE OF HUMANITY, HE LIVED IT. BEFORE HE WAS THE BARD OF AVON, HE WAS A SPY.

A VERY POOR SPY.

ENGLAND, 1586. SWEPT UP IN THE SKIRTS OF A MYSTERIOUS STRANGER, WILL SHAKESPEARE BECOMES ENTANGLED IN A DEADLY AND HILARIOUS MISADVENTURE AS HE ACCIDENTALLY UNCOVERS AN ATTEMPT TO MURDER QUEEN ELIZABETH HERSELF. AIDED BY THE MERCURIAL WIT OF KIT MARLOWE, WILL ENTERS LONDON FOR THE FIRST TIME, CHASED BY REBELS, SPIES, HIS OWN GOVERNMENT, HIS PAST, AND A BEAR.

"I loved Her Majesty's Will, a delightful romp through Elizabethan England. When Will Shakespeare and Kit Marlowe stumble onto a plot to assassinate Queen Elizabeth, the fun is non-stop, an irresistible mix of suspense, surprises, and humor I just hope we get to see this zany team again." - SHARON KAY PENMAN, The Sunne In Splendour and Lionheart

"I LOVE this book! I'm laughing and on the edge of my seat and turning the e-pages so fast, I'm gonna fry my iPad." - C.W. GORTNER, The Queen's Vow and The Tudor Secret

EVE OF IDES

THE NIGHT BEFORE HIS ASSASSINATION AT THE HANDS OF CONSPIRATORS, JULIUS CAESAR ATTENDED A FEAST. WITH HIM WERE BRUTUS, CASSIUS, AND ANTONY. DURING THE MEAL, CAESAR WAS ASKED WHAT HE THOUGHT WAS THE BEST WAY TO DIE. CAESAR ANSWERED, 'WHAT DOES IT MATTER, SO LONG AS IT'S QUICK?' BASED ON HISTORY AND THE WORKS OF SHAKESPEARE, EVE OF IDES REVEALS THE UNEXPLORED RELATIONSHIP BETWEEN THE MAIN PLAYERS OF THE AGE - CAESAR, BRUTUS, AND ANTONY. HISTORY WAS NEVER SO ALIVE.

MORE DAVID BLIXT
FROM SORDELET INK

The Star-Cross'd Series

THE MASTER OF VERONA
VOICE OF THE FALCONER
FORTUNE'S FOOL
THE PRINCE'S DOOM

VARNISH'D FACES & OTHER SHORT STORIES

The Colossus Series

COLOSSUS: STONE & STEEL
COLOSSUS: THE FOUR EMPERORS

and coming soon

COLOSSUS: WAIL OF THE FALLEN
COLOSSUS: TRIUMPH OF THE JEWS

HER MAJESTY'S WILL
plus Essays on Shakespeare

ORIGIN OF THE FEUD
TOMORROW AND TOMORROW

Visit
WWW.DAVIDBLIXT.COM
for more information.

Plays From SORDELET INK

The Count of Monte Cristo
by Christoper M Walsh
adapted from the novel by Alexandre Dumas

The Moonstone
by Robert Kauzlaric
adapted from the novel by Wilkie Collins

The Woman in White
by Robert Kauzlaric
adapted from the novel by Wilkie Collins

Season on the Line
by Shawn Pfautsch
adapted from Herman Melville's Moby-Dick

Hatfield & McCoy
by Shawn Pfautsch

It Came From Mars
by Joseph Zettelmaier

The Gravedigger
by Joseph Zettelmaier

Ebenezer - a Christmas Play
by Joseph Zettelmaier

The Scullery Maid
by Joseph Zettelmaier

Once A Ponzi Time
by Joe Foust

Eve of Ides
by David Blixt

And coming in 2016 a new novel

The Dragontail Buttonhole
by Peter Curtis

Visit www.sordeletink.com

Made in the USA
Charleston, SC
11 June 2015